THE FEASTS OF ISRAEL

THE FEASTS
OF ISRAEL

Kevin J. Conner

Available from:

BIBLE TEMPLE PUBLISHING
7545 N.E. Glisan Street
Portland, Oregon 97213
(503) 253-9020

ISBN 0-914936-42-5
Printed in U.S.A.
at
Bible Press
Portland, Oregon

THE FEASTS OF ISRAEL

"Three times in a year shall all thy males appear before the Lord thy God in the place which He shall choose; in the Feast of Unleavened Bread, and in the Feast of Weeks, and in the Feast of Tabernacles: and they shall not appear before the Lord empty: Every man shall give as he is able, according to the blessing of the Lord thy God which He hath given thee". *(Deuteronomy 16:16,17)*

"Blessed — happy, fortunate (to be envied) — are the people who know the joyful sound (who understand and appreciate the spiritual blessings symbolized by the Feasts); they walk, O Lord, in the light and favour of Thy countenance" *(Psalm 89:15. Amplified)*

"What will ye do in the Solemn Day, and in the Day of the Feast of the Lord?" *(Hosea 9:5).*

A JEWISH FOLK TALE

God's world is great and holy. Among the holy lands in the world is the Holy Land of Israel. In the land of Israel the holiest city is Jerusalem. In Jerusalem the holiest place was the Temple, and in the Temple the holiest spot was the holy of holies.

There are seventy peoples in the world. Among these holy peoples is the people of Israel. The holiest of the people of Israel is the tribe of Levi. In the tribe of Levi the holiest are the priests. Among the priests, the holiest was the high priest.

There are 354 days in the year. Among these the holidays are holy. Higher than these is the holiness of the Sabbath. Among Sabbaths the holiest is the Day of Atonement, the Sabbath of Sabbaths.

There are seventy languages in the world. Among the holy languages is the holy language of Hebrew. Holier than all else in this language is the holy Torah, and in the Torah the holiest part is the Ten Commandments. In the Ten Commandments the holiest of all words is the Name of God.

And once during the year, at a certain hour, these four supreme sanctities of the world were joined with one another. That was on the Day of Atonement, when the high priest would enter the holy of holies and there utter the Name of God. And because this hour was beyond measure holy and awesome, it was the time of utmost peril not only for the high priest but for the whole of Israel. For if, in this hour, there had, God forbid, entered the mind of the high priest a false or sinful thought, the entire world would have been destroyed.

Every spot where a man raises his eyes to heaven is a holy of holies. Every man, having been created by God in His own image and likeness, is a high priest. Every day of a man's life is a Day of Atonement, and every word that a man speaks with sincerity is the Name of the Lord.

Folk tale adapted from a version in The Dybbuk by Saul An-Ski

"The Jewish Catalogue"

FOREWORD

INTRODUCING THE FEASTS OF THE LORD

The more a believer reads and studies the Word of God, the greater the discovery that the Bible is a vast mine of treasures of truth. "Surely there is a vein (or, a Mine) for the **silver,** and a place for the **gold** where they fine (or, refine) it. **Iron** is taken out of the earth, and **brass** is molten out of the stone." *(Job 28:1-2)*

As it is in the natural realm, so it is in the spiritual realm. Silver and gold, iron and brass are not to be found on the surface of the earth but these things are formed under pressure and then dug from beneath the earth's surface. Then they go through the refining process before their beauty and usefulness is seen.

So it is with the truths of the Word of God. Many truths of the Scriptures are not to be found by a mere surface reading of the Word but have to be dug out and brought to the surface in order that their beauty and usefulness may be discovered.

Solomon the wise Preacher said: "It is the glory of God **to conceal** a thing: but the honour of kings is **to search** out a matter" *(Proverbs 25:2)*; so God's glory is concealed through His Word but the believer as a king-priest may see His glory revealed by searching out the matter.

One of the greatest, richest and deepest gold and silver mines is that which pertains to the Feasts of the Lord, outlined more especially in Leviticus Chapter 23.

It is a mine that has rarely been dug into and many priceless gems are to be found therein.

The Church in general has walked over a vast wealth of truth in this subject. This has either been done through ignorance of the wealth therein or through lack of interpretative keys to understand, or else through fear of fanciful or extreme interpretations of the subject or else through plain neglect.

Because of these things the Church, as a whole, has been robbed of much historical, prophetical, typical and practical truth.

It is impossible to read the New Testament scriptures (for so many believers glory in the fact that they are "New Testament believers and not Old Testament oriented"), or understand large portions of them without a reasonable knowledge and understanding of the Old Testament. The New Testament is simply the fulfilment of the Old Testament. Each Testament is incomplete without the other. The Old made way for the New. The New completes the Old. The Old was preparatory to the New. The New is the fulfilment and the answer to the Old.

The New Testament has many quotations, references and allusions to the Old Testament Feasts of the Lord. The Student will perceive this as he reads and meditates in the subsequent chapters of this Text.

It is in the light of these references that it can be seen how impossible it is to understand such without a working knowledge of the Feasts alluded to.

When the Lord brought Israel out of "the house of bondage" unto Himself, He gave them the complete order of approach to His presence. This order was set forth in the Mosaic Covenant. At Mt. Sinai God brought the people into Covenant relationship, this Covenant being more particularly called "The **Old** Covenant *(Hebrews 8:13)*. Read also *Exodus 19:1-6; Exodus 24.*

There were five major things involved in this Covenant. These were:

1. The Law, Moral and Civil *(Deuteronomy 4:10-13; 5:1-21)*
2. The Tabernacle of Moses *(Exodus chapters 25-40).*
3. The Sacrificial Offerings *(Leviticus chapters 1-7)*
4. The Aaronic and Levitical Priesthood *(Exodus 28-29; Leviticus chapters 8-9)*
5. The Feasts of the Lord *(Leviticus 23; Deuteronomy 16)*

Each of these constitutes a book in itself because of the vastness of the material in the subjects suggested thereby.

There are authors who have written on the Tabernacle of Moses, the Offerings, the Priesthood and the Feasts, as well as the Law Covenant. However, the material on these subjects seems to be somewhat limited in its scope. This is especially true concerning the fifth area belonging to the Mosaic Covenant, which area concerns the Feasts of the Lord.

It is with this area of truth that the present Text is concerned.

Companion Books entitled *"The Tabernacle of Moses"* and *"The Tabernacle of David"* have been published already. This Text will follow the same format so that it may be used as a reference source.

It is the author's desire that all who read and study and meditate on the truths therein will experience the same joy and blessing of which the Psalmist spoke:

"Blessed is the people that know the joyful sound: they shall walk, O Lord, in the light of Thy countenance" *(Psalm 89:15).*

"Blessed, happy, fortunate (to be envied), are the people who know the joyful sound, **who understand and appreciate the spiritual blessings symbolized by the Feasts:** they walk, O Lord, in the light and favour of Thy countenance" *(Psalm 89:15. Amplified Old Testament).*

Kevin J. Conner

TABLE OF CONTENTS

Chapter One
WHY STUDY THE FEASTS

Many Christians, the moment they hear someone speak of the Feasts of the Lord ask: "Why study the Feasts?"

They are like many in Israel, who, as Hosea lamented "I wrote for him the ten thousand things of My law, but they are counted as a strange thing (as something which does not concern him)" *(Hosea 8:12. Amplified Old Testament)*. The intricate details of the Mosaic economy become meaningless unless all is seen through the Cross in relation to Christ and the church.

The answer to the question is the same answer which is given as to why we study the Tabernacle of Moses, the Tabernacle of David, the Temple of Solomon, the Priesthood and the Offerings. The Scriptures given in answer to this question are applicable to any question as to why New Testament believers should study Old Testament revelation along with the New Testament revelation.

We note some of the major scriptural reasons why the Feasts should be studied.

1. **The Feasts should be studied** because they are a part of the Scriptures given by inspiration of the Holy Spirit which are profitable for doctrine, reproof, correction and instruction in righteousness *(II Timothy 3:16-17)*.

2. **The Feasts should be studied** because they are "a shadow of things to come" *(Colossians 2:16-17; Hebrews 10:1-2)*. They point to Christ Who is the substance.

3. **The Feasts should be studied** because they were prophetic types and ensamples, foreshadowing in Israel's history future events. They shadowed forth that which Christ would fulfil in Himself and in the Church, which is His Body *(I Corinthians 10:6, 11; Matthew 5:17-18; 11:13)*. They were written for our admonition. Part have found fulfilment, and part are yet to find fulfilment.

4. **The Feasts should be studied** because the believer will find that there are things written therein for his learning *(Romans 15:4)*.

5. **The Feasts should be studied** because Christ came to fulfil all that was written of Him in "the Law, the Psalms and the Prophets" *(Luke 24:26-27, 44-45; John 5:45-46; Acts 3:22-23)*.

6. **The Feasts should be studied** because this part of the Law was also a "schoolmaster to bring us to Christ" *(Galatians 3:24)*.

7. **The Feasts should be studied** because Jesus said: "In the volume of the Book it is written of Me" *(Hebrews 10:7; Psalm 40:6-8; 29:9)*. All the intricate details point to some aspect of the person, work and glory of the Christ of God.

8. **The Feasts should be studied** because there was knowledge and truth in the external form of the Law. We study the external form to discover the internal knowledge and truth that was hidden therein *(Romans 2:20, Amp. N.T.; Hebrews 1:1-2, Amp. N.T.)*

9. **The Feasts should be studied** because they set forth "patterns" of heavenly things on earth *(Hebrews 8:5; 9:9, 23-24)*.

10. **The Feasts should be studied** because they set forth the total ministry of Christ relative to the plan of redemption. They set forth in their time element the present Dispensation, from the first coming of Christ (Passover), through the Church Age (Pentecost to the second coming of Christ (Tabernacles).

11. **The Feasts should be studied** because the truths therein are part of "present truth" which the Holy Spirit is quickening to the Church in these "last days" *(II Peter 1:12; Matthew 4:4)*.

12. **The Feasts should be studied** because there has never been a generation who have experienced all three Feasts, but the end-time generation will experience such, even as did that generation under King Solomon's glorious reign *(II Chronicles 8:13)*. This generation will hear what the Spirit is saying to the Churches *(Revelation 2:7)*.

The things involved in the Feasts of the Lord pertained to the material, the natural and the temporal. It is a principle of God's dealings with His people that it is "First the natural, afterwards that which is spiritual" *(I Corinthians 15:46-47)*.

It is first the animal-lamb, then the Divine-human Lamb of God; first the natural loaves and leaven, then the spiritual loaves and leaven; first the earthly Sanctuary, then the heavenly Sanctuary.

When the Lord Jesus Christ came, He came to fulfil and abolish the natural, the external and temporal, and bring in the Spiritual, the internal and the external *(II Corinthians 4:18)*. The Letter of the Law was swallowed up in the Spirit of Life.

In the Feasts of Israel, as in the Tabernacle of Moses and its Priesthood and Offerings, God used the language of creation as the language of redemption. When we know the Creator we will understand the language of creation. When we know the Redeemer we will understand the language of redemption. Considering the things which are visible, the things which have been made, will help us to understand the invisible things, even His eternal power and Godhead *(Romans 1:20)*.

These then are the scriptural reasons why we should study the Feasts of the Lord.

Chapter Two
PRINCIPLES OF INTERPRETATION

Any preacher, teacher or author who sets out to expound the sacred scriptures musts needs be governed, guided and controlled by certain basic principles of interpretation.

This is especially so when it comes to interpreting and expounding those portions of scripture that have to do with historical and typical things.

If these principles are not followed and used properly, then the Scriptures, and more particularly the types, can be made to say anything that the expounder may want them to say.

Many times, when exposition is given concerning typical things as under the Mosaic Covenant, such as the Tabernacle, the Priesthood and Offerings, the hearer will ask: "How does the speaker arrive at that conclusion?" The same question is asked concerning the interpretation of the Feasts of the Lord.

Hence because of these honest enquiries, we set forth some of the basic principles of interpretation which will be used throughout this Text, and by which the author arrives at various conclusions.

(For a fuller treatment of these Principles, the reader is directed to the published Text *"Interpreting the Scriptures"* by Kevin J. Conner and Ken Malmin, available from the Publishers of this text).

1. The Context Group of Principles

The Context Group of Principles involves the First, Comparative, Progressive and Complete Mention Principles.

The Context Principle is that principle by which the interpretation of any verse of scripture is determined upon a consideration its context, either verse, passage, book or Testament context.

In studying the Feasts we will note the verses, passages, and the book and Testament in which the Feasts are spoken of. All will be considered in the light of the whole Bible. We will consider the historical setting of the Feasts, where and what was their literal fulfilment in the Nation of Israel. Only by doing this can we then move to the typical and spiritual significances that are to be found in Christ and the church, the people of God today.

In using **The First Mention principle** we will check and see what was meant in the first mention of anything pertaining to the Feasts. Generally the first mention gives the truth in seed form.

In using **The Comparative Mention Principle** we will compare scripture with scripture and bring the passages together that may be contrasted or compared, in order to help our understanding of the Feasts. This will be so especially in the light of the Old Testament and the fulfilment in the New Testament. This is "comparing spiritual things with spiritual" *(I Corinthians 2:13),* after seeing "First the natural, then that which is spiritual" *(I Corinthians 15:45-46)*

And in using **The Progressive Mention Principle** we will consider God's progressive revelation which God gave in the Feasts. The progressive principle is conveyed to us in the Word of the Lord concerning Israel "precept upon precept, precept upon precept; line upon line, line upon line; here a little, there a little" *(Isaiah 28:13).*

By use of **The Complete Mention Principle** we will have considered every direct reference to the Feasts of the Lord in the Bible. By putting all the fragments together we will be able to see more fully the truth which God scattered about throughout His Word in both Testaments.

2. Theological Principles

There are certain Principles which arise out of Theology, and these principles may be grouped together because they have to do with the purposes of God.

These principles are the Election, Covenantal, Ethnic and Chronomentrical Principles. They are especially seen in the Old Testament relative to the Nation of Israel, and then in the New Testament relative to Christ and the church. In using these principles the interpreter works from part to whole, and whole to the individual parts.

The Election Principle shows how God elected Moses and Israel in the Old Testament and Christ and His church in the New Testament to fulfil His purposes.

The Covenantal Principle is especially used in this text as it pertains to the two major Testaments: the Old Covenant (Moses), and the New Covenant (Jesus). The Old Covenant economy under which the Feasts were given finds fulfilment spiritually and eternally in the New Covenant economy, in Christ and the church. It is important to recognize that God takes nothing of the Old Covenant and places it on the New Covenant but all passes through the cross of Jesus Christ.

The Ethnic Principle is an important principle also. It has to do with God's purposes in the nations, Hebrew, Gentile and especially in the church composed of Jew and Gentile, which is now God's "holy nation" (I Peter 2:5-9). A proper application of this principle will help us to understand that the Feasts of the Lord concerned Israel in the Old Covenant but they were Feasts of the Letter, after the external form. The Feasts of the Lord in the New Testament concern the church, but after the Spirit, and the spiritual and internal form.

Using **The Chronometrical Principle,** which has to do with time, will help us to understand and discern "the Times and Seasons" as set forth in the Feasts of the Lord and their respective months and days.

3. The Christo-centric Principle

The scriptures show that Christ is the central Person of the Bible. The Written Word revolves around Him who is the Living Word. He is the hub of the wheel of truth and all truths are as spokes relating to Him. Thus we will see how the Feasts point first to Christ, the hub of Divine revelation, and then to His church. "In the volume of the book it is written of Me" Jesus said (Psalm 40:6-8). Thus in using **The Christocentric Principle** we will see Christ in the Feasts.

4. The Moral Principle

The Moral Principle has to do with the practical lessons or principles which may be applied to a person's life, general conduct and behaviour. In interpreting the Feasts there will be seen many practical lessons and principles which can be applied to the believer in Christ, who enjoys these spiritual Feasts in Him.

5. The Figures of Speech Group of Principles

There are several specialized principles which may be grouped together because they have to do with figures of speech or extensions of them. Three of these principles are especially noted here, these being the Symbolic, Numerical and Typical Principles.

The Feasts abound with symbolic elements and these elements can only be understood by using **The Symbolic Principle.** By use of the symbol God used one thing to represent another. In discerning the common link between the symbol and that which is symbolized we discover the truth God meant to convey. In the Feasts we have symbolic objects, creatures, actions, etc. All have to be interpreted.

In using **The Numerical Principle** we will discover the truth God has hidden in His use of certain numbers. Numbers belong to the symbolic grouping also. Thus the Feasts of the Lord took place in specific months, on specific days — all of which set forth truth which the use of the Numerical Principle will discover.

The Typical Principle is also of great importance in helping one to arrive at the truth in the Feasts of Jehovah. For the Festival occasions were types, that is, prophetic foreshadowings of something to come. A type is an anticipative figure, a prophetic symbol.

In the Feasts there are typical persons, offices, institutions and events. It is not that doctrines are built on these types, but types are used to illustrate doctrine. The Typical Principle may be used to interpret portions of the Feasts in the form of an extended analogy between the Feast itself and the Person and Work of Christ. This will be seen in the course of this Text.

These are the basic Principles of Interpretation applied in this Text and the Student would do well to keep such in mind as the study continues.

Chapter Three
THE FEASTS IN OUTLINE

"Three times in the year shall all thy males appear before the Lord, in the place which He shall choose; in the Feast of Unleavened Bread, and in the Feast of Weeks, and in the Feast of Tabernacles; and they shall not appear before Me empty; every man shall give as he is able" *(Deuteronomy 16:16)* Read also *Exodus 23:14-19*.

Just as there are three major colours in the rainbow, and these **three** are **manifest in seven** primary colours, so it is with the Feasts of the Lord in Israel. There are **three** major Feasts, yet these Feasts may be broken up into **seven** Feasts.

As will be seen in detail, the Feasts are typical and prophetical of that which finds its fullest expression and completion in Christ and His church, the true Israel of God *(I Corinthians 10:6, 11; Galatians 6:16)*.

Israel, the chosen nation, was spoken of as "the church in the wilderness" *(Acts 7:38)*. Therefore, the New Testament church can find numerous things in Israel's history and the dealings of God with Israel which find their spiritual counterpart in New Testament times.

The twenty-third chapter of Leviticus sets forth the most suitable outline of the three, yet seven, Feasts. Other corroborating scriptures will be brought in throughout the text.

I   (1.   The Feast of Passover — *Lev. 23:4-5*
    (2.   The Feast of Unleavened Bread — *Lev. 23:6-8*
    (3.   The Feast of the Sheaf of Firstfruits — *Lev. 23:9-14*

II   (4.   The Feast of Weeks (Pentecost) — *Lev. 23:15-22*

III   (5.   The Feast of Trumpets — *Lev. 23:23-25*
    (6.   The Feast Day of Atonement — *Lev. 23:26-32*
    (7.   The Feast of Tabernacles — *Lev. 23:33-44*

The Feast of Passover took place in the first month; the Feast of Pentecost took place in the third month, and the Feast of Tabernacles found fulfilment in the seventh month.

In Diagramatic form:

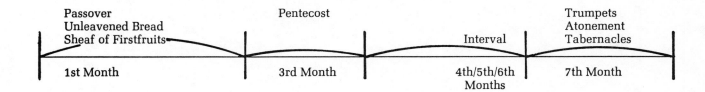

Passover Unleavened Bread Sheaf of Firstfruits	Pentecost		Interval	Trumpets Atonement Tabernacles
1st Month	3rd Month		4th/5th/6th Months	7th Month

Chapter Four
OUR STUDY APPROACH

Our study approach will be three-fold, as set out in the following questions and diagram.

1. What happened in Israel **historically** in these Feasts? What did it mean to them? Under this we will observe what took place in the literal and historical fulfilment of the Feasts.

2. How did Christ fulfil **prophetically** that which was foreshadowed in these Feasts? The historical was typical and the typical was therefore prophetical of that which was to find fulfilment in Christ first and then in His church.

3. What spiritual and practical truths can be seen **experientially** in these Feasts, first relative to the believer individually, and then to the church corporately?

FULFILMENT OF THE FEASTS OF THE LORD		
IN ISRAEL	**IN CHRIST**	**IN THE CHURCH**
Historically Literally	**Historically Personally**	**Historically Spiritually**
Prophetically Typically	**Actually Antitypically**	**Experientially Practically**
What God did in Israel	**What God did in Christ**	**What God does in the church**
Observation	**Interpretation**	**Application**

Chapter Five
FULFILMENT — LITERAL AND/OR SPIRITUAL?

Consistency of interpretation requires that the three Feasts be interpreted by the same principles. The question is asked: "Should the Feasts be interpreted literally or spiritually, or part literally and part spiritually?"

Some expositors believe that Passover and Pentecost have had a literal fulfilment and now find spiritual fulfilment in the church, while the Feast of Tabernacles has yet to find literal fulfilment in the Jewish nation.

It is held that the Feast of Tabernacles, as do the other Feasts, must find an earthly, literal and natural fulfilment in Israel, and not in the church. It is because of this that the spiritual meaning and fulfilment of Tabernacles is obscured as far as the church is concerned.

The **Key** to discovering and understanding the answer to this question is **The Cross** of Jesus and the finished work of Calvary in relation to the **Old Covenant!**

Under the Old or Mosaic Covenant, all that pertained to the Feasts was historical and literal. Actual days, literal animal sacrifices, literal and material Sanctuary services and ceremonies played their part in the fulfilment of the Feasts.

However, the historical and literal were typical and prophetical of that which was to come in the Person of Christ. The actual things used in the Feasts were also symbolical of Christ who was to come, or the church, the Body of Christ.

When Christ came, He fulfilled in Himself **historically, personally** and **antitypically** all that was shadowed forth **historically, typically** and **symbolically** under the Old Covenant. Thus He **fulfilled**—and by fulfilment **abolished**—the temporal, literal and symbolic things used in these Feasts and brought in that which is spiritual and eternal.

Christ therefore fulfilled historically and personally the Feasts of Passover and Pentecost and Tabernacles. The literal aspects have been fulfilled and abolished. The external form is done away with (II Corinthians 4:18; Hebrews 8:13; Romans 2:20). What then remains? The things which remain are the spiritual and eternal truths hidden in the previous external forms. These truths are to become experiential in the believer's life. It is these which constitute the **New Covenant!**

The Old Covenant Feasts were fulfilled historically and literally in Israel up to the time of Christ. In the Cross, Christ fulfilled historically and personally the types and shadows in the Feasts. Since the Cross, the Feasts are spiritual and experiential in the believer individually, and in the church corporately.

Thus Passover, Pentecost and Tabernacles must be experienced spiritually by the believer in Christ.

It is inconsistent, since the Cross, to have the first two Feasts spiritual and the last one literal. The Feast of Tabernacles, for instance, could not be fulfilled literally in the Jewish nation, for it would necessitate a literal rebuilt temple, a restoration of animal sacrifices, and a restoration of the Aaronic Priesthood as well as the whole of the Mosaic economy. To have such would be a violation of the Book of Hebrews. It would be a repudiation of the New Covenant Sanctuary, the Sacrifice of Christ, and His eternal Priesthood after the order of Melchisedek. It would be a rejection of Jesus Christ Himself. It would be taking one back to the other side of the Cross, and repudiating the New Covenant to reinstate the Old Covenant. It is here that the Covenantal Principle of interpretation needs to be applied.

Hence, consistency of interpretation, as well as proper Biblical theology, demands that the three Feasts **before the Cross** found their historical and literal fulfilment in natural Israel under the Old Covenant, while they found their historical and personal fulfilment in Jesus **at the Cross** under the New Covenant. And again, they find spiritual and experiential fulfilment **after the Cross** in the church, spiritual Israel (Romans 4:13-16; 9:6-9; Galatians 3:22; Ephesians 2:12-14; 3:3-6; I Peter 1:9-12; 2:5-9).

The Diagram illustrates this truth:

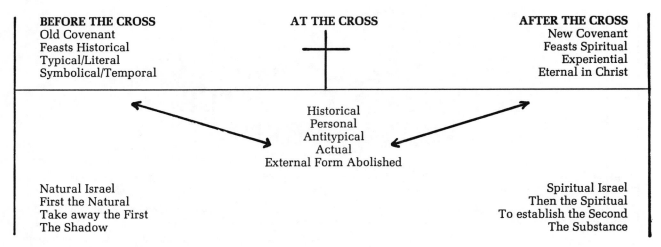

BEFORE THE CROSS	AT THE CROSS	AFTER THE CROSS
Old Covenant		New Covenant
Feasts Historical		Feasts Spiritual
Typical/Literal		Experiential
Symbolical/Temporal		Eternal in Christ

Historical
Personal
Antitypical
Actual
External Form Abolished

Natural Israel	Spiritual Israel
First the Natural	Then the Spiritual
Take away the First	To establish the Second
The Shadow	The Substance

Read *I Corinthians 15:46-47; Hebrews 10:9.*

Chapter Six
GENERAL OBSERVATIONS

I. DEFINITION OF THE WORD

A. English — **"Festival"** — "a religious festival of rejoicing as opposed to a fast."

B. Hebrew — **"Chagag"** — "to dance", indicating occasions of joy and gladness. "To move in a circle", i.e., (spec.) to march in a sacred procession, to observe a festival; by implication, to be giddy (S.C. 2287).

Gesenius says concerning keeping the festival that it comes from the idea of leaping and dancing in sacred dances *(Exodus 5:1; Leviticus 23:41)*, especially of a public assembly *(Psalm 42:5)*. This Hebrew word is translated "a festival, celebrate, dance, keep or hold a solemn feast (holiday), reel to and fro".

C. Greek — **"Heorte"** — of uncertain affinity "a festival". It is translated "Feast, holyday" (S.C. 1859).

Other definitions of the word "Feast" state that it means "an appointed day" or "an assembly", or "a fixed time or season", "times of assembling" or "solemnities" *(Isaiah 33:20)*.

Thus these Feast days were occasions when Israel kept Divine appointments; times when they assembled before the Lord, times of gladness and joyousness, times of festivity. All their worship centered around these three religious festivals.

So for the believer. The Lord our Redeemer has made some set appointments and He expects His people to keep them. Any believer who loves and desires to serve the Lord his God will not fail to keep these appointments with the Lord.

The saints are not to forsake the assembling of themselves together in keeping the Lord's Feasts *(Hebrews 10:25; I Corinthians 1:2, 9-10; I John 1:3-6)*.

II. THREE TIMES IN A YEAR

The Lord commanded Israel to keep these set appointments three times in the year *(Exodus 23:14, 17; 34:23; Deuteronomy 16:16-17)*. Three times in the year all were to appear before the Lord and keep His appointments. These three festivals, though having various names, were primarily the Feast of Passover, the Feast of Pentecost and the Feast of Tabernacles.

As all these things ordained in Israel happened unto them for types and ensamples, we see "first the natural, then the spiritual" *(I Corinthians 15:46)*. Israel experienced the natural fulfilment under the Old Covenant whereas the believer will experience the spiritual fulfilment under the New Covenant. All find their fullest expression in Christ and His church.

Three is the number of the eternal Godhead. It is also the number of a complete or perfect testimony and witness. Thus in keeping the three Feasts the believer will come to have a complete and perfect testimony and witness in the things of God. In the Feasts one comes to know the fulness of the Godhead, for the Father, Son and Holy Spirit are seen at work in these particular Feasts.

III. THE FEASTS AND THEIR APPOINTMENTS

The Feasts and their appointments originated with the Lord, not with the children of Israel. It was God's desire to meet with His people, on His terms, and on His grounds of approach. They were **His** Feasts. The Lord was the Host and Israel was His guest, invited to feast with Him.

For this reason the Lord not only gave the intricate details of the Feasts themselves, but also the set times and the place, and the sacrifices which would be involved in the keeping of them.

All of these appointments were the Lord's appointments. We consider these Festival appointments in relation to the appointed nation, the appointed times and seasons, the appointed place and the appointed sacrifices and offerings.

A. The Appointed Covenant Nation

It was to a redeemed people, redeemed from the slavery of Egypt and separated unto the Lord, that the instructions concerning the Feasts were given. Israel was a people near unto Him *(Exodus 19:4; Psalm 148:14)*.

These Feasts were not given to any Gentile nation. The only way any Gentile could participate in the Festivals was to become a proselyte to the faith of Israel in the one true God. He could be initiated into the Israel of God by forsaking all sin of idolatry and immorality and by being brought into covenant relationship with Jehovah through the rite of circumcision.

These were the Feasts of the **Lord** and only by being in covenantal relationship with the **Lord** could these Feasts be enjoyed.

Hence God enjoined the rite of circumcision upon Israelite or stranger before they could partake of the Paschal lamb *(Exodus 12:43-50)*. Circumcision was the sign and seal of the Abrahamic Covenant *(Genesis 17:1-14)*, and only as one was in covenantal relationship with the Lord were they entitled to the promises and privileges of the covenant.

Israel was the covenant nation and as such could enter in and experience the wonderful Feasts of Jehovah.

Paul in writing to the Ephesians speaks of the condition of the Gentiles outside of Christ.

"Wherefore remember, that ye being in time past Gentiles in the flesh, who are called Uncircumcision by that which is called the Circumcision in the flesh made by hands; That at that time ye were without Christ, being aliens from the commonwealth of Israel, and strangers from the covenants of promise, having no hope, and without God in this world: but now, in Christ Jesus, ye who were sometimes far off are made nigh by the blood of Christ" *(Ephesians 2:11-13)*.

It is "in Christ" that both Jew and Gentile may now together enjoy and partake of the Feasts of the Lord, in the **Lord** Jesus Christ. It is "in Christ" that both are now in **New Covenant** relationship with God. Only covenant people can partake in the Festivals which the Lord has commanded.

None can partake of the Feast of Tabernacles without the Feast of Pentecost. None can partake of the Feast of Pentecost without having first partaken of the Feast of Passover, by being in covenant relationship with God through Christ.

That which happened literally in Israel, the Old Covenant people, pointed in principle to that which happens spiritually in the Church, the New Covenant people of God *(I Corinthians 10:6, 11; 15:46; Acts 7:38)*. Israel shadowed forth as "the church in the wilderness" the New Testament Church. The New Testament Church is now that "holy nation" *(I Peter 2:5-9)*.

The Lord gave certain instructions concerning these Feasts as well as a tremendous promise to those who would keep them. We note these two instructions and the special promise given to the obedient ones.

1. All the Males to keep the Feasts — *Deuteronomy 16:16; Exodus 23:17; 34:23.*

The Lord's instruction was that all the males were to keep the Feasts. This was especially for those who lived at a distance from the Sanctuary of the Lord *(Deuteronomy 12:21)*.

Certain Festivals involved the whole family, when the father and mother, the sons and daughters, along with the stranger, the widow, the Levite and the fatherless, were to rejoice before the Lord. However, on certain Festival occasions, because of distance, only the males could attend, and keep the Feasts of Jehovah.

The **Male** here is used to represent headship, representing the whole family before God. The husband is the head of the wife and children. He symbolizes love and care, protection and provision, authority and responsibility for his family before the Lord. He would come to the Feast, learn the ways of the Lord and in turn take it back to his family and teach them diligently what he had learnt *(Deuteronomy 6:3-15)*.

In spiritual sense "in Christ", there is neither male nor female, and every New Testament believer is to keep the Feasts *(Galatians 3:28)*. Yet, in natural sense, there is still the family order of the husband and wife and children. It is the responsibility of the husband to take the spiritual leadership and oversight as priest in his home. It is his responsibility before the Lord to instruct and teach his wife and family the things of God as found in the great Festival occasions *(Ephesians 5:23-33; 6:1-4; Colossians 3:18-21)*.

2. None to appear before the Lord empty — *Deuteronomy 16:16-17*

When the males came to appear the Lord and keep the Feast they were not to appear before Him empty handed. All were to give as they were able. The things brought were free-will offerings *(Deuteronomy 16:10-12)*, and these were according to the blessings of the Lord. None could be excused for coming empty handed because all had the blessing of the Lord on their lands and inheritances. The freewill offerings were simply evidences of God's blessing on them *(Exodus 23:15; 34:20)*. To appear empty handed would be a reproach on the blessing of the Lord or an evidence of selfishness.

These freewill offerings were in turn distributed to the Levite, the stranger, the widow, the fatherless, the poor and the needy. So when the New Testament believers gather together, we are also to give to the Lord and His service, as we are able, according as God has prospered us *(II Corinthians 8-9; I Corinthians 16:1-2, 3)*. The early believers ministered to the poor and needy also in their free-will offerings *(A .ts 4:32-37; Acts 11:27-30; I Corinthians 16:1-3)*.

3. Promise of Inheritance Preservation — *Exodus 34:24*

The Lord gave the nation a great promise of preservation if all the males would keep the set Feasts. He promised that He would cast out enemy nations before them and enlarge their borders. He also promised that no enemy would desire their land when they went up to keep these Feasts in the set times of the year. Therefore all the males had assurance that their inheritances and their families would be looked after by the Lord while they attended the Festivals. None need have any fear of enemy attacks on their lands or households.

The promise holds true for New Testament believers also. If the husband as head of the family will put God and His kingdom first *(Matthew 6:24-34)*, then all the necessary things of life will be added to him. The Lord will preserve him and his family. The Lord will preserve his going out and coming in as he keeps the set Feasts of the Lord his God *(Psalm 121:1-8; Deuteronomy 28:1-6)*.

B. The Appointed Times and Seasons

Not only did the Lord set out these Feasts for His covenant people, but He also ordained the set times and seasons in which they were to be kept.

Again, as it is in the natural, so it is in the spiritual. There were natural times and seasons in Israel, and these pointed to spiritual times and seasons in the redemptive plan of God. Times and seasons in creation point to times and seasons in redemption. Let us note the Scriptures which speak of these things:

1. The Sun, Moon and Stars were given for signs and seasons, for days and years. The sun and the moon actually governed the Festival seasons *(Genesis 1:14-19; Psalm 104:19; Jeremiah 33:20; Psalm 81:3; Deuteronomy 16:6)*.

2. There is a "time and a season" for every purpose of God under the heaven *(Ecclesiastes 3:1, 17; 8:6)*.

3. God is the one who arranges and sets in order the "times and the seasons" *(Daniel 2:21)*.

4. The former and latter rains were given to Israel in their proper "times and seasons" *(Jeremiah 5:24; Ezekiel 34:26; Leviticus 26:4; Deuteronomy 11:14; 28:12; Acts 14:17)*.

5. The Feasts of the Lord were to be kept in their "times and seasons" also *(Leviticus 23:4)*.

   Passover was to be kept in its appointed season *(Exodus 13:10; Numbers 9:2, 3, 7, 13)*. This is applicable to each of the Feast days.

6. The sacrifices were to be offered to the Lord in due season also *(Numbers 28:2)*.

7. Trees bring forth in their seasons *(Psalm 1:3; Matthew 21:41; Mark 12:2)*.

8. Before Jesus' ascension, He told the disciples that it was not for them to know "the times and the seasons" which the Father had put in His own power *(Acts 1:7)*.

9. Paul later on, however, reminded the Thessalonian believers that they had no need to be told again of these "times and seasons" *(I Thessalonians 5:1)*. Evidently Paul had taught them of these things since the ascension of the Lord Jesus.

10. Peter the apostle also spoke of the "times and seasons" of refreshing which would come from the presence of the Lord before Jesus Christ would return the second time *(Acts 3:19-21)*. Peter linked these with the "times of restitution" spoken of by the prophets.

These Scriptures show the importance of the times and seasons in the mind of the Lord as well as in the history of natural Israel. The Preacher said "To every thing there is a season, and a time to every purpose under heaven" *(Ecclesiastes 3:1)*. God laid out His purposes in the Feasts of Israel, and this shadowed forth His eternal purpose in Christ and the church *(Ephesians 3:10-11)*.

Passover was to be kept in the **First** month of the sacred year. The Feast of Pentecost was to be kept in the **Third** month of the year, and Tabernacles was to be kept in the **Seventh** month of this same year. Passover and Pentecost were seasons of rain and harvest; corn harvest. Tabernacles also was a season of rain and harvest; fruit harvest. They were joyful seasons, and times of celebration before the Lord God.

It will be seen that just as Israel knew the times and seasons of the Lord's appointed Festivals and prepared themselves to enter into them, so the New Testament shows the fulfilment of these Feasts, and that in their appointed times. The New Testament believer has the privilege of entering into and enjoying these glorious Feasts.

A glance at the history of the church from the Gospels and Acts unto the present time show the times and the seasons when the Feasts find fulfilment. There is no excuse or reason why any believer need not experience the truths typified in the Lord's Feasts. It is only as one fails to "discern the signs of the times" *(Matthew 16:1-3)* that they can fail to enter into the Festival experiences which the Lord has provided for them.

It should be the prayer of God's people in these "last days" that they be like the men of Issachar which had "understanding of the times" to know what God's people ought to do *(I Chronicles 16:32)*. Thank God that there are those in the church who discern that it is the time and season of the Lord for latter rain outpouring and a keeping of the final Feast, the Feast of Tabernacles *(Zechariah 10:1-2)*.

C. The Appointed Place

Again we see that the Lord commanded Israel to keep the Feasts in a certain place. The Feasts were not only to be celebrated in their appointed times and seasons but in the place which God appointed. This place was where **The Name of the Lord** was recorded. God was very particular about this. The Festivals were not to be held in any or every place, or the places where the heathen had celebrated their idolatrous Festivals. The Lord said that He would choose a place and that place would be a set place, a place where His redemptive Name would be recorded. We note some of these chief Scriptures which confirm this fact.

1. Israel was commanded to utterly destroy **all places** where the idolatrous Canaanites served their gods *(Deuteronomy 12:2, 3)*.

2. The Lord said: "But unto **the place** which the Lord your God shall choose out of all your tribes to put **His name** there, even unto His habitation shall ye seek and thither shalt thou come . . ." *(Deuteronomy 12:5)*.

3. And again: "Then there shall be **a place** which the Lord your God shall choose to cause **His Name** to dwell there . . . *(Deuteronomy 12:11)*.

4. God links **"the place"** and **"His Name"** together in these verses also *(Deuteronomy 12:13, 14, 18, 21; 14:23-24)*.

5. In Deuteronomy 16 God reiterates that all offerings and worship must be at the place where His Name was placed. "But at **the place** which the Lord thy God shall choose to place **His Name** in, there thou shalt sacrifice the Passover at even, at the going down of the sun, at the season that thou camest out of Egypt. And thou shalt roast and eat it in the place which the Lord thy God shall choose: and thou shalt turn in the morning, and go unto thy tents." See also *Deuteronomy 16:2, 6, 7, 11, 15*.

6. And finally it says in *Deuteronomy 16:16*, "Three times in a year shall all thy males appear before the Lord thy God in **the place** which He shall choose; in the Feast of Unleavened Bread, and in the Feast of Weeks, and in the Feast of Tabernacles: and they shall not appear before the Lord empty."

The place where **His name** was placed, put, set, dwelt and recorded was **the Tabernacle** of Moses, the Sanctuary of the Lord.

The whole purpose of building the Tabernacle was that God might have a place where He could dwell in His Presence and Glory; a place where He could record His Name. The same is true of the Temple built by Solomon (Read — *Exodus 25:8; II Samuel 6:2; I Kings 8:12-21, 29, 33, 35, 43, 44*).

The New Testament clearly shows the fulfilment of the Tabernacle of Moses and the Temple of Solomon. First in Christ and then in the church, His body *(John 1:14-18; 2:18-21; I Corinthians 3:16-17; 6:19-20; Ephesians 2:19-22; II Corinthians 6:14-18)*.

The Name of the Godhead Bodily dwells in Christ and also now in the church. The Fulness of the Divine Name is the Name of the Lord Jesus Christ, the most comprehensive redemptive Name ever to be revealed, in this world and the world to come *(Matthew 28:19; Acts 2:36; Colossians 1:19; 2:9)*. Jesus Himself said: "Where two or three are gathered together (drawn together, make a harmony, a symphony) in (into) My Name, there **I am** in the midst of them." Note *Matthew 18:20* with *Exodus 3:15-16*.

It is in the New Testament Church that the Sanctuary of God finds it expression and it is that the Godhead Name is to be found. It is first "in Christ" and then in His church where God has placed His Name. It is to this Name that believers gather to keep the Feasts of the Lord. Not in any or every place, but in **the place** where **His Name,** His Presence, is recorded and dwells.

D. The Appointed Sacrifices and Oblations

Not only were these Feasts kept by a covenant people, in their appointed times and seasons, and in the appointed place where His Name was recorded, but they were also to be celebrated with specified sacrifices and oblations.

The intricate details of the Levitical offerings are recorded for us in Leviticus Chapters 1-7. The interpretation of the significance of such would require another book itself. However, we will note the appointed Festival sacrifices in a brief outline for the present, and then consider the basis truth set forth therein.

1. Specific offerings were to be presented at the Feast of Passover in the first month *(Numbers 28:11-25)*.

2. In the Feast of Weeks (Pentecost) specific offerings were also presented to the Lord *(Numbers 28:26-31)*.

3. The Feast of Tabernacles especially, had sacrifices and offerings presented to the Lord. There were more offerings in this Feast than any other. The details are given in the following Scriptures:

    Note: The Feast Day of Trumpets *(Numbers 29:1-6)*.
    The Feast Day of Atonement *(Numbers 29:7-11)*.
    The Feast of Tabernacles *(Numbers 29:12-40)*.

The significance of these additional sacrifices which were offered besides the regular "daily sacrifice" will be considered under their respective Feast. Sufficient for the present is to mention the basic truth involved in these sacrifices.

The prominent truth that the Lord endeavoured to teach Israel was that of **blood atonement.** The approach to God can only be upon the foundation of blood, sacrificial blood. There can be no Feasting with the Lord or His people except on the basis of bloodshed, blood atonement. The principle of *Exodus 12:13* is applicable here: "And the blood shall be to you **a token** upon the houses where ye are: and when I see **the blood** I will pass over you, and the plague shall not be upon you to destroy you . . . ." And again: "For the life of the flesh is in **the blood,** and I have given it to you upon the altar to make an atonement for your souls: for it is the blood that maketh **atonement** for the soul" *(Leviticus 17:11)*.

God has nothing to say to man apart from blood atonement, apart from the blood of Jesus Christ. All of God's communications to the believer in Festival relationship is upon the foundation of the sacrificial blood of Jesus. God speaks to us through the blood of His Son, and upon this basis we can celebrate the Feasts of Jehovah. "And when Moses was gone into the Tabernacle of the Congregation to speak with Him, then he heard the voice of One speaking unto him from off the mercyseat that was upon the ark of the testimony, from between the two cherubims: and he spake unto him" *(Numbers 7:89)*.

The Blood of Jesus is the perfect and only one and once-for-all sacrifice in the New Testament times which God accepts. It fulfills and abolishes in itself all the untold millions of animal sacrifices and oblations of the Old Testament. His sacrifice is never to be repeated. Christ died once for all never to die again. His one perfect vicarious death fulfills all the multitudes of dying victims of the Old Covenant. Thus all the sacrifices and oblations of the three Feasts are all fulfilled in the **one sacrifice and oblation** of the Lord Jesus Christ at Calvary. It is upon this foundation of New Covenant blood that all believers can experience and enjoy the Feasts of the Lord *(Matthew 26:26-28; Hebrews 9:10-28; 12:24; Colossians 1:20; I John 1:7; 5:6-8; Revelation 12:11)*.

It is for this reason that one can never expect a literal fulfilment of the Feast of Tabernacles in a rebuilt temple and a reinstated Mosaic economy with animal sacrifices and oblations. The **body** and **blood** of Jesus, the God-Man, forever abolishes animal body and animal blood. God will never return to that which, though He ordained and commanded, was never ever pleased with. When He saw His only begotten Son declared as "the Lamb of God which taketh away the sin of the world", then He declared from heaven" This is My beloved Son, in whom I am well pleased" *(John 1:29, 36; Matthew 3:15-17)*.

E. The Sabbath Days and Feast Days

It is worthy to note that the Lord, in giving the outline of the Feasts does so in connection with the Sabbath days. The instructions concerning the Feasts are introduced with Sabbath day instruction. *Leviticus 23* clearly shows this relationship between the Sabbath days and the Feast days, with certain differences, which we define here.

1. **The Sabbath Days** — *Leviticus 23:3, 11, 15, 16, 38.*

    The Israelites worked six days but the seventh day was the Sabbath of rest. No work was to be done on this day. They were to rest in their dwellings. The Sabbath days were holy convocations, or holy assemblies. Here the people were summoned to gather and worship the Lord when near His sanctuary. The Sabbath was given as the sign and seal of the Mosaic Covenant *(Exodus 31:12-18)*. It was given to a people in covenant relationship with the Lord for a perpetual covenant. It was the queen of all Sabbaths and for any person to work on this day meant being put to death. The man who gathered sticks on a Sabbath day was stoned to death and it illustrates the absolute sacredness of the covenant Sabbath *(Numbers 15:32-41)*.

2. **The Feast Days** — *Leviticus 23:1-2, 4*

    The set Feasts or appointed seasons of the Lord were also known as holy convocations, or Sabbath days. No work was to be done on these days either. All were to gather together unto the Lord at His Tabernacle and keep the Divine Festivals. The Feasts days as extra Sabbaths are called "holy convocations" as seen in verses 2, 4, 7, 8, 21, 24, 27, 35, 36, 37. The Feast days as extra Sabbaths are called "Sabbaths" as seen in verses 24, 32, 32, 39, 39. The difference between the Sabbath and the Feasts days may be seen in the following.

The Sabbath Days		The Feast Days
Kept weekly	—	Kept annually
Rest in their dwellings	—	Gathering of all males
with their families		at the appointed place
Or, later, attend the Synagogue services		or Sanctuary of the Lord

3. No servile work to be done

The thing that connects the Sabbaths and Feast days is that no work was to be done on these occasions. This is especially repeated in *Leviticus 23:*

a. Vs. 3. **No work** was to be done on the weekly Sabbaths.

b. Vs. 7. **No servile work** was to be done on the first day of Unleavened Bread.

c. Vs. 8. **No servile work** was to be done on the seventh day of Unleavened Bread.

d. Vs. 21. **No servile work** was to be done on the Day of Pentecost.

e. Vs. 25. **No servile work** was to be done on the Day of Trumpets.

f. Vs. 28, 30-31. **No manner of work** was to be done on the Day of Atonement or else the person would be cut off from God's people.

g. Vs. 35. **No servile work** was to be done on the first day of the Feast of Tabernacles.

h. Vs. 36. **No servile work** was to be done on the eighth day of Tabernacles either.

At least eight times in this chapter God tells the Israelites that no work was to be done on the Sabbath or Feast-Sabbath days. This also meant that sometimes there would be two Sabbaths in the same week; that is, the weekly Sabbath and the Festival Sabbath. It is this which will help the believer to understand the events of the week of Christ's crucifixion, which will be considered under the appropriate section.

The spiritual truth which the Lord sought to teach Israel was that which pertained to **rest.** The physical day or days of rest pointed to the spiritual day or days of rest. "Servile work" spoke of the labours of man, man's efforts to provide for himself what was needed and what needed to be done for his own sustenance. Sabbath **rest** spoke of man ceasing from his own works and entering into and enjoying the work of God, as exemplified in the work of the High Priest on these particular days. For the Israelites it was **rest** first, then **feasts** followed! There could be no true Feasting without true resting!

So it is for the believer in Christ. We are called to cease from our own works, works of the flesh (*Galatians 5:19-21*), and works of the law (*Romans 3:27-28; 9:30-32*), and find rest in Jesus Christ. Jesus Himself called to those who were labouring, who were weary and heavy laden and come to Him and He would give them rest, and if they would learn of Him they also would find rest (*Matthew 11:28-30*).

Those who believe cease from their own works and enter into rest (*Hebrews 4:1-8*). Unbelief will not cease from self-effort. Faith alone enters into rest (*Hebrews 4:10-11*). The Christian can cease from his own works, believe and enter into rest because of the **finished work** of Christ (*John 17:1-3; 19:30*). He knows that he is not saved by works of righteousness which he has done but by grace through faith (*Ephesians 2:8-10*). Jesus Christ is our great High Priest and only His work of redemption brings true rest. There can be no true and complete rest until sin has been dealt with in the atonement. Thus the believer ceases from all servile work, and keeps the Feasts of the Lord. If a Christian is working, he is not resting; and if he is not resting, he is not feasting! It is first resting in Christ, and then feasting on Christ! This is the beautiful truth symbolized in the relationship between the Sabbath days and Feast days.

4. Sabbath Day Offerings — *Numbers 28:9-10*

Another thought the Lord brings to the attention of the Israelites relative to the Sabbath days as well as the Festival Sabbaths is that of the sacrificial offerings. The Sabbatical offerings were two lambs for a burnt offering, with a meal offering of two-tenths deal of flour with oil, and also its drink offering of outpoured wine. These were offered besides the daily sacrifice. It taught Israel once again that rest was only on the basis of sacrifice.

For the believer the three aspects of truth are brought together. That is, **sacrifice, rest,** and **feast.** For the church, only the perfect sacrifice of Christ makes resting and feasting possible and available.

F. Feasts of the Lord or Feasts of the Jews?

When the Lord gave the revelation of the Feasts of Moses and Israel they were originally the Feasts of the Lord. "Concerning **the Feasts of the Lord** . . . even these are **My** Feasts" (*Leviticus 23:2*). "These are **the Feasts of the Lord** . . . " (*Leviticus 23:4, 44*).

The children of Israel were told to "keep it a **Feast unto the Lord**" (*Leviticus 23:39, 41; Deuteronomy 16:15*). As long as Israel served the Lord as a redeemed and holy people and kept His laws and ordinances they were certainly the Feasts of the Lord — **His Feasts.**

But the time came, when, because of backsliding and apostacy, the prophets lamented the fact that the Feasts were no longer the Feasts of Jehovah. True, the Israelites kept the external form of the Feasts but they missed the internal reality of them. They therefore became but hypocritical observances and empty ritualism; performances of a profane people. While keeping the Letter of the Feasts they missed the Spirit of the Feasts. The Prophet Isaiah cried: "... the new moons and Sabbaths, the calling of assemblies, I cannot away with; it is iniquity, even the solemn meeting. **Your new moons** and **your appointed Feasts** My soul hateth: they are a trouble unto Me; I am weary to bear them *(Isaiah 1:13-14* with verses *10-16* and *Lamentations 2:6).*

The very things that God ordained, commanded and blessed now become an abomination to Him once His people lapse into external and hypocritical observances of them *(Matthew 23).* The Gospel of John alludes to the same degeneration which was evident in Messiah's times. He spoke also of the Feasts as having become "a Feast of the Jews" — **not** "the Feast of the Lord" as it once had been, and should have been *(John 5:1, 16-18; 7:2).*

The times of Christ prove most fully the point. While the Jews were keeping the Letter of the Law, going through the external, the formal, the ritual, they missed the Spirit of the Law, the internal, spiritual, and eternal. It is ironical that John records the fact that, while the religious leaders were crying for the unjust crucifixion of Jesus, they would not go into "the judgment hall, lest they be defiled; but that they might eat the passover" *(John 18:28).*

Thus Jewry kept the external Passover and missed the true Passover, Christ Himself. They kept the external Pentecost, and missed the true Pentecost in the upper room where Christ's disciples were. They carried on the empty ritualism of the Day of Atonement before a veil which God Himself had rent, and missed entering within the veil through Christ Jesus!

The practical lesson that all should learn from this is that it is not the external, the formal or the ritual observances of the Feasts that God accepts. It is the internal, the spiritual and the reality of such that alone pleases God. The believer is to serve God and experience the Feasts in "newness of spirit" and not in "oldness of the letter" *(Romans 7:6).* It is the Spirit which quickens, makes alive. The letter kills. The flesh profits nothing *(II Corinthians 3:6; John 6:63).*

Chapter Seven
THE FEAST OF PASSOVER

As seen in the outline of the Feasts, Passover had three particular parts to it:

1. The Feast of Passover
2. The Feast of Unleavened Bread
3. The Feast Day of the Sheaf of Firstfruits.

In this chapter we will deal in detail with the first part, the Passover itself. The scriptures in the Old Testament where this Feast is dealt with are *Exodus 12:1-14, 21-29; Leviticus 23:4-5; Numbers 33:3; Deuteronomy 16:1-8.* The scriptures in the New Testament where this Feast finds fulfilment are *Matthew 26:1-2, 17-75; 27:1-66; Mark 14-15; Luke 22-23; John 18-19; Hebrews 11:28.*

The Gospel writers record for us the details of the crucifixion of Jesus, therefore the chapters mentioned above should be read by the student as he approaches this particular Feast. It is there we see the antitypical fulfilment of the historical and typical Passover in the nation of Israel. History and prophecy parallel each other; type and antitype remarkably correspond together. The antitype is always greater than the type, even as the substance is greater than the shadow. The Apostle Paul, in one summarized and interpretative verse says: "For even Christ our Passover is sacrificed for us." *I Corinthians 5:7.*

I. THE STORY IN BRIEF:

When the time came for the deliverance of the nation of Israel out of Egypt, "the house of bondage" *(Exodus 13:3, 14; Joshua 24:17)*, God gave Moses specific instructions concerning the means of deliverance. It was in the message of the Passover lamb that Moses actually preached the Gospel to the Israelites, and all could either accept or reject the Gospel message.

The heads of each household were to take a lamb of the first year on the tenth day of the first month and set it aside until the fourteenth day. In the evening of the fourteenth day the lamb was to be killed, and its blood sprinkled on the lintel and two side posts of the household door. The household itself was to feast upon the body of the lamb roasted with fire, with bitter herbs and unleavened bread. They were to eat it in haste, and be dressed ready to leave Egypt at the midnight hour.

At midnight the death angel would pass through the land and every house that did not have the token of blood on the door and lintel would suffer judgment. This judgment was the death of the firstborn, of both man and beast. The Lord said "When I see the blood, I will **pass over** you and the plague shall not be upon you to destroy you, when I smite the land of Egypt" *(Exodus 12:12)*. Thus the Feast of **Passover** originated in the "passing over" of the angel of death over the blood sprinkled doors of the Israelites or any of the Egyptians who cared to believe the Gospel word.

The very title (Hebrew **"Pesach"**) translated "Passover" means "a passing over", or "to pass or hover over". It was the Passover Festival. The Greek title (Greek **"Pascha"**) is derived from the Hebrew title also *(Exodus 12:27; Hebrews 11:28)*. A double thought is involved in this word. There is the thought of the "passing over" in judgment of the death angel, but also the thought of "hovering over" in Divine protection. Thus judgment and mercy are linked in this Passover Feast according to the faith and obedience or the unbelief and disobedience of the persons in each household, be they Israelites or Egyptians. All were forbidden to go outside the door of the house until the Lord brought them forth in the hour of deliverance.

The Lord also told them that they were to celebrate this Feast yearly and explain to their children what the whole service meant in its original setting.

In order for us as New Testament believers to understand the significance of the **Feast of Passover**, we set out the details in outline form, considering them first in the historical and the type, and then in fulfilment in the antitype and reality, as in Christ and the church.

A. Passover, The Beginning of Months — *Exodus 12:2*

The Feast of Passover was the **beginning** of months for Israel. It became the first month of the sacred year to the nation. Here God changed the calendar for them. The past or previous six months were forgotten as God introduced the new calendar for them, in a new beginning. This Feast was therefore the **foundation** of their experience in God. The very fact that it took place in the first month, the beginning of months, showed that God had more in mind for them in the months that lay ahead. This is seen in the subsequent Feasts.

Thus:

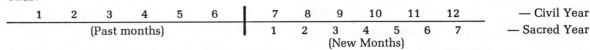

1	2	3	4	5	6		7	8	9	10	11	12		— Civil Year
		(Past months)					1	2	3	4	5	6	7	— Sacred Year
									(New Months)					

So for the believer in Christ. Receiving Christ as the Lamb of God is but the beginning of one's experience in God. It is the first, the foundation experience. There is more to follow. New birth is the beginning of New Covenant relationship *(John 3:5; II Corinthians 5:17)*. No believer should stop at this Feast, but move on to the others also.

B. The Four Days of the Hidden Lamb — *Exodus 12:3-6*

God commanded Israel to take a lamb on the tenth day and set it aside until the fourteenth day of the first month. That is to say, the lamb was taken and kept aside for death for four days. It was ordained to die in due time. One wonders if the children of Israel ever understood the significance of the lamb being kept aside for four days, from the tenth until the fourteenth day. However, as the believer sees God's plan of redemption we can see what God had in mind by the antitypical fulfilment. This may be considered in two ways; that is, weekly and dispensationally.

1. Weekly

In the events of the week of crucifixion, Jesus entered Jerusalem on the tenth day and was slain on the fourteenth day, four days later *(Luke 19:37; Matthew 22:15-24)*.

2. Dispensationally

The Scripture shows that "a day unto the Lord is as a thousand years and a thousand years as one day" *(Psalm 90:4; Genesis 2:17; II Peter 3:8)*. When Adam sinned, God set His lamb, Jesus Christ, aside for death. Jesus Christ was foreordained to die. From Adam to Christ we have four days of the Lord, or four thousand years: that is, four days in the Lord's time. The scripture speaks of the Lamb of God being set aside to die for man.

"Forasmuch as ye know that ye are not redeemed with corruptible things . . . But with the precious blood of Christ, as of a lamb without blemish and without spot: Who verily was **foreordained before** the foundation of the world, but was **manifest in these last times** for you" *(I Peter 1:18-20)*. "And all that dwell upon the earth shall worship him (the Beast), whose names are not written in the book of life of the Lamb slain **from** the foundation of the world" *(Revelation 13:8; 17:8)*. "Behold the Lamb of God which taketh away the sin of the world" *(John 1:29, 36)*. Read also *Ephesians 1:3-5, 9-12; 3:10-11*.

C. A Lamb of the First Year — *Exodus 12:5; 11:4-7; 12:29-30*

This signified that it was a firstborn lamb. The firstborn were especially to be set aside and given to God. The Lord gave specific instructions concerning the firstborn of man and best *(Exodus 13:11-13)*.

The theme of the "Firstborn" runs throughout the whole of scripture. Cain is set aside for Abel; Ishmael is set aside for Isaac; Esau is set aside for Jacob; and here Egypt is set aside for Israel. God said that Israel was His firstborn *(Exodus 4:22-23)*.

This setting aside of the firstborn after the flesh (after that which is natural,) and the bringing in of God's firstborn (after that which is spiritual,) points to the distinctions in the first or natural birth, and the second or spiritual birth. The first birth constitutes us as sinners; the second birth constitutes us as saints.

This setting aside pointed back to the fact that it was the First Adam who brought in sin and death, placing mankind in the house of bondage to Satan. It also pointed forward to the fact that Jesus Christ, the Lamb of God would be His Firstborn Son. Jesus was the Firstborn of Mary, the Firstborn of God's new creation *(Matthew 1:21-25; Revelation 3:14; Colossians 1:15, 18; Romans 8:29)*.

D. A Male — *Exodus 12:5.*

The lamb must be a male; not, in this case, as sometimes in other sacrifices, a female. The scriptures declare "By **one man** sin entered the world and death by sin, and so death passed upon all men" *(Romans 5:12)*. Adam, as the first male, sinned, and so a male must die for sin. Adam, as the male, was the seed-bearer of the whole unborn human race. In him is constituted Federal Headship. When he sinned and fell, all the race as yet in his loins sinned and fell. We did what Adam did, for we were "in Adam" (*I Corinthians 15:22; Romans 5:12-21*).

E. Without Spot or Blemish — *Exodus 12:5*

The Israelites were to inspect the lamb that was to die for them, and see that it came up to God's standard: that it was perfect, and without spot or blemish (*I Peter 1:18-20*).

In wonderful fulfilment we see how all who inspected Jesus Christ—God's Lamb—found Him to be perfect, without fault, without spot or blemish. It speaks of the perfection of Christ, the sinlessness of the Lamb of God. We note some of those who inspected God's Lamb.

1. Pilate — *John 18:28, 38; 19:4-6; Matthew 27:1-25.*
2. Herod — *Luke 23:8-12.*
3. Annas — *Luke 3:2; John 18:13, 24.*
4. Caiaphas — *John 11:49-53; 18:13-14, 19-24, 28.*
5. Judas — *Matthew 27:3-10.*
6. The Centurion — *Matthew 27:54.*
7. The repentant thief — *Luke 23:39-43*

All have to confess there is no fault, spot or blemish in Him. Before these men, Jesus was the lamb of God, slaughtered before His shearers (*Isaiah 53:7; Acts 8:32-33; Psalm 38:11-15; 39:1-2; Matthew 26:62-63; 27:12-14*).

F. A Lamb for an House — *Exodus 12:3-5*

God's intention was that all come to experience "household salvation". It was "a lamb for an house". Those who would know the saving benefits of the Passover lamb could do so by being in and of the household of faith. God promises, on His terms, that salvation for a household is also available to New Testament believers in the Lamb of God. Read *Genesis 7:1; Joshua 24:15; Genesis 18:19; John 4:46-54; Acts 16:15, 31; 18:3, 8; Luke 19:5-10.*

Note also the progressive revelation of "the lamb" in Scripture.

1. A lamb for an house — *Exodus 12:3-4.*
2. A lamb for a nation — *Exodus 29:38-42.*
3. A Lamb for the world — *John 1:29, 36; Revelation 5:12.*

Isaac asked his father "Where is the lamb?" and John the Baptist answers his question saying "Behold **the Lamb** of God which taketh away the sin of the world" (*John 1:29, 36 with Genesis 22:8*).

G. Kill it in the Evening — *Exodus 12:6* Literally "Between the two evenings".

The lamb must be killed in the evening of the fourteenth day. It was not the spotless life of the lamb that brought deliverance, but its death.

The perfect, sinless and spotless and blemishless life of the Lamb of God — Jesus — only condemns the sinner. It is His substitutionary **death** that brings salvation. It is first His saving death, then His saving life (*Romans 5:8-10*).

Jesus was slain "between the two evenings" in the week of the crucifixion. He was slain the fourteenth day at evening, as well as on the fourth Day of the Lord (*Mark 15:33*). The hours of crucifixion, 9 a.m. - 3 p.m. were the hours which fulfilled "between the two evenings".

H. The Whole Assembly shall Kill it — *Exodus 12:6*

The whole congregation of Israel was involved in the death of the Passover lamb. The Gospels show how the Sanhedrin, the Priests, and the people of Israel all clamoured for the crucifixion of Jesus and for His blood to be shed (*John 19:15; Luke 23:23; Mark 15:33; Matthew 27:4, 25*).

I. The Blood must be Applied to the Lintel and Door Posts — *Exodus 12:7, 13, 22*

The blood was the evidence that death had taken place. Then the blood had to be sprinkled on the lintel and the two side posts of the door. What was done with the blood was very important to the Lord.

1. The blood must be shed. This was the evidence of death.
2. The blood must be sprinkled. This was the evidence of application.

3. The blood must be applied in a triune manner; on the lintel, and on the two side posts. It svmbolized that the triune God was involved in man's triune salvation (*Acts 20:28; Hebrews 9:14; I Thessalonians 5:23*). Salvation is through a triune Name — the Lord Jesus Christ.

4. The blood was to be the token on the door of every house in order for deliverance to be effective. The absence of blood brought judgment by the death angel.

5. The blood must be applied with hyssop. Hyssop comes from a lowly shrub. It speaks of the humility and lowliness of faith, which applies the blood of Jesus (*Ephesians 2:8; Hebrews 11:28*).

6. The blood must be applied in faith and obedience to the Word of the Lord through the Gospel given to Moses.

In fulfilment, we see that when Jesus died on the Cross, He was both the Lamb and the blood-sprinkled door. In His death He is the Lamb, but in His resurrection He is the **door** — the only entrance ot the Household of God, the Household of faith (*John 10:9*).

His blood must be lifted up, exalted, for the triune God was involved in the work of redemption (*Acts 20:28; Matthew 26:26-28; Hebrews 9:14*).

It is by faith that the sinner accepts the sprinkled blood of Jesus as the token of his deliverance. The blood must not be trodden under foot (*Colossians 1:13-14; Hebrews 9:22; 11:28; 10:29*).

J. The Body of the Lamb must be Eaten — *Exodus 12:8-10*

The Lord God was also particular about the body of the lamb, even as of the blood. Both the body and blood pointed to the body and blood of Jesus, the Lamb of God (*Matthew 26:26-28*).

1. It was to be eaten in the one and the same night.

2. It was to be eaten with unleavened bread. No sin was in Jesus.

3. It was to be eaten with bitter herbs. Calvary was a bitter experience. Sin is a bitter bondage to Satan also.

4. It was not to be eaten raw. It was to be roast with fire. So Jesus must experience the sufferings of the fire of God's holiness at Calvary. Not His perfect life, but His sacrificial death saves.

5. It was not to be sodden with water. So the Gospel of Jesus is not to be "watered down". Water-sodden meat cannot be roasted.

6. Any thing remaining over was to be burnt after the Feast. No Egyptian must touch the body of the saving lamb.

The antitypical fulfilment is seen in the fact that Jesus Christ, our Passover Lamb, suffered and died in the same night. He experienced the burning fires of Calvary (*Hebrews 12:29*). He was without sin, un-leavened by any taint of evil. He also experienced the bitter sufferings of the cross. Therefore the Gospel is not to be presented as if Christ was merely a martyr, or watered down in any manner. It must be exactly as it took place in the sight of God and man (*I Corinthians 5:7-8; 11:23-30; John 6:53-55; 19:29*). The Israelite must feed on the virtues of the lamb. The head, the legs and the purtenence were to be fed upon. So the believer feeds on Christ's mind (the head), the walk of Christ (the legs) and the inward motives and affections of Christ (the inward parts).

K. How the Lamb was to be Eaten — *Exodus 12:11*

The Passover lamb was not to be eaten in any casual manner or slovenly manner. It was to be eaten in haste, ready for departure from the House of Bondage.

1. Loins were to be girded—*Ephesians 6:14; Luke 12:3-5; I Peter 1:13; Jeremiah 1:17*.

2. Shoes must be on their feet — *Ephesians 6:15; Isaiah 52:7*.

3. Staff must be in their hand — *Hebrews 11:13*.

4. The lamb must be eaten in haste — *Hebrews 11:13; Exodus 12:11*.

Thus all was to be done as ready for departure, in a state of readiness.

So the believer has his loins girt about with truth, his feet shod with the preparation of the Gospel of peace, and the sword of the Spirit in his hand, as he partakes of Christ (*Ephesians 6:13-17*).

Eating the lamb, the bitter herbs and the unleavened bread in haste made sure that their dough had no time to leaven. There is no time for the believer to play around in the Egypt of this world. The believer is a pilgrim and stranger en route for the heavenly country and heavenly City of God (*Hebrews 11:10-16; 13:14; I Peter 1:13; 2:11*).

L. **The Lord's Passover** — *Exodus 12:11-13, 23*

The Lord told Israel that He would pass through the land of Egypt and smite all the houses with death if there was no blood seen. He would "pass over" the houses of both Israelites and Egyptians if blood was sprinkled. Hence the title "Passover" for this Feast.

There is the double truth implicit in this title. The "pass-over" for the one meant death and judgment on the firstborn. The "pass-over" for the obedient meant divine protection and life. The destroying angel would not touch any house where the blood was. The covering blood was the token of faith and obedience.

The believer in Christ also passes over from death to life through faith in Christ's sacrificial blood *(Romans 3:24-25; I John 3:14)*. Not any plague will come our dwelling as faith in the blood is exercised *(Psalm 91:1-10)*.

M. **A Memorial** — *Exodus 12:14*

The Passover was to be a memorial and ordinance for ever in all their generations. It was to be kept as a Feast unto the Lord. It was a memorial of redemption and deliverance from Egypt's life of sin and bondage.

Jesus instituted the ordinance of the Lord's Supper to replace the Passover Supper. The Table of the Lord is a memorial Feast for He asks us to "do this in remembrance of Me" *(Matthew 26:26-28)*.

N. **The Midnight Hour** — *Exodus 11:4-6; 12:29-30*

The Feast was to be held just before the midnight hour, for at that time, the death-angel would go through Egypt and smite the firstborn of man and beast if no blood was evident.

The "Midnight Hour" is always significant of the end of the age. It is the darkest hour before the dawn of a new day. At midnight there would be a great cry made as the death-angel struck in every house which had rejected the Passover Lamb.

Note in these Scriptures what happened at the "Midnight Hour" and see how God works in connection with such *(Matthew 25:6; Job 34:20; Judges 16:3; Mark 13:35; Luke 11:5; Exodus 11:4-6)*. All point to the end of age.

O. **At the Going down of the Sun** — *Deuteronomy 16:2, 6*

When the Lord gave further instructions concerning the Passover Feast He stressed that it was to be at the going down of the sun.

The Prophet Amos foretold a day when God would cause the sun to go down at noon, and thus turn their Feasts into mourning *(Amos 8:9-10)*. How remarkably both these Scriptures were fulfilled is evidenced at the crucifixion. When Jesus died on the cross, the sun was darkened at midday for three hours; thus from noon to the evening. This turned the Jews' Feast of Passover into mourning for "the only Son" *(Mark 14:33-34; Matthew 27:45-46)*. The sun, the natural light of the world, was darkened in connection with the **Son,** the spiritual light of the world.

P. **Where His Name was Recorded** — *Deuteronomy 16:2, 6; 12:5-14, 18, 21.*

The Passover was also to be kept in the place where God would place His Name. This place was the Tabernacle of the Lord once they came into the land of promise. It was later on at the Temple of the Lord in the city of Jerusalem. Here God recorded His Name.

Thus the true Passover was kept just outside the city of Jerusalem in the full view of the Temple of God where He had recorded His Name. It was in this Temple that God rent the veil in connection with the death of **His Lamb** *(I Kings 8:12-30; Matthew 27:50-51)*.

Q. **Not a Bone was to be Broken** — *Exodus 12:46; Psalm 34:20*

In the eating of the Passover lamb, God commanded that no bones were to be broken. Undoubtedly the full significance of this was not understood until the death of Jesus Christ. The soldiers brake the legs of the two thieves in order to hasten their deaths., But when they were about ot break the legs of Jesus they found that He was already dead, for He had surrendered His spirit to the Father in death. He was not a disobedient sheep needing His legs to be broken, as were the two thieves.

Thus God watched His Word to fulfil it, both type and prophecy, as in the Law and the Psalms. Men unwittingly fulfilled the same *(Acts 13:27; John 19:33-37)*. Type and prophecy came together in remarkable fulfilment.

R. Unleavened Bread to be Eaten Seven Days — *Exodus 12:15-20, 34, 39*

The full significance of this is dealt with fully under the next part of this Feast. For the present it should be noted that all leaven was to be put away. No leaven was to be found in their habitations or else that person in whose possession it was found, be the Israelite or stranger, would be cut off from the congregation of the Lord. For seven days they were to be feeding upon unleavened bread, beginning the night of the Passover. The putting away of leaven for seven days speaks of complete separation from all sin, and all evil or leavening influences that work as such in a believer's life. No leaven was to be seen in the household of faith.

Refer to comments on the Feast of Unleavened Bread.

S. Safety in the House inside the Door — *Exodus 12:22-24*

One of the strong commandments of the Lord was that which pertained to the security of the Israelite or stranger.

None were to go outside the door of the house until God commanded it. Thus safety and security were conditional upon obedience, by staying inside the blood-sprinkled door and the household of faith, feeding on the lamb. If any Israelite dared to presume and leave the house, stepping outside that blood-sprinkled door, there was no guarantee of safety. He would undoubtedly have been met by the death-angel in the land.

Thus the believer's security is to stay inside the blood-sprinkled door (Christ, *John 10:9*), and in the church (which is His house, *I Timothy 3:15; Ephesians 2:18-22; Hebrews 3:1-5*). Any disobedience borders on the great sin of presumption, and treading under the blood of the covenant *(Hebrews 10:26-29)*. All must stay under the "covering blood".

T. Explanation of the Service — *Exodus 12:25-28*

The Lord commanded Israel to keep this service forever and especially when they came into the land of Canaan. When the children would ask in time "What mean ye by this service?" they were to explain its origin and purpose in keeping it.

So it is the responsibility of leadership to explain the New Testament fulfilment of the Old Testament Passover, both as to the work of Christ on the Cross, as well as in the Lord's Table where this service or Feast is commemorated *(I Corinthians 5:6-8; 11:23-34; Matthew 26:26-28)*.

U. Redemption makes Division and Difference — *Exodus 11:7; 8:23.*

In the process of delivering Israel from the house of bondage, the Lord said that He would put "a difference" between the Israelites and the Egyptians. This difference is also called "a division" and "a redemption", as noted in marginal readings.

So it is that redemption makes the difference between the believer and the unbeliever, creating the division in the human race into just two classes *(Romans 3:22; 10:12)*.

V. Spoiling the Egyptians at the Exodus — *Exodus 12:31-36, 40-42*

With the death of the firstborn of man and beast, Pharaoh called for Moses and Aaron and told them to get quickly out of Egypt. In their haste to get rid of the Israelites, they were spoiled. The Israelites took from the Egyptians jewels of gold and silver, and raiment, and anything else they required, "And they spoiled the Egyptians."

This was in fulfilment of the prophetic word given to Abraham over 400 years before *(Genesis 15:13-21)*. It was also Israel's "pay day" for many years of work and slavery. In due time the Israelites would give of this spoil, this substance, to the Lord for the building of the Tabernacle of the Lord *(Exodus 25:1-9)*.

So it is that Christ spoiled principalities and powers in His triumph on the cross, and at His "exodus", and the believing church partakes of these spoils won through His death *(Colossians 2:10; Isaiah 53:12; Judges 5:12; Psalm 68:18; Ephesians 4:8-10)*.

W. Must be Circumcised to Eat the Passover — *Exodus 12:43-51*

The Lord laid down certain prerequisites for all who ate the Passover lamb.

1. A stranger was not to eat of it.

2. A foreigner was not to eat of it.

3. A hired servant was not to eat of it.

4. An uncircumcised person was not to eat of it.

Be they Israelite or foreigner, all must therefore experience the rite of circumcision to partake of the Passover. Circumcision was the sign and seal of the Abrahamic Covenant (*Acts 7:8; Genesis 17*). If a person was not circumcised, he was not in Covenant relationship with the Lord, and therefore not entitled to the promises, privileges and blessings of the Abrahamic Covenant.

The New Testament shows that the person who is in New Covenant relationship with Christ is qualified then to partake of the Lord's Supper. The true circumcision is that of the heart, in the spirit; and not of the flesh or after the letter (*Matthew 26:26-28; Romans 2:24-29; Galatians 6:15; Romans 4:11-12; Colossians 2:11-13*).

"In Christ" we are no longer strangers and foreigners but fellow-citizens of the household of faith and of the commonwealth of Israel (*Ephesians 2:12-19*).

X. A Holy Convocation — *Exodus 12:16*

The Passover, like the Feast of Unleavened Bread and all other Feast days, was a holy convocation, or an extra Sabbath. No manner of work was to be done. All were to rest in the finished work of the lamb.

The believer finds true rest and spiritual Sabbath in ceasing from his own works and resting in the finished work of Jesus Christ, God's Lamb (*Matthew 11:28-30; Ephesians 2:8-9; John 17:1-4; 19:30*).

Y. The Exodus on Eagle's Wings — *Exodus 12:40-42; 19:1-6*

Israel as a nation had been preserved through the various plagues which fell on Egypt. Now, at the midnight hour, they experienced the great exodus. Exodus means "going out". This going out was into the wilderness. The Lord reminded them at Mt. Sinai that this delivering power from Egypt was the power of "eagle's wings". There He brought them unto Himself in the wilderness.

All of this rich symbolism finds its ultimate fulfilment in the church of the "last days" when it is taken out into "the wilderness" on the power of the "wings of a great eagle". This wilderness is a place of preservation, a place prepared by God. The church in the end times shall know the preserving power of God in the midst of great plagues of wrath on a godless world (*Acts 7:38; Revelation 12:6, 14*). The Lord likens Himself to a great eagle caring for its own (*Deuteronomy 32:11; Luke 17:32-37; Isaiah 40:31; Psalm 103:1-4*).

Z. Healing Power in the Lamb — *II Chronicles 30:13-20; Psalm 105:37.*

As the children of Israel feasted on the body of the slain and roasted Passover lamb, it seems as if there was a great manifestation of the healing power of the Lord. The Psalmist tells us that there was not one feeble person among them when He brought them forth.

It is wonderful to note also that when Hezekiah restored the Feast of Passover back to the nation (having it in the second month, as permitted by the Law on special occasions), that the Lord healed the people.

If healing took place under the typical lamb, how much more shall the people of the Lord find healing in the true Lamb, the Lord Jesus Christ, as they feast upon Him (*Exodus 15:26; III John 2; Isaiah 53*). Read also *Mark 16:15-20.*

AA. The Song of Moses and the Lamb — *Exodus 15:1-19; Revelation 15:1-4.*

There is no recorded song in scripture until we come to the "Song of Moses" after the deliverance from Egypt by the power of the Passover lamb. It is the first song recorded in the Word for us. Surely there is significance in this.

Similarly none can sing the song of the redeemed until redeemed by the Lamb of God from Satan's bondage (*Revelation 5:9-10*). The saints who come out of great tribulation and stand on the Sea of Glass sing the song of Moses and the lamb. The New Testament believers sing the song of Jesus who is the Lamb (*John 1:29, 36*).

BB. The Church of the Firstborn — *Exodus 4:22-23; Hebrews 12:22-24*

The nation of Israel is spoken of as the "church in the wilderness" (*Acts 7:38*). It is also referred to as God's son, His firstborn. As seen earlier, the emphasis that God placed on the "firstborn" is important. The firstborn lamb must die. Those who rejected the firstborn lamb had their firstborn slain. All Israelites and all Egyptians must face the truth of the firstborn.

Thus the fulfilment is seen in the following:

1. Jesus Christ is God's firstborn lamb, the firstborn of Mary.

2. He is the firstborn from death, the firstborn of the dead, and the firstborn of all new creatures.

3. The first Adam sinned and brought all his unborn race under death.

4. God sets aside the firstborn after the fleshly birth, and brings in His firstborn after the new and second and heavenly birth.

5. God sets aside Egypt as the first of the nations, and brings in Israel as His firstborn, the firstborn church.

Thus the writer to the Hebrews speaks of "the church of the firstborn" who have come to the blood of Jesus, which speaks better things than that of Abel's. One only becomes a member of the church of the firstborn by accepting Jesus Christ, God's firstborn Lamb, and by the new and spiritual birth.

Thus, the details of this glorious Feast find wonderful fulfilment in Christ who is our Passover Lamb, sacrified for us (I Corinthians 5:6-8). The historical and actual Feast for Israel becomes typical, and the typical is prophetical. As the substance is always greater than the shadow, and the antitype greater than the type, so Christ our Passover Lamb supercedes and transcends all Old Testament Passover lambs.

II. FOR THE STUDENT:

In concluding our study on this Feast, we note that there are eight major references to the Passover in Scripture, the eighth being the true Passover, even Christ Himself. We list these out for the Student to enlarge upon for himself:

A. The original Passover, instituted at the Exodus of Israel as a nation from Egypt under Moses at the beginning of the journey to Canaan land (Exodus 12).

B. The second Passover, after they were come out of Egypt in the setting up of the Tabernacle of the Lord (Numbers 9:1-5)

C. The Passover at the end of the wilderness journey, under Joshua and the new generation, as they enter the promised land (Joshua 5:10-11).

D. The Passover in the second month, held under godly King Hezekiah (II Chronicles 30 with Numbers 9:6-14).

E. The great Passover, kept under godly King Josiah (II Kings 23:21-23; II Chronicles 35:18-19).

F. The Passover restored and kept under Ezra, after the close of the 70 years Babylonian captivity (Ezra 6:19).

G. The Passover seen in the vision of Ezekiel's Temple (Ezekiel 45:21).

H. The true Passover Lamb, the Lord Jesus Christ Himself, fulfilling in Himself all the glorious details of the Old Testament type (Matthew 26-27; Mark 14-15; Luke 22-23; John 18-19; "Christ our Passover is sacrificed for us." I Corinthians 5:6-8:

Jesus established the Lord's Supper at the time of the Passover Supper, when He Himself was about to be slain as the true Lamb of God. Thus He closed off the old ceremony of the body and blood of the lamb and established the new with the bread and wine of His communion table. The great tragedy was that the Jews carried on the old Passover, and missed the true Passover in Christ (Acts 12:4. Note here that "Easter" should be translated by its Greek word as "Passover" — **not** "Easter").

Chapter Eight
THE FEAST OF UNLEAVENED BREAD

The next part of the Feast of Passover, and the main burden of it, is called the Feast of Unleavened Bread. This in fact became the most common name for the Feast of Passover. Undoubtedly this was because of the duration of the Feast which was to last for seven days *(Exodus 23:14-15)*.

The main portions of scripture dealing with the details of this Feast are found in *Exodus 12:8, 15-20, 31-39; 13:3-10; Deuteronomy 16:1-8; Numbers 28:17-25; Leviticus 23:6-8.*

The New Testament references which should be read in connection with the Old Testament references are to be found in *Matthew 26:17-19; Mark 14:12-21; Luke 22:1-2; I Corinthians 5:6-8.*

Paul's interpretative verse summarizes the truth for us when he wrote: "Therefore let us keep the Feast, not with old leaven, neither with the leaven of malice and wickedness; but with the unleavened bread of sincerity and truth." *(I Corinthians 5:8)*.

I. THE STORY IN BRIEF:

With the coming of the Passover Festival, the head of the house must cleanse his house of all leaven. For seven days no leaven was to be seen in his dwelling. All in the house must eat of unleavened bread from the first day until the seventh day. Anyone found with leavened food in the house would be cut off from the congregation of Israel. This ordinance was to be kept each year in all households. It seems that the full significance of this Feast was never fully understood in Israel as a nation. However, a consideration of the Old Testament historical and typical Feast with New Testament Scriptures, as well as Old Testament Scriptures, gives us the understanding and interpretation of this Feast.

A. The Feast of Unleavened Bread — Exodus 23:14-15; 34:18

The title for this Feast is the Feast of Unleavened Bread. It was an integral part of the Passover Feast, so much so, that the titles were used interchangeably or almost synonymously.

B. Kept for Seven Days — Exodus 12:15-19

The Feast began on the evening of the fourteenth day of the first month and lasted until the twenty-first day of the same month. In *Leviticus 23:6* it states that the Feast began on the fifteenth day of the first month. The apparent discrepancy is understood when we realize that the Hebrew day was from "even to even". Thus the evening of the fourteenth day would be the beginning of the fifteenth day as far as Hebrew time was concerned, for Hebrew time was from sunset to sunset or from 6 p.m. to 6 p.m. *(Numbers 28:17)*.

The number **seven** is significant of fulness and completion. The number seven is used several hundreds of times in Scripture. The first use is at the close of the days of creation, for on the seventh day all work was completed, and thus God rested and sanctified the seventh day. The believer who keeps this Feast keeps it fully unto the Lord, and sets himself aside completely to Him. The seven-days-Feast speaks of complete separation from all things that are leavened to feed upon Christ who is the believer's bread.

C. A Sabbath Day — Exodus 12:16; Leviticus 23:7; Numbers 28:18.

As every Feast day was a Sabbath, so was the Feast of Unleavened Bread. It was a holy convocation, a Sabbath or an High day. This meant that in the Passover month or week that there was an extra Sabbath besides the weekly Sabbath. It is this which explains the Sabbath or High day besides the weekly Sabbath in the week of Christ's crucifixion *(John 19:31)*.

The Sabbath was a day when no manner of work was to be done. It was a day of rest, a cessation from work, and so the believer ceases from his own works and enters into spiritual rest in Christ as he keeps the Feast *(Hebrews 4:3, 9-10)*.

D. Importance and Significance of Unleavened Bread in Israel

The importance and significance of unleavened bread in Israel may be seen in the various occasions when the Lord commanded it to be used. The spiritual truth becomes more evident as these Scriptures are considered.

1. Unleavened Bread was used in the **consecration** of the Priests to their office and ministry *(Leviticus 8:2, 26; Exodus 29:2, 23)*.

2. Unleavened bread was also used in the **vow of separation** of the Nazarite unto the Lord *(Numbers 6:1-12)*.

3. Unleavened Bread was also used in the **food** of the Priests, especially in the Meal offering, as well as the Peace offering *(Leviticus 2:4-5; 6:14-18; 7:11-13)*.

4. Unleavened Bread was used in all the **Feasts** of the Lord, except that in Pentecost leavened bread was offered *(Exodus 34:18; Leviticus 23:5-8)*.

5. Unleavened Bread was used when the Angel of the Lord appeared to Gideon in his **call to service** *(Judges 6:11-24)*.

6. Unleavened Bread was to be used in the Passover Feast as Israel was about to be **separated** from Egypt's life of slavery and bondage *(Exodus 12:17, 31-34)*.

Thus the symbolical truths in unleavened bread are **"consecration"** and **"separation"** unto the Lord. These speak of the doctrine of sanctification where the believer is separated from all that would corrupt, and consecrated unto the service of the Lord.

E. All Leaven to be Put Away — *Exodus 12:15, 19, 20*

Every house must put away all leaven. It was a time of great cleansing, of separation from leavening influences.

We consider the symbol of leaven as to the natural and the spiritual significance. (Read also *Exodus 23:18; 34:25; Leviticus 2:11; 6:17; 10:12*).

1. Leaven Naturally —

Leaven (or yeast) is a little bit of sour dough, and when placed in a batch of dough has the action of fermentation. Leaven puffs up. It works silently, secretly and gradually, until the whole is leavened. All the dough is affected by its mysterious operation and fermentation. It causes the dough to rise. Its influence permeates the whole until all is leavened, until all becomes like itself.

Thus "a little leaven leaventh the whole lump." The "principle of leaven" is used politically and religiously in various forms of propaganda in all nations, permeating and influencing societies, cultures and concepts either for good or evil.

2. Leaven Spiritually—

Almost without exception leaven in scripture is used to symbolize that which is evil, either in doctrine or practice. Both Old and New Testaments set this forth. The Old Testament use of leaven is evidently symbolic of that which must be put away. The New Testament however, clearly interprets the symbol for us. Thus the literal leaven pointed to the spiritual leaven.

There are five distinct references to leaven in the New Testament and a consideration of the contextual use of each will show that leaven is indeed evil and that which has to be put away. Leaven is seen to be symbolic of sin, human weaknesses, infirmities, false doctrine or corrupt practices.

a. The Leaven of Herod — *Mark 8:15; 6:14-28*

A study of the references to Herod show that he was a very sinful and worldly man. He feared the Word of God in John's mouth but was not prepared to repent. He was sly as a fox, sensual, proud and murderous. He was controlled by the spirit of the world. Jesus warned the disciples to beware of the **leaven of Herod, the spirit of worldliness.**

b. The Leaven of the Sadducees — *Matthew 16:6-12*

Jesus also warned the disciples to beware of the leaven of the Sadducees. There was no mistaking what the leaven of the Sadducees was. It was their doctrine. The Sadducees did not believe in the supernatural, in spirit, in angels, or in the bodily resurrection *(Matthew 3:7; Mark 12:18; Acts 5:17; 23:6-8)*.

The doctrine of the Sadducees works like leaven, corrupting and influencing all those who receive it. **Modernism** is the counterpart of the **leaven of the Sadducees** today.

c. The Leaven of the Pharisees — *Matthew 16:6-12; Luke 12:1*

The Lord Jesus also warned His own to beware of the leaven of the Pharisees. No mistake could be made here because Jesus interprets the symbol of the **leaven of the Pharisees** as **hypocrisy.** (Read also *Luke 11:37-44; 12:1; Matthew 23:3*).

The Pharisees "say and do not". They do not practice what they preach. Thus, although the Pharisees were religious, fasted, tithed, believed in the supernatural, in the sacred Scriptures, they were as whited sepluchres. Externally clean but inwardly they were rotten, as dead men's bones.

Hypocrisy works like leaven in a believer's life unless it is purged out and put away. It causes one to be puffed up.

d. The Leaven of Corinth — *I Corinthians 5:1-13.*

This chapter clearly shows that the **major leaven** in the Corinthians Church was **sensuality.** The whole Epistle shows other forms of leaven at work in the Church also. Note how Paul refers to the action of leaven in which the Corinthians were "puffed up" *(I Corinthians 4:18-19; 5:2; 8:1; 13:4).* To be "puffed up" is also symbolic of pride and inflation.

A study of this Epistle shows that the sin of fornication, along with other sins, had not been dealt with in Corinth. It worked like leaven affecting other members (Compare *II Corinthians 12:20-21).* Paul exhorts the church to "put away" the person who is having such a leavening influence in the church. He told them to "purge out" the old leaven, reminding them that a little leaven would leaven the whole lump.

This purging out of the leaven as seen here is the proper exercise of church discipline. Paul spoke of the **leaven of malice and wickedness,** which was **"old leaven"** and needed purging out. All churches need to purge out sin and its leavening influence.

e. The Leaven of Galatia — *Galatians 5:9*

A study of the context of this Epistle to the Galatian Church clearly shows that the **leaven of Galatia** was **legalism,** a mixture of Law and Grace. Having Christ in one hand and Moses in the other hand. It was a confusion of the Old Covenant and the New Covenant revelation. It was a mixture of flesh and spirit, bondage and liberty, works of the Law and faith in Christ. The Galatians having received Christ by faith now sought to go back to the beggarly elements of the Law, hoping to be perfected by legalistic works.

The Judaizing teachers of the Law put their "leaven of legality" in all of the churches which Paul planted. Paul warned the believers of the leavening influence of this teaching unless they arrested its action by purging it out and putting away the subtle influences of such.

Various groups of believers are influences by this same leaven of the Galatian Church and such needs purging out in order that the church may be a new lump, unleavened by corrupting influences.

Thus Jesus and Paul clearly interpret for us the symbol of leaven, both in the Gospels and the Epistles. Although the symbol of leaven was never specifically interpreted for us in the Old Testament, it is in the New Testament. All leaven therefore must be put away in order to keep the Feast of Unleavened Bread.

f. How to Keep the Feast — *I Corinthians 5:7-8*

In verse 7 Paul says "Christ our **Passover** is sacrificed (slain) for us." In verse 8 he exhorts us "to keep the Feast (holy day) . . . with the **Unleavened Bread** of sincerity and truth." Thus the Feasts of Passover and Unleavened Bread are brought together in his letter to the Corinthian Church.

This Feast must be kept:

1) In Sincerity — that is, in clearness, in purity; the opposite to the corrupting influences of impurity and hypocrisy.

2) In Truth — that is, truly; the opposite to deceit and lying. These two words are used in contrast to the "leaven of malice and wickedness."

The believer keeps this Feast when he puts away all evil doctrine and all evil practices, when he lives a sanctified life. The separated life is the unleavened life; not allowing secret or corrupting influences of evil to puff up the believer or any area of his relationship with Christ, the Passover Lamb of God *(Galatians 5:19-26; Ephesians 4:17-32; Colossians 3:1-17).*

The believer also keeps the Feast in the Lord's Supper, the holy communion. There he partakes of the bread of Christ, and there he is also part of that one bread, the church, the body of Christ *(I Corinthians 5:7-11; 10:15-21; 11:20-34; Acts 20:6-7).* As he keeps himself from evil and partakes of the Table of the Lord in sincerity and truth, he indeed keeps the Feast. Christ is to him the bread of healing, the bread of life *(Psalm 105:37; II Chronicles 30:13-20; Mark 7:24-30).*

For Israel, the keeping of the Feast meant a complete separation from Egypt's gods, religion, bondage, food, works and slavery, as well as its glory and wisdom and might. The putting away of leaven therefore is the practical separation from all known evil, and all that has corrupting influence in the life of the believer.

This is why the children of Israel took their dough before it was leavened. They could not tarry in Egypt. There was no time to let the leaven get in and work *(Exodus 12:34, 39)*. The believer has no time to tarry in the Egypt of this world but needs to move right on into separation, the moment he receives Christ as his Lamb.

g.   Eating the Lamb, the Bread and the Bitter Herbs — *Exodus 12:8; Numbers 9:11.*

The Lord commanded Israel to keep the Passover Feast eating three things in the course of the Feast.

1)   The **flesh** of the lamb was to be roasted and eaten.

2)   It must be eaten with **unleavened bread.**

3)   Both must be eaten along with **bitter herbs.**

All is fulfilled in Christ Jesus.

The believer is to partake of Christ the slain Lamb, and the bread which He gives is His flesh. We do this as we remember the bitterness of Gethsemane and Calvary's sufferings and death *(John 6:51-56)*.

Christ is the Lamb *(John 1:29, 36)*; Christ is the Bread *(John 12:24; Isaiah 28:28; John 6:51-56)*; Christ experienced the bitter cup and the bitterness of our sins and bondage to Satan, the bitterness of judgment and death *(Isaiah 53:8; Luke 22:42)*.

This bread was called "the bread of affliction" *(Deuteronomy 16:3-4, 8)*. Jesus was afflicted for us to become the Bread of Life *(Isaiah 53:4; John 6:30-35)*.

h.   A Memorial — *Exodus 12:14; 13:3, 9.*

The Feast was also celebrated as a memorial of their deliverance and separation from Egypt, the House of Bondage. Jesus established the Last Supper also and asked us to remember Him who delivered us from so great a bondage *(Luke 22:19-20)*.

i.   Explanation of the Feast — *Exodus 13:8-9.*

The Lord commanded the Israelites to explain the Feast to their children. When the sons and daughters would ask what the sign of putting away of leaven meant, the head of the house was to tell them of the law of the Lord. He would explain how God brought Israel out of bondage with a strong hand, separating them from the leavening influences of Egypt. Israel was to be a new lump of dough unto the Lord, unleavened *(Romans 11:16)*.

So the law of the Lord, the work of sanctification, has to be taught and explained to the spiritual Israel of God. The Lord's Supper as the New Testament also needs explanation as it is kept *(Galatians 6:16; Ephesians 2:10-12; I Corinthians 11:23-34)*.

j.   The Additional Offerings — *Numbers 28:17-25.*

As seen previously, each of the Feast days had special offerings besides the regular daily sacrifice. In this Feast of Unleavened Bread additional offerings were presented to the Lord. These were as follows:

1)   Burnt Offerings — Two bullocks, one ram and seven lambs.

2)   Sin Offering — One goat.

3)   Meal Offerings — Fine flour and oil were to be presented with the burnt offerings totalling 6/10ths deal of fine flour with oil.

4)   Then the daily sacrifice, which consisted of the morning and evening lamb for the burnt offering, and its attendant meal and drink offering.

The truth is the same as seen in the whole sacrificial system. The nation of Israel can only be acceptable to God through blood atonement.

The burnt offering speaks of the complete and total consecration of Christ to the Father's will.

The sin offering speaks of Christ's substitutionary and atoning work on Calvary.

The meal and drink offering speak of Christ's perfect and sinless humanity, His sinless body and blood presented as a sweet savour to God.

God accepted Israel in the perfections of the sacrifice. So God accepts the church in the perfections of Christ. In Him we keep the Feasts.

28

II. FOR THE STUDENT:

Following is an outline of references showing the importance of bread in Israel. Bread is the staff of life. All pointed to Christ as the Bread of Life, unleavened indeed, for no sin or evil was found in Him. Nothing that puffs up was ever seen in His holy, perfect and sinless humanity. The believer therefore must feed on the perfections of Christ as his food. He is the Bread which came down from Heaven, bread that a man can eat and never die. This is true spiritual communion.

A. Abraham presented three unleavened cakes to the Lord (Genesis 18).

B. Israel fed on the unleavened bread as they left Egypt (Exodus 12-13).

C. The Lord fed Israel with Manna from heaven for the 40 years they wandered in the Wilderness (Exodus 16).

D. The Meal Offering was of fine flour, and leaven and honey were forbidden to be baked therein (Leviticus 2).

E. The Table of Shewbread in the Tabernacle of Moses had 12 loaves of bread thereon as the food for the priests. It was called the Shewbread (Leviticus 24:5-9; Numbers 4:7; II Chronicles 2:4).

F. A golden pot of manna was placed in the Ark of the Covenant for a memorial (Hebrews 9:4).

G. Abraham received bread and wine from Melchisedek at the time of the covenant (Genesis 14:18; Hebrews 7:1-12).

H. The Angel of the Lord who appeared to Gideon accepted his sacrifice of unleavened cakes on the altar (Judges 6:19-21).

I. In the Feast of Pentecost the Lord commanded Israel to offer two wave loaves baken with leaven. This was in direct contrast to that which was commanded under the Feast of Passover and Unleavened Bread (Leviticus 23:15-17). The significance of this will be considered under the interpretation of that Feast.

J. Godly kings and leaders in Israel always brought the people back to the keeping of the Feasts of Passover and Unleavened Bread (II Chronicles 8:13; 30:13-21; 35:17; Ezra 6:22; Ezekiel 45:21).

Chapter Nine
THE FEAST DAY OF THE SHEAF OF FIRSTFRUITS

The final part of the Feast of Passover is spoken of as the Feast Day of the Sheaf of Firstfruits. The only specific scripture which deals with this Feast Day is found in *Leviticus 23:9-14*. The New Testament clearly interprets this simple but beautiful Feast Day in *I Corinthians 15:20-23*, while the Gospels show the fulfilment of the same in the resurrection of Christ. Again Paul in a summary statement in Corinthians interprets this ordinance by referring to "Christ the Firstfruits." The day of the Sheaf of Firstfruits is a remarkable prophetic type of the resurrection of the Lord Jesus, His ascension to heaven to the Father and also symbolic of the coming resurrection of all saints of all ages.

I. THE STORY IN BRIEF:

When Israel eventually entered into the promised land, they were commanded to keep this Feast day then. It involved the harvest period under Passover and Pentecost. It could not be kept in the Wilderness as that was a place of wandering, feeding on the manna from heaven. It was not a place of harvest or feeding on the fruit of the land *(Joshua 5:10-12)*.

The custom was carried out in this manner. The standing ripe harvest, barley and wheat, would soon be reaped. A person would go to the standing harvest, take one sheaf and bring it unto the priest. The lone sheaf was called "the sheaf of the Firstfruits". The priest was then to take this one sheaf and wave it before the Lord in His house. This was to be done on "the morrow after the Sabbath". Certain prescribed offerings were also to be presented along with this sheaf. None could eat of the bread or roasted grain of the corn harvest until that sheaf had been presented to the Lord and accepted for Israel.

It may be asked: How many of the Israelites really understood the symbolic truth and significance of this simple but beautiful ceremony? The New Testament historical fulfilment is that which interprets the ceremony for us and helps the believer to understand and appreciate the Feast Day of the Sheaf of Firstfruits.

A. Bring a Sheaf of the Harvest — *Leviticus 23:10*

A sheaf in Scripture is generally used to typify persons or a person.

1. Joseph dreamed a dream in which he saw eleven sheaves bow down to his sheaf. The interpretation was clear. It was a prophetic dream which showed that his eleven brothers would bow down to him in the appointed time *(Genesis 37:5-11)*. This shows that the sheaf was symbolic of a person.

2. The Song of Degrees found in *Psalm 126* is also a prophetic psalm. It speaks of the sower going forth to sow in tears. Then he comes back later in the harvest time bringing his sheaves with him. This prophetic psalm could be applied to the Lord Jesus Christ. He is the Lord of the Harvest. In His first coming He went forth weeping bearing precious seed. In His second coming He will come rejoicing in the harvest time, bringing His sheaves with Him. The sheaves in this harvest time are the redeemed souls which come to fruition by the Gospel.

3. The single sheaf, presented to the Lord here on this Feast day speaks of the person of our Lord Jesus Christ. He is the sheaf of firstfruits *(I Corinthians 15:20-23)*.

B. The Sheaf of the Firstfruits — *Leviticus 23:10.*

This one sheaf is distinctly called "the sheaf of the firstfruits". The nation of Israel was familiar with the concept of the firstfruits, or the firstborn. Both taught the same truth. The firstfruits were always the choicest, the foremost, the first, the best, the pre-eminent of all that was to follow. The firstfruits were holy to the Lord. The same truths were also applicable to the firstborn of both man and beast.

1. The firstborn of both man and beast were **sanctified** and presented to the Lord. They were distinctly and uniquely His *(Exodus 13:2, 11-13; 22:29)*.

2. The firstfruits of all the earth were to be **presented** to the Lord, at His altar in praise and thanksgiving. Sometimes they were presented to the priests and Levites *(Deuteronomy 26:1-11; 18:3-5; Leviticus 19:23-25)*. Read also *Nehemiah 10:34-39*.

Thus, the firstfruits belonged exclusively to Jehovah. They were holy, sanctified and presented to Him.

3. The New Testament shows beautifully how the Lord Jesus is the fulfilment of all that truth symbolized in the firstfruits and especially here as the Sheaf of firstfruits.

    a. He is the firstborn of Mary *(Matthew 1:23-25).*

    b. He is the first-begotten of the Father *(Hebrews 1:6).*

    c. He is the firstborn from the dead *(Colossians 1:18).*

    d. He is the first-begotten of the dead *(Revelation 1:5).*

    e. In all things He is the pre-eminent One *(Colossians 1:18).*

    f. He is the beginning of the creation of God *(Revelation 3:14).*

    g. He is the firstborn among many brethren *(Romans 8:28).*

    h. He is the firstfruits of the resurrected ones *(I Corinthians 15:20, 23).*

Christ Jesus is indeed the "most holy One", the One sanctified by the Father, the first, the choicest, and the pre-eminent One. He is both the firstborn and the firstfruits unto God, exclusively belonging to the Father. He is the **sheaf of the firstfruits.**

C. The First of the Firstfruits — *Exodus 23:19; 34:26*

The **sheaf** of the firstfruits needs to be distinguished from the **harvest** of the firstfruits *(Exodus 23:16; 34:22),* or that which took place under the Pentecost harvest. This sheaf was a forerunner sheaf, a sample sheaf of the coming harvest. The harvests of Passover (barley) and Pentecost (wheat) were a kind of first-fruits harvest because the final harvest was to come in the end of the year under Tabernacles (fruit). Hence this sheaf was but **the first** of the firstfruits, and the harvest would follow.

It is the Father's will that His Son be **first** and have the pre-eminence in all things in the church *(Colossians 1:18).* The believer is to seek **first** the kingdom of God as personified in Christ the King *(Matthew 6:33).* The believer is to maintain **first** love, **first** works and **first** faith in Christ also *(Revelation 2:4, 5; I Timothy 5:12).*

D. A Representative Sheaf of the Harvest — *Leviticus 23:10*

This sheaf was a representative sheaf, symbolic of the coming harvest. It was not the whole harvest but a part of the whole, yet the whole was represented in that one sheaf. So Christ Jesus in His resurrection represented the great harvest of resurrected ones yet to come.

It is worthy to note that the Gospel of Matthew, when recording the message of the resurrection tells us that "the graves were opened; and many bodies of the saints which slept arose, and came out of the graves **after** His resurrection" *(Matthew 27:52-53).* Thus Christ was the **first** here in resurrection life of this resurrected company of saints.

It is possible that the sheaf of Firstfruits could be viewed in a double sense.

1. Christ the sheaf of firstfruits in His own personal resurrection.

2. The company of saints raised bodily with Him at His resurrection could together with Him be looked upon as being "the sheaf".

Whichever way it is viewed, Christ Himself is indeed the representative sheaf, the earnest, the first-fruits, the promise, the forerunner of the great harvest of resurrected ones at the close of the age *(I Corinthians 15:20-23, 51-57; I Thessalonians 4:13-18; Romans 8:29).* There are more to come, exactly like Him *(Philippians 3:20-21):*

    —The Apostle James speaks of the early Church believers as "a kind of firstfruits" *(James 1:18).*

    —The Apostle Paul said that the believers had "the firstfruits of the Spirit" *(Romans 8:23).*

    —Paul also referred to the converts in Achaia as "the firstfruits" *(I Corinthians 16:15).*

    —The Apostle John spoke of the 144,000 redeemed Israelites as being "the firstfruits unto God and the Lamb" *(Revelation 14:4).*

Jesus Christ therefore is the representative sheaf and the saints down through the ages will be the harvest of the end of the age, gathered into the heavenly garner *(Matthew 13:36-43).*

E. Wave the Sheaf before Jehovah — *Leviticus 23:11; Exodus 23:19*

This one sheaf was to be taken to the house of the Lord and waved in presentation before Jehovah. It speaks of Christ's ascension to the heavenly Father's house, the true tabernacle and temple. When He was about to ascend after His resurrection, He told Mary not to touch Him for he had not yet ascended to the Father (John 20:17).

While the Jews kept the letter of the law concerning this Feast day, and that before a rent veil, Christ fulfilled the reality and spirit of it as He ascended to the Father's house and presented Himself as the sheaf of the firstfruits in His resurrection and glorified body. The empty tomb testified to the fact that the sheaf of firstfruits had been reaped and waved before the Lord in His heavenly sanctuary.

F. To be Accepted for You — *Leviticus 23:11*

The sheaf waved before Jehovah was accepted for Israel. Paul told the believers that they were "accepted in the Beloved" *(Ephesians 1:6)*. So we may say that as the sheaf was accepted before Jehovah for Israel and Israel was accepted of Jehovah in that sheaf, so Christ is accepted before God for us and we are accepted of God in Christ.

It was sin that made man unacceptable to God. The only way man can find and experience acceptance of God is through Christ the resurrected One, the sheaf of firstfruits. The church, which is His body, is accepted in the Head which is Christ.

G. The Morrow after the Sabbath — *Leviticus 23:11; Numbers 28:26.*

This one sheaf was to be waved in the house of the Lord "on the morrow after the Sabbath". It is a most remarkable prophecy of the resurrection day. No set date is mentioned in Leviticus for the waving of the sheaf of firstfruits, under the historical-typical command. However, when we come to the New Testament historical-antitypical fulfilment we find the dates to be implicit in the Old Testament command.

If we take the Passover week, or the week of the crucifixion of Jesus we discover the following dates:

Day		Date	Event	
Saturday		10th	Lamb taken and set aside	Jesus enters Jerusalem
Sunday	Kept for 4 days	11th		
Monday		12th		
Tuesday		13th		
Wednesday		14th	Passover/Crucifixion day *Luke 23:54; Mark 15:42; John 19:42*	Jesus crucified Day of Preparation *John 19:31.*
Thursday		15th	Feast of Unleavened Bread Sabbath or High Day *Luke 23:54; Matthew 27:62 John 19:31*	3 Nights & 3 Days *Matthew 12:40*
Friday		16th	Secular Day/Spices prepared by the women *Luke 23:55-56*	
Saturday		17th	Weekly Sabbath/rested according to fourth Commandment. *Luke 23:56; Matthew 28:1; Exodus 20:8-11*	
Sunday		18th	The "morrow after the Sabbath" or first day of the week Day of Resurrection. Day of Sheaf of Firstfruits waving. *Matthew 28:1; Mark 16:1-6; John 20:1; Luke 24:1*	Jesus resurrected

Thus this event remarkably fulfils Christ's own prophetic word that He would be dead for 3 days and 3 nights and then be raised after that (*Matthew 12:38-40; 16:21; Luke 24:7, 46; Matthew 27:63; Mark 8:31; 16:9; Matthew 28:1*).

From the 14th day to the close of the 17th and beginning of the 18th day we have a time period of 3 days and 3 nights, counting the Hebrew reckoning of time from "even to even".

Other shadows of the "Three Days & Three Nights" Bible theme are seen in these scriptures (*Genesis 22:1-6; Hebrews 11:17-19; Exodus 3:18; 5:3; 8:27; 15:22-27; Esther 4:17; Jonah 1:17*).

Note: Failure to recognize that there were **two Sabbaths** in the Passover week has brought much confusion and misunderstanding as to the day of Christ's crucifixion, as well as the day of His resurrection. It has distorted the truth of Christ's statement concerning His being 3 days and 3 nights in the heart of the earth.

The Unleavened Bread was a High Day or extra Sabbath, and then there was the weekly Sabbath also, thus making two Sabbaths in the week of the crucifixion (*John 19:30-31; Luke 23:50-56*).

Each of the Gospels confirm the fact that the resurrection of Christ took place at the close of the weekly Sabbath and early the first day of the new week. This is to say that the resurrection took place on "the morrow after the Sabbath". Type and antitype meet together in wonderful fulfilment.

Thus one of the foundation stones of the Christian Faith — the resurrection of the Christ — was established on the **first** day of the new week, **not** the Sabbath!

The Christian rejoiced in a new day, the first day of the new week, the resurrection day. It was for this reason that the early believers gradually moved away from keeping of the Sabbath to the keeping of the first day of the week (*John 20:1; Acts 20:7; I Corinthians 16:2; Revelation 1:10*).

The Jews kept a Christless Sabbath! The keeping of the first day of the week, the resurrection day, was foreshadowed by Israel while they were keeping weekly Sabbaths. One wonders how many of them ever understood why God instituted this simple ordinance of the sheaf waving to take place on "the morrow after the Sabbath". The New Testament believer rejoices in the knowledge of the truth.

H. Offerings Presented with the Sheaf — *Leviticus 23:12-13*

Besides the daily evening and morning sacrifices there were other specified sacrifices to be offered with this sheaf. These offerings were:

1. A lamb without blemish of the first year to be offered as a Burnt Offering. Thus sacrificial body and blood were involved here.

2. The Meal Offering and its accompanying Drink Offering also to be offered as a sweet savour to the Lord. Here we see bread and wine involved.

3. The Sheaf of the Firstfruits offered.

The thoughts and truths combined here are those which speak of Christ's death (Burnt Offering), His resurrection (the sheaf), and the communion that results from both (Meal Offering) in the bread and the wine (*John 6:51-58; Matthew 26:26-28; I Corinthians 11:23-34*). It is significant that there was no Sin Offering presented with the sheaf. All here speaks of Christ Himself in His sinlessness and His resurrection. On that basis death could not hold Him (*Acts 2:24*).

The **death** and the **resurrection** of Christ are brought together for each is inseparable from the other. The Lamb sets forth Christ's death. The sheaf sets forth His resurrection. The Bread and Wine sets forth the communion, the Lord's Table in which the believer remembers Christ's death and resurrection.

I. A Statute Forever — *Leviticus 23:14*

The Israelites were not to eat bread, corn or parched ears, until the day that the sheaf was presented to the Lord. It was to be a statute forever in all their generations in their dwellings. A statute is an established rule or law.

It was symbolic of the fact that the true Israel of God, the church (*Galatians 6:16*) could not partake of the food of God, the fruit of the promised land until after the resurrected Christ had been accepted in the Father's house in His ascension. Since Christ's death, burial, resurrection, ascension, presentation to and acceptance by the Father, the believer can enjoy the fruit of Canaan land (*Joshua 5:10-12*). The memory of His death and resurrection will be a statute eternally.

L. The Harvest Time — *Leviticus 23:10; Matthew 13:39; Revelation 14:12-14*

As noted earlier the one sheaf was representative of the great harvest of sheaves yet to be gathered in. Jesus said that the harvest would be the end of the age. In the Epistle to the Corinthian church Paul spoke of the coming resurrection of all saints at the second advent of Christ. He declares that there will be an order in the resurrection. The order he sets forth is as follows:

1. Christ the firstfruits risen from the dead — The one Sheaf.

2. Those that are Christ's at His coming — The harvest of Sheaves.

Christ died and is risen again. The saints who have died over the centuries and are still dying today will come to that time when all the dead in Christ shall rise again. The resurrection of the saints is spoken of as the **first resurrection** *(Revelation 20:1-6)*. This takes place at the second coming of Christ and it will constitute the great harvest of the redeemed and resurrected believers of all ages. All the saints, having died in the faith of the resurrection, will stand in their "lot" in the end of the days *(Daniel 12:13)*. *The student is referred to a fuller treatment of "the harvest" under the next Feast, the Feast of Pentecost.*

Thus in the Feast of Passover, which speaks wholly of Christ, we see the foundations of the Christian Faith. We see typified His death, burial, resurrection and ascension to the Father. It is the first Feast, the foundation Feast, and every person who comes to God through Christ must partake of this Feast, experiencing the truths therein.

II. CONCLUSION

In concluding our study of this Feast we see how this Feast is set forth in symbolic manner in the Lord's Supper, the **communion table.**

It is significant that the Lord's Supper was established at the time of the Passover Supper *(Luke 22:1; Matthew 26:17)*. The Lord Jesus therefore in fulfilling the Old Covenant Passover and instituting the Lord's Supper of the New Covenant shows that the one pointed to the other, and the latter replaces the former. It is in the Lord's Supper that the three parts of the Feast of Passover are symbolized. A consideration of these Scriptures confirm this fact *(I Corinthians 10:16-17; 11:20, 23-34; Luke 22:1-20; Matthew 26:26-28)*.

The following comparison and contrast brings this truth into sharper focus:

The Passover Supper	—	**The Lord's Supper**
The Old Covenant Feast	—	The New Covenant Feast
The Passover lamb	—	The lamb of God
The flesh and unleavened bread	—	The bread which is His flesh
The bitter herbs	—	The sufferings of Calvary
The blood of the lamb	—	The blood of Christ
The sheaf of firstfruits	—	The resurrected Christ
Until the cross	—	After the cross
Until He come — **first coming**	—	Until He come — **second coming**
Memorial service	—	Do it in remembrance of Me
Deliverance and redemption	—	Deliverance and redemption
from Pharaoh and Egypt, the	—	from Satan and the world, the
house of bondage	—	**kingdom of darkness**

Chapter Ten
THE FEAST OF PENTECOST

The next great Feast that the Lord commanded Israel to keep was the Feast of Weeks or the Feast of Pentecost, as the New Testament calls it. It is this Feast which the Lord seemed to have in mind when he told Moses that Pharaoh was to let the people go, so that they could "hold a Feast to Me in the wilderness" *(Exodus 5:1; 10:9).*

The major scriptures dealing with the things pertaining to this Feast are found in *Exodus 19-20,24; Deuteronomy 16:9-12; Exodus 23:16-17; 34:22-23; Leviticus 23:15-21* and *Numbers 28:26-31.* The student should read these Scriptures and familiarize himself with the content thereof as the following material is drawn from these passages.

The New Testament Scriptures showing the antitypical fulfilment of this Feast are found in *Acts 2; II Corinthians 3,* and *Hebrews 8.*

A study of this Feast shows that it pointed to the coming of the Holy Spirit to form the church of Jesus Christ, and write upon the hearts and minds of the believers the New Covenant commandments. This will be seen by our consideration of the historical-typical enactment in Israel and then in the historical-antitypical fulfilment in the church.

I.   THE STORY IN BRIEF:

The Exodus of Israel from Egypt took place under the Feast of Passover in the first month, the month of Abib or Nisan. After crossing the Red Sea and being led by the pillar of fire they were brought to the foot of Mt. Sinai. Here at Sinai they experienced the Feast of Pentecost, in the third month, which was Sivan. At Sinai the Law of 10 Commandments was written and given to the nation. Here the Tabernacle of the Lord, the Aaronic priesthood and the sacrificial system was given. Here the nation was established as "the church in the wilderness" *(Acts 7:38).* Later on, when Israel entered the promised land, special and peculiar offerings were presented to the Lord as Israel gathered in the Pentecostal harvest amidst great joy and rejoicing.

The full significance of this Feast Day can only be understood and appreciated by considering the details laid down in the relevant scriptures. Again we will consider first the natural and then the spiritual; first the type, then the antitype; first the shadow, then the substance; first the temporal under the Old Covenant Israel, then the eternal under the New Covenant Israel *(II Corinthians 4:18).*

A. Names of the Feast

This particular Feast day is known by different names, each of which set forth some facet of truth, which will be interpreted as the study proceeds. It was called:

1.   The Feast of Harvest — *Exodus 23:16*

2.   The Feast of Weeks — *Exodus 34:22; Deuteronomy 16:10, 16*

3.   The Day of Firstfruits — *Numbers 28:26; Exodus 34:22*

4.   The Feast of Weeks of the Firstfruits of Wheat Harvest — *Exodus 34:22*

5.   The Feast of Harvest, the Firstfruits of Israel's labours — *Exodus 23:16*

6.   The Feast of Pentecost, in the New Testament. Pentecost being the transliteration of the Greek word for "fifty" — *Acts 2:1; 20:16; I Corinthians 16:8.*

As mentioned, this was the Feast the Lord wanted them to hold unto Him in the wilderness *(Exodus 5:1, 3; 7:16; 10:9).* It will be seen by these various titles for the Feast that it actually involved a particular 24 hour day, as well as a period of time. Thus it is the **day** of Pentecost, as well as the Feast of **Weeks!**

B. Pentecost in the Third Month — *Acts 2:1; 20:16; I Corinthians 16:8; Exodus 19:1-2.*

The Greek name for this Feast Day is known as "Pentecost", a simply meaning "fiftieth". This word is not used in the Old Testament but it is used 3 times in the New Testament. This Feast took place on the fiftieth day after the waving of the sheaf of firstfruits *(Leviticus 23:15-16).* This brought Israel into the third month after their exodus from Egypt's bondage.

We consider the Old Testament historical-typical fulfilment and then see how the New Testament fulfils this period of time.

1.   The Old Testament Fiftieth Day

a.   Passover to Pentecost

From Passover to Pentecost can be traced the required 50 days. Passover took place on the 14th day of the first month *(Exodus 12:18; Numbers 28:16; Leviticus 23:4-5).* Israel left Egypt on the 15th day of the same month, in the Feast of Unleavened Bread *(Leviticus 23:6; Numbers 28:17-18; Exodus 12:18).*

After the exodus they crossed the Red Sea, following the cloudy pillar to Mt. Sinai coming to the mount apparently the first day of the third month *(Exodus 16:1; 19:1).* Here at Mt. Sinai the Lord spoke to Moses to tell Israel to sanctify themselves against the third day. Then Moses went up again to the mount on this day and it was on this day that the Lord wrote the Ten Commandments on tables of stone. In all we have 50 days, which maybe seen as follows:

First month, Abib or Nisan — 15 days
Second month, Zif   — 30 days
Third month, Sivan   — 4 days
                    49 days or 7 Weeks (7x7-49)

Then we come to the next day which was the 50th day when the Lord wrote with His finger the Ten Commandments. Hence the Jews today look upon the Feast of Pentecost as the celebration or the commemoration of the giving of the Law.

b. **The Feast of Weeks** — *Leviticus 23:15-16*

The "time element" is set forth more expressly in this passage. It links Passover and Pentecost together. Here the Lord commanded Israel, when they arrived in the land and had harvest time, to count from the day of the waving of the sheaf of firstfruits 49 days, or seven sabbaths complete. Then they were to count the day following, which was the 50th day, the morrow after the seventh sabbath, and this was the day of Pentecost. Thus we have: 7 x 7 Sabbaths or 49 days

The morrow after the seventh sabbath, was the 50th day. On this day they were to offer specified offerings. Thus we have a double witness concerning the Feast of the 50th day; that which was fulfilled historically in Israel from Passover to Pentecost, and then that which was to find fulfilment when they came into the promised land.

2. **The New Testament Fiftieth Day** — *Acts 1:3; 2:1*

The Lord Jesus came to fulfil all the intricate details of the Law *(Matthew 5:17-18; 11:13).* The Book of Acts shows the fulfilment of this time period of 50 days unto the Feast Day of Pentecost.

After Christ's resurrection at the close of His 3 days and 3 nights in the tomb, He was seen of His disciples for 40 days, speaking to them of the things pertaining to the kingdom of God. At the close of this period of 40 days He ascended back to the Father. The disciples tarried in Jerusalem in the upper room for 10 days and then "when the Day of Pentecost was fully come" the Holy Spirit was outpoured on the believing and waiting disciples. Thus we have:

40 days post-resurrection ministry of Jesus
10 days tarrying of the disciples
50 days to Pentecost.

As Israel experienced the giving of the Law at Mt. Sinai 50 days after leaving Egypt under Passover, so the disciples experienced the coming of the Holy Spirit to write His laws 50 days after the completion of Passover by the resurrection of Christ. And again, as the Feast of Pentecost was celerated 50 days after the waving of the sheaf of firstfruits, so the Holy Spirit was poured out on the 50th day after the resurrection of Christ Jesus. Truly a remarkable fulfilment of the Feast of the Fiftieth Day in the third month!

C. **Significance of the Number Fifty**

The number 50 is used symbolically to represent liberty, freedom or deliverance. This is seen in the fact that every 50th year (or, 7x7=49 + 1=50) in Israel was called the year of Jubilee. It was a year of release, of liberty and freedom. Slaves were set free, debts were cancelled, families were reunited, and liberty was proclaimed throughout the land by the sound of the Jubilee trumpets *(Leviticus 25:8-17).* Priests also served the Tabernacle of the Lord from 25 or 30 years until the age of 50 years, then they were at liberty to cease from such service *(Numbers 4:1-3; 8:23-26).*

For the nation of Israel, the Feast of Pentecost on the 50th day after their deliverance from Egypt was a celebration of liberty from the house of bondage. They were free slaves, now at liberty to serve the true God, the Lord their redeemer.

For the New Testament believers, the Day of Pentecost meant liberty and freedom from Old Covenant bondages of ceremonialism of the Law. It meant freedom in the liberty wherewith Christ had set them free. It meant that they were at liberty to serve the Lord, not in the oldness of the letter but in newness of the Spirit (*Romans 7:1-6*). Liberty however, does not mean licence (*Galatians 5:1; Romans 6:18*).

Other uses of the number fifty may be seen in *Genesis 6:15; I Kings 18:4, 13; II Kings 2:7; Leviticus 27:1-5, 16; Mark 6:40; Luke 9:14.*

D. The Morrow after the Sabbath — *Leviticus 23:15-16*

Here again this Feast, as the Day of the Sheaf of Firstfruits was celebrated on "the morrow after the sabbath", but on this occasion, after the seventh Sabbath. The same truth is applicable here as noted under the Sheaf of Firstfruits The Day of Pentecost took place, **not** on the weekly Sabbath, but on the **first day** of the new week, or "the morrow after the sabbath".

It is worthy to note that two of the Feast days in the Old Testament by-passed the weekly sabbath and took place on the first day of the week. Thus even under the Law Covenant they shadow forth the two foundational events of the New Covenant Church.

1. The Sheaf of Firstfruits was waved on "the morrow after the sabbath" which was the first day of the week. The New Testament antitypical fulfilment is seen in the fact that the Son of God rose from the dead on "the morrow after the sabbath" on the first day of the week. The New Testament believer worships the Lord on this day as the resurrected Christ of God!

2. The Day of Pentecost took place on "the morrow after the Sabbath", on the first day of the new week. The New Testament antitypical fulfilment is seen in the fact that the Blessed Holy Spirit descended from heaven on this day to fill the believers with Himself.

Thus two Persons in the eternal Godhead — the Son of God, and the Holy Spirit — by-passed the Old Testament sabbath day, and acted on the **first day** of the week, or "the morrow after the sabbath". The two foundational events of the church, the **resurrection of Christ,** and the **outpoured Holy Spirit,** both took place on the **first day** of the week! It is for this reason that the New Testament believer keeps the Lord's day and not the Old Testament sabbath.

The very fact that these two Feast days were kept on the morrow after the sabbath actually prophesied an end of sabbath keeping as of the Mosaic Law. It is the fulfilment of the prophetic word through the prophet Hosea when the Lord said that He would "cause all her mirth to cease, her Feast days, her new moons, and her sabbaths, and all her solemn Feasts" (*Hosea 2:11*). The Apostle Paul shows how all these typical things were caused to cease by their fulfilment in Christ, and then spiritually in the church (*Galatians 4:10; Romans 14:4-7; Colossians 2:16-17*).

True sabbath rest is in Christ's finished work and in the Spirit (*Matthew 11:28-3); Acts 20:7; I Corinthians 16:1-2; Hebrews 4:1-11*).

The Sabbath was the sign and seal of the Old or Mosaic Covenant. The New Covenant sign and seal is the Baptism in the Holy Spirit. One was a **day** of rest; the other is the **Spirit** of rest. To return to sabbath keeping is to confuse the covenantal seals. God does not take the sign and seal of the Old Covenant and put it on the New Covenant. Once the believer knows which covenant he is under then all confusion ceases as to the keeping of days.

E. What Happened at Mt. Sinai?

Although the Feast day took place on the 50th day, there were other important things which transpired on and subsequent to this day. The Old Testament and New Testament Pentecosts can be beautifully compared and contrasted as to these events.

1. Supernatural Manifestations

As Moses entered the mount of God, supernatural manifestations took place. The Presence of God was evidenced by the sound of the trumpet, by thunders, lightnings, thick clouds, fire and a voice. The result was trembling, fear and quaking by Moses as well as the Israelites (*Exodus 19:16-19; Deuteronomy 4:32-40; Hebrews 12:18-21*). Elijah experienced similar manifestations at Mt. Horeb when he saw and heard the earthquake, wind and fire, and then the still small voice (*I Kings 19:8-14*).

On the Day of Pentecost, after Jesus, the Mediator of the New Covenant had entered the heavenly Mt. of God — Mt. Zion (*Hebrews 12:22-29; Revelation 14:1-4*), there were great manifestations of His Presence in the upper room. The Holy Spirit descended as a mighty rushing wind, the place was filled with His Presence, tongues of fire sat on the heads of the disciples and they all spake with other tongues as the Spirit gave them utterance (*Acts 2:1-4; 4:31*). When this was noised abroad, thousands of Jews, out of every nation, gathered to hear the Word of the Gospel of grace. Thus wind and fire, the sound from heaven, and then the speaking in other tongues were manifestations of God's Presence. Fear and wonder fell on the hearers as the Gospel was preached.

At Sinai we have Moses, fire, darkness, trumpet voice, quaking, thunder and lightning. This was the Old Testament Pentecost.

At Jerusalem (or Mt. Zion), we have Jesus, tongues of fire, rushing mighty wind, shaking and conviction. This was the New Testament Pentecost.

2. The Giving of the Law Covenant — *Exodus 19:16-20; Deuteronomy 4-5; Exodus 31-34.*

The Jews refer to this day as "The Feast of the Giving of the Law" or the Birthday of Judaism.

On the 50th day it seems that the Lord wrote with His finger on the two tables of stone the Ten Commandments. Relative to the giving of the Old Covenant commandments, and the people breaking the same by idolatry, 3000 people were slain. When the Tables were renewed, the face of Moses, their Mediator, shone with the Glory of God.

Events relative to the New Testament Pentecost show the great comparison and contrast to the Old Testament Pentecost. This was the Birthday of the New Covenant church.

The New Covenant commandments are now to be written by the Spirit (the finger of God, *Luke 11:20; Matthew 12:28*), on fleshy tables of the heart and mind *(Jeremiah 31:31-34; Hebrews 8)*. At Pentecost, after Peter's preaching, 3000 people were saved unto life by the ministration of the Spirit.

Paul tells us that the Glory of God in the face of Jesus Christ is the greater Glory than that on the face of Moses. Jesus is the New Covenant Mediator. The Glory of the Old Covenant is done away, while the Glory of the New Covenant remains. Paul deals with this comparison and contrast relative to the Feast of Pentecost and the Law in II Corinthians Chapter 3. This may be seen more clearly when columnized.

Old Testament Pentecost		New Testament Pentecost
The Fiftieth Day	—	The Fiftieth Day
Writing of Ten Commandments on two Tables of Stone	—	Writing of Commandments of love on Tables of Heart and Mind *(Matthew 22:34-40; Romans 13:8-10; Matthew 5-6-7)*
By the Finger of God	—	By the Spirit of God *(Luke 11:20; Matthew 12:28)*
Three thousand people slain	—	Three thousand people live *(Acts 2:41)*
A ministration of death	—	A ministration of life
The letter	—	The Spirit
Glory on the face of Moses	—	Glory on the face of Jesus
Face veiled so people could not behold the Glory	—	Unveiled face so we can be changed into same Glory
Glory to be done away	—	Glory that remaineth
Ministers of Old Covenant	—	Ministers of New Covenant
Mt. Sinai	—	Mt. Zion *(Hebrews 12:22-24)*

3. The Book of the Covenant — *Exodus 24; Hebrews 8-9.*

Relative to the Feast of Pentecost was the giving of the Book of the Covenant. The Book of the Covenant contained other civil and ceremonial Laws besides the Ten Commandments. This Book was blood-sprinkled, even as were the people. Under Passover the blood was sprinkled on the door. Under Pentecost the blood was sprinkled on the people and the Book. Compare *Exodus 24:8* with *Matthew 26:28*. Both Moses and Jesus speak of the "blood of the Covenant".

This Book of the Covenant was kept in the side of the Ark of the Covenant *(Deuteronomy 31:9-15, 24-26)*. It was the responsibility of the Priests and Levites to teach the 12 Tribes the Laws of the Lord, as the church in the wilderness, or the Old Covenant church *(Acts 7:38)*.

The New Testament fulfilment is in the writing of the New Testament Books, subsequent to the outpouring of the Holy Spirit at Pentecost. The New Testament Books are blood-sprinkled, sprinkled by the blood of Jesus. The New Covenant people are also blood-sprinkled, for it is the Spirit who applies the blood of cleansing. It is also the responsibility and ministry of the church to teach God's people the New Covenant commandments of the Lord Jesus Christ *(Matthew 26:26-28; Hebrews 9:11-22; Ephesians 4:9-16)*.

4. The Revelation of the Tabernacle Order — *Exodus 25-40*

Subsequent to the Feast Day of Pentecost was the revelation to Moses of the Tabernacle of the Lord, and the whole order of approach and worship therein.

Here at Mt. Sinai, God established His church *(Acts 7:38)*, the Aaronic priesthood, the sacrificial system, the Tabernacle, the sabbath days and the Festival occasions. Here Israel was taught how all must approach God in sacrifice and worship as a redeemed and holy people. The details of these things are enumerated for us in *Exodus, Chapters 25-40; Leviticus, Chapters 1-27*; as well as in certain chapters of the book of Numbers.

The New Testament antitypical fulfilment is seen in the teaching of the Apostles concerning the priesthood of all believers, the spiritual sacrifices offered in a spiritual house, and the spiritual experience of the Feasts of the Lord.

The New Testament church, as a redeemed and holy nation approaches God through the perfections of Christ Jesus, by the Spirit (I Peter 2:5-9; Revelation 1:6; 5:9-10). The Epistles lay out for us the New Testament church order.

F. The Two Leavened Wave Loaves — *Leviticus 23:15-21; Numbers 28:26-31.*

The most peculiar ceremony which took place on the Day of Pentecost was the presentation before the Lord of the two leavened wave loaves. It was a ceremony not fully understood by the Hebrews for it seemed to be a contradiction of the previous commandments of the Lord. We will consider the pertinent details.

1. A New Meal Offering Baken with Leaven

The Lord commanded Israel on this Pentecostal day to "offer a **new meal** offering unto the Lord."

They were to bring out of their dwelling places **two wave loaves** of two-tenths deals of fine flour. And they were to be **baken with leaven!**

In the Feast of Passover, leaven was absolutely forbidden on pain of excommunication (Exodus 12:15, 19, 20, 31-34; 13:3-10).

In the regular daily Meal Offering no leaven or honey was permitted. Nothing leavened could be offered with blood sacrifices on the altar of the Lord (Leviticus 2).

We have seen that leaven is symbolical of evil, or that which is false, corrupting in its influence, and pointed to the fact that Jesus Christ was perfect and sinless as our Unleavened Bread, our Meal Offering.

But here in Pentecost the Lord commanded the very opposite, saying that Israel should make a **new** Meal Offering of fine flour and bake it with leaven. Why? Why is there no leaven to be seen in Passover and yet there is leaven seen in Pentecost? What truth was God setting forth symbolically here?

The reason is that Passover wholly speaks of Christ and His sinless perfections, while Pentecost has to do with the church, which has not as yet attained to sinless perfection.

Only two particular offerings were offered with leaven in them; these being the Peace Offering offered with leavened bread (Leviticus 7:11-13), and these two Pentecostal Wave Loaves (Leviticus 23:15-22).

The significance of leaven has already been dealt with. It is worth remembering that Paul wrote his epistles to the Corinthian and Galatian believers, as also other churches, and they certainly were "Pentecostal leavened wave loaves." He wrote to arrest the action of the leaven and also to have it purged out (Read again I Corinthians 5:6; Galatians 5:9; Mark 8:15; Matthew 16:6-12; Luke 12:1).

We may say therefore that leaven in the two Pentecostal wave loaves is God's recognition — and the believer's — that the root of sin has not yet been eradicated, even though the believer is indwelt by the Holy Spirit. The coming of the fire of the Holy Spirit is to arrest the action of sin in the believer's life (Romans 6:11, 16-22; Ephesians 4:17-32; 5:3-13; Colossians 3:1-13; Romans 8:1-4).

In summary then it may be seen that Passover speaks of Christ, the Lamb of God, and the believer has faith in the blood and stays under its protection and provision.

In Unleavened Bread, Israel was to put away leaven and in a practical way feed on the unleavened food. In fulfilment the believer practically puts away all works of the flesh and outworking of sin.

In the Sheaf of Firstfruits, Israel and the believer in the church rests in the fact that God has accepted them in the One Sheaf, Christ.

In Pentecost, the two wave loaves baken with leaven, speak of the fact that sin has not yet been eradicated from the church, in spite of the indwelling of the Holy Spirit. The believer, because of human frailities still renders imperfect service to the Lord. It will be seen, however, that **no leaven** is found in the Feast of Tabernacles. Under this Feast the church is brought to maturity and perfection by the atoning blood of Jesus, the Word of God, and the ministry of the Holy Spirit.

2. Two Wave Loaves

There were **two** wave loaves offered to the Lord on this Feast Day of Pentecost. It was a dual offering, both loaves being of the same measure before the Lord. The truth of the dual offerings may be seen through the whole of the Levitical system.

a. Two loaves were offered on the Day of Pentecost (Leviticus 23:17-21)

b. Two birds were used in the sacrifice and cleansing of the leper (Leviticus 14:1-7 with 1:14 and Genesis 15:9).

c. Two trumpets of silver were used in the various callings of the camp of Israel and more especially in the Feast of Trumpets (*Numbers 10:1-10; 29:1*).

d. Two tables of stone had the Ten Commandments written on them by the Spirit (Finger) of God (*Exodus 20:1-17; 31:18*).

e. Two goats were used in the great day of Atonement ceremonies (*Leviticus 16*).

When one is with one, making two, then we have agreement and two is therefore the number of witness, the number of testimony. Jesus sent the 12 apostles and the 70 disciples out two by two to witness and testify in every city whither He Himself would come (*Luke 9:1-6; 10:1-2*).

The Lord Himself also said that in the mouth of two or three witnesses must every word be established (*Deuteronomy 19:15; Matthew 18:16-20*). Thus the two wave loaves speak of witness and testimony. They can also be used to symbolize the two ethnic divisions on which the Holy Spirit was poured out in "Pentecostal effusion", make of both **one new man,** even the Jew and the Gentile (*I Corinthians 12:13*). Both Jew and Gentile testify to the unregenerate world of the power of the Gospel of Christ and the work of the Holy Spirit (*Ephesians 2:11-20; Acts 2; Acts 10*).

They may also be used to symbolize Christ and His church, who, together declare the same testimony. Although two, yet they are one in witness. God speaks to the world by the testimony of Christ and His church (*Hebrews 2:11; Ephesians 5:31*).

3. Two-Tenths Deals of Fine Flour — *Leviticus 23:17*

Both wave loaves were to be of one and the same measure of fine flour, that is, two-tenths deal.

The measure of two-tenths deal is found in Israel on several occasions, showing that the Lord had some significant truth in mind when He commanded this measure.

a. The Manna which fell in the Wilderness wanderings had two-tenths deal in it, for, on the sixth day Israel was to gather twice as much to carry them over the Sabbath (*Exodus 16:22, 36*). The two-tenths deal here speak of the **double portion.**

b. The Meal Offering presented on the Feast Day of the Sheaf of Firstfruits was also to be made of two-tenths deal of fine flour (*Leviticus 23:13*).

c. The twelve loaves of Shewbread on the golden table were also to be made of two-tenths deal of fine flour (*Leviticus 24:5-7*). Thus again we have **the double portion** of life and health in the "Bread of His Presence" as the Shewbread literally means.

d. The two wave loaves offered here at Pentecost were also to be made of two-tenths deal of fine flour (*Leviticus 23:17*).

e. In the two tables of stone on which the Ten Commandments were written we also have the thought of two-tenths, for the **Ten** Commandments find their fulfilment in the **two** Commandments of Jesus, as given in the New Testament (*Matthew 22:34-40*).

The two-tenths deal of fine flour find their fulfilment in the double portion of the Spirit upon both Jew and Gentile, who are of the same body.

They also can find fulfilment in the fact that the Old Covenant was stamped with the Ten Commandments on Two Tables of Stone, while the New Covenant shows that the Ten Commandments are fulfilled in the Two Commandments of love. Love to God and love to one's neighbor fulfil the Law of Commandments.

It is under the Feast of Pentecost that the Holy Spirit, who is the Finger of God, writes the commandments of Jesus on the tables of the heart and mind (*Jeremiah 31:31-34; II Corinthians 3*).

As the **New** Meal offering, the Jew and Gentile come together in the **New** Covenant, receive a **new** name, and speak in **new** tongues and finally are brought to the **new** Heavens and **new** Earth and the **new** Jerusalem. God makes all things **new** (*II Corinthians 5:17-18; Revelation 21:1-8; Mark 16:15-20; Matthew 26:26-28*).

4. Of Fine Flour — *Leviticus 23:17*

The two wave loaves were to be of fine flour. Fine flour originates in the whole wheat. This wheat must be taken and put through the grinding and crushing process to become fine flour. Only then can it become suitable to become bread.

Fine flour speaks of the trials, testings, temptations and sufferings of the believer, as the corn of wheat, in order to become the bread of God, even as for Jesus Christ (*John 12:24; Isaiah 28:28; 52:14; 53:1-6; Psalm 147:14; John 6:51-56*).

Jew and Gentile believers together would experience the crushing process in order to become "one bread". Paul says concerning Christ and the church that they are **bread**! "The bread which we break, is it not the communion of the Body of Christ? For we being many are one bread, and one body: for we are all partakers of that one bread" (I Corinthians 10:16-17).

The two Wave Loaves being made of fine flour then speak of the oneness of the Jew and Gentile, blended together by the unifying power and ministry of the Holy Spirit.

5. Baken with Leaven — Leviticus 23:17

No one can eat fine flour by itself. In order to make fine flour into bread and make it palatable, it must be baked. The fire and the baking process intensify the unity of the loose fine flour.

So the fire of the Holy Spirit (Hebrews 12:29; Matthew 3:11-12) intensifies the unity of Jew and Gentile as the bread of God, suitable to be waved before Him (Luke 3:16; Hebrews 9:14).

This also speaks of the fiery trials of faith for all saints to bind them together in one loaf, whether Jew or Gentile (Job 23:10; James 1:12; I Peter 1:6-7; Proverbs 17:3).

6. The Firstfruits unto the Lord — Leviticus 23:17

The truth of the firstfruits has already been considered under the Sheaf of the Firstfruits. There it was seen that the firstfruits spoke of the choicest, the first, the best. They were peculiarly the Lord's and presented to Him. They were sanctified to His service. This is true whether it speaks of Christ or His church. Read Exodus 23:16, 19; 34:22, 26; Leviticus 2:12-14; Numbers 18:12; 28:26; Deuteronomy 26:10; II Kings 4:42; Nehemiah 10:35-37; 12:44; Proverbs 3:9.

The New Testament writers particularly see the early converts, both Jew and Gentile as "a kind of firstfruits" unto the Lord (James 1:18; I Corinthians 15:20, 23; 16:15; Revelation 14:4). They also realized they had but received "the firstfruits" of the Holy Spirit's operations (Romans 8:23; Ephesians 1:13-14). The firstfruits speak of more to come; the great harvest yet to be reaped and brought in. Thus as the two wave loaves presented to the Lord were but the firstfruits of a great harvest of corn and bread yet to be harvested, so the early church converts, Jew and Gentile, were but the firstfruits of a great harvest to be reaped during this entire church era. Believers are also called the "church of the firstborn". (Hebrews 12:23).

7. A Wave Offering — Leviticus 23:17, 20

The Hebrew word **"Tenoofaw"** meaning **"to wave"** (S.C.8573 frm S.C.5130) has also the thought of "to quiver" (i.e., vibrate up and down, or rock to and fro); a brandishing" and specially the official undulation of sacrificial offerings. It is translated "offering, shaking, waveoffering".

On the Day of Pentecost the 120 disciples, filled with the Holy Spirit, were God's "wave offering", for men thought they were drunk by the way they acted and spoke (Acts 2:1-15).

Jews and Gentiles, baptized by the same Spirit into the same body are indeed God's "wave offering" (I Corinthians 12:13; Ephesians 2:11-22).

8. Holy to the Lord for the Priest — Leviticus 23:20

Even though the two wave loaves were leavened, yet the Lord counted them holy unto Himself for the priest.

So the Lord God counts the church holy, separated and sanctified unto Himself, for His Christ, even though at present imperfect. The church is acceptable to God through Christ. The believer is "holy in Christ" (Ephesians 1:4; 5:27).

9. A Holy Convocation — Leviticus 23:21

The Day of Pentecost was also a sabbath day, a holy convocation. No servile work was to be done on this day of rest. It prophesied of the fact that "the morrow after the sabbath", or the first day of the new week would become the New Testament "sabbath" or "day of rest". The disciples came through the transition from the Old to the New Covenant and came to keep the first day of the week as these scriptures indicate (Matthew 28:1; Acts 2:38; 20:7; I Corinthians 16:1-2; Revelation 1:10).

10. A Statute For Ever — Leviticus 23:21

The keeping of the Feast Day of Pentecost was a law that was to be kept in all generations. This finds its fulfilment in the fact that the Holy Spirit has come to dwell with the believer forever (John 14:16-17. The believer has a continual "Pentecostal Feast" thereby.

G. **The Feast of Harvest of Firstfruits** — *Exodus 23:16; 34:22; Deuteronomy 16:10; Numbers 28:26.*

As seen earlier this Feast Day was called the "Feast of Weeks", or the "Feast of Harvest", or the "Feast of the Firstfruits. Thus this Feast not only involved a special and literal 24 hour day, it also involved a period of time. There are several other things therefore of significance involved in this Feast besides the special set day ceremonies.

1. **The Early Rains** — *Deuteronomy 11:10-15; Leviticus 26:4; Deuteronomy 28:12; Joel 2:23; Zechariah 10:1*

There can be no harvest without the rains to cause it to grow and mature. The Lord promised Israel that He would bless their land, that He would give the "first rain and the latter rain" in order that they would be able to gather in the corn, wine and oil in the appointed seasons. Thus under Passover and Pentecost, there was the "latter rain" or "spring rain", according to the reckoning of the sacred year of Israel.

Rain in Scripture is symbolical of revival and refreshing. Spiritually speaking it pointed to the outpouring of the Holy Spirit as the "early and latter rain". The Lord promised that He would come to His people as the rain *(Hosea 6:1-3)*.

The Jews always understood that the outpouring of rain or water was symbolical and prophetical of the coming outpouring of the Holy Spirit on their own nation as well as other nations. The outpouring of the Holy Spirit on the Day of Pentecost and onward was indeed "the first rain" or "the spring rain". The Prophet Joel, who is the Prophet of Pentecost, alluded to this in *Joel 2:21-32*, where he links the outpouring of early and latter rains with his prophecy of the outpouring of the Holy Spirit on all flesh.

2. **The Harvest Time** — *Deuteronomy 16:10; Exodus 23:16; 34:22.*

With rain comes harvest time. The rains were necessary for both sowing and harvest periods. As in any agricultural year two harvests take place, so in the land of Canaan. There were two periods of harvest: corn harvest and fruit harvest. Thus:

a. Passover and Pentecost: — **corn** harvest.

b. Tabernacles: — **fruit** harvest.

Passover was **barley** harvest and Pentecost was **wheat** harvest *(Ruth 1:22; 2:23; Exodus 34:21-22; Judges 6:11; I Samuel 6:13; II Samuel 21:9-10)*.

The first harvest of the year, in the beginning of Israel's sacred year was **corn** harvest, which came as the result of the early or the Spring rains. However, the corn harvest pointed to the fruit harvest, the harvest in the end of the year *(Leviticus 23:33-44; Deuteronomy 16:6-17; Exodus 23:16; 34:22; Numbers 29:12-40)*.

The final harvest will be considered under the Feast of Tabernacles. Sufficient for the present is to see that the reason why this Feast is called the Feast of Weeks, or the Feast of the Harvest of Firstfruits is because of the corn harvest brought in during this period of time, in these weeks. The Day of Pentecost was actually a "Harvest Festival" or "Thanksgiving Day".

The antitypical fulfilment of this is seen in the Book of Acts. Under the early outpouring of the Holy Spirit as rain there was also a great harvest of souls. Great numbers, great multitudes came to the Lord. There were 3000 souls, then 5000 souls, and then multitudes of men and women who came in during this harvest period *(Acts 4:4; 5:14; 2:41-42)*. Later on, as the rain of the Holy Spirit continued to be poured out there was a great harvest of Gentile converts reaped. It was the fulfilment of the great harvest which Jesus saw *(Matthew 9:37-38; John 4:35)*.

It has been suggested by various expositors that the barley harvest represented the Jewish converts, as barley harvest comes first, and the wheat harvest represented the Gentile converts. To the Jew first came the Gospel, and then to the Gentile. Together they constitute the "corn harvest" of the early Church ingathering period.

3. **The Harvest of Firstfruits** — *Exodus 23:16; 34:22; Numbers 28:26*

Sufficient has been said concerning the significance of the firstfruits. However, it needs to be noted that the Feast of Weeks was but the firstfruits harvest.

The firstfruits always point to more to come. Hence the harvest of Passover and Pentecost pointed to the harvest of the Feast of Tabernacles. This harvest was to come in **the end of the year!** It speaks prophetically of the harvest in **the end of the age** *(Matthew 13:30, 39; Mark 4:29; Revelation 14:15)*. This harvest will necessitate the final outpouring of the Holy Spirit as rain according to the word of James *(James 5:7)*.

4. **Harvest of Freewill Offerings and Rejoicing** — *Deuteronomy 16:9-12, 16-17; 28:47.*

With the harvest in, the Lord commanded Israel to bring freewill offerings unto Him, according to the blessing of the Lord upon them. They were to rejoice before the Lord for His goodness. The freewill offerings were to be given to their sons and daughters, their servants, the strangers, the fatherless, the widow and the Levites (Note also *Deuteronomy 12:4-12*). The New Testament shows the same spirit of joy and giving upon the early believers, as distribution was made to the needy saints *(Acts 4:32-34; 6:1; 13:52; I Corinthians 16:1-2; II Corinthians 8-9)*.

Thus the believer must experience the glorious Feast of Pentecost, even as Passover. Passover is but the beginning, introducing one to the Lamb of God, Jesus Christ. The believer must continue on in the Feasts of the Lord and enter into Pentecost. Pentecost brings one into the blessed ministry of the Holy Spirit and into the church, the Body of Christ. However, this Feast is not the ultimate. There is another Feast into which the believer and the church must enter. This is the Feast of Tabernacles.

Every time a sinner receives Christ as his own Saviour, he experiences Passover. It is not that the historical Passover is repeated again, but the historical fact and truth becomes experiential truth. The same is true of Pentecost. Pentecost is an historical fact and truth, never to be repeated as such again. However, every time a believer receives the Holy Spirit baptism there is an experiential Pentecost. It is this balance between historical and experiential truth that needs to be kept in mind in studying the Feasts, and especially so as we move on to that glorious Feast, the Feast of Tabernacles.

Chapter Eleven
INTRODUCING THE FEAST OF THE SEVENTH MONTH — TABERNACLES

We come now to the third and final and most glorious Feast of the Lord—the Feast of Tabernacles. It is a Feast about which the people of God seem to know or understand very little. Believers who have studied the Feasts of the Lord differ as to the interpretation of this final Feast. It will be found that this Feast is alluded to in the Major and Minor Prophets more than the other Feasts combined. It was, for Israel, the consummation of the sacred year, and was the "Feast of all Feasts" as far as the Hebrew mind was concerned. Before studying the Feast of Tabernacles and its integral parts and significant details, some broad observations should be considered.

I. THE FEAST OF PROPHECY — ISRAEL OR THE CHURCH?

A. The Feast of Prophecy

Between Pentecost and Tabernacles there was an interval of time of 3 months, these being the 4th, 5th and 6th months. Passover and Pentecost were linked together by a few weeks but Tabernacles stood alone at the end of the sacred year, separated from the previous Feasts by several months. These months were dry months, when generally no rain fell. There were no holy convocations when the nation gathered before the Lord and His Sanctuary.

Most expositors of the Feasts of the Lord recognize that there is definite significance in the time lapse between Pentecost and Tabernacles, the dry months. Hence, this Feast is generally recognized as the Feast of Prophecy — that is, a Feast which has yet to find fulfilment. However, it is at this point that the difference of opinion arises concerning to **whom** this Feast pertains: whether to the nation of Israel, or the New Testament church.

B. Feasts for Israel or the Church?

It is important to understand who this Feast is for, and who it concerns. There are basically three schools of interpreters who seek to answer this important question.

1. Feasts for Israel Only

One school of interpreters holds that the Feasts strictly pertain to the chosen nation Israel and have nothing to do with the New Testament church. Passover and Pentecost are spoken of as being the Jewish Feasts and then the Mystery Body of Christ comes in between the first two Feasts and the Feast of Tabernacles.

This school holds that after Pentecost God's "prophetic clock" stopped because of Jewish unbelief. During the period of the church age, the Jews have been set aside and God is doing a new thing in the formation of the church. It is said that the church comes in during a parenthetical period of time, while the Jews have been set aside. Once God has finished with the church, then He will turn again to the Jews and they will have their eyes opened to accept Christ in the Feast of Tabernacles.

The following diagram illustrates this school of interpretation.

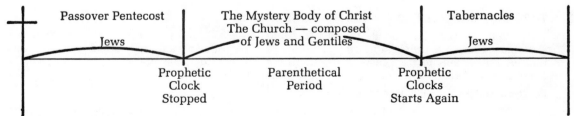

2. Feasts for the Church and Israel

The general teaching of the second school is that Passover was fulfilled in Christ, Pentecost was fulfilled in the church, while the Feast of Tabernacles finds fulfilment in Israel. Or, the first four Feasts pertain to God's heavenly people, the church, while the last three Feasts pertain to God's earthly people, the Jews.

The three parts of the final Feast are interpreted in the following manner.

a. **The Feast of Trumpets** finds fulfilment in the future regathering of long-dispersed Israel. The interval between Pentecost and Trumpets is likened to the present dispensation and the work of the Holy Spirit. When the present era is ended and the church or "Pentecostal" period expires, then the elect of Israel will be regathered to keep the Feast of Trumpets in Jerusalem (*Matthew 24:31; Romans 11:25; Joel 2:1; 3:21; Leviticus 23:23-25* are used to support this interpretation). It is further held that the Feast of Trumpets finds its fulfilment in the "catching out" of the church and then the regathering of Israel as the second coming of Christ.

b. **The Day of Atonement** is interpreted to be symbolic of the national day of cleansing from sin for Israel after their regathering. It is held that under the Trumpets Israel will be gathered back to the land, unconverted, and under the Day of Atonement will repent, turn to God and experience national cleansing (*Leviticus 16; Zechariah 12:9-14; 13:1; Joel 2:11-15* and *Hebrews 9:11-14* are used to support this interpretation).

c. **The Feast of Tabernacles** is interpreted to be both a memorial as well as prophetic; memorial to Israel's redemption out of Egypt, and prophetic as to the kingdom rest after her regathering and restoration. The Feast, coming at the end of harvest when the people dwell in booths is understood to be the fulness of Israel's Millennial rest unto the New Heavens and New Earth. It is also held that the Feast of Tabernacles will be kept in the Millennium by Israel and other nations, who will be forced to keep it or be plagued (*Zechariah 14:16-20; Leviticus 23:33-44; Deuteronomy 16:13* are used to support this view).

Undoubtedly there is a measure of truth in this view as to the nation of Israel's coming back into relationship with the Lord God. However, the major weakness in this view is seen in these remarks: None could experience Tabernacles without Pentecost, and none could experience Pentecost without Passover. All must follow God's order in the Feasts according to their respective months. Again, it was Jewish **believers** who experienced the first historical Passover and Pentecost in the Gospels and the Acts. These believers actually consisted or constituted **the Church!** Hence it becomes inconsistent to take two of the Feasts and apply them to Christ and the Church, and then take the third Feast and apply it only to the nation of Israel.

No unbelieving Jew or Israelite could experience the last Feast without partaking of the first Feast. The Jew must know Christ as his personal Saviour and experience Christ as the Passover Lamb first, then he can experience his personal Pentecost in the baptism of the Spirit which sets him in the church, the Body of Christ. And then, and only then, can he proceed on in God to experience the truth of the Feast of Tabernacles. This is true for both Jew and Gentile. There can be no Feast outside of Christ. Everything since the Cross is "in Christ".

3. Feasts for the Church

The next major school of interpretation holds that the Feast of Tabernacles must find its fulfilment in Christ and in His church. The author of this Text holds to this final view, though recognizing that the Jew will, under an outpouring of the Holy Spirit in the end-times, come to experience "in Christ", all three Feasts. The major reason this view is held is that the Feasts of Passover and Pentecost at or after their historical fulfilment found experiential fulfilment only in **believers** in Christ, whether Jew or Gentile. In Christ there is neither Jew nor Gentile, bond nor free, male or female, but only the new creature. The new creation composes the New Testament church. This is now the true Israel of God (*Galatians 6:15-16; Ephesians 2:11-20*). Hence, consistency of interpretation demands that as Passover and Pentecost found historical **and** experiential fulfilment in Christ and His church, so the Feast of Tabernacles will find the same kind of fulfilment. It is this view which will be pursued in this Text.

II. THE FEAST UNFULFILLED IN ISRAEL'S WANDERINGS

Paul tells us that many of the things which happened to Israel were for types and examples to the New Testament Church (*I Corinthians 10:6, 11*). One of the most remarkable historical-types in Israel's history is that which pertains to the Feasts of the Lord. We will consider both the type and antitype, Old Testament Israel and New Testament Israel, as to the fulfilment of the Feasts of the Lord.

A. Natural Israel — The Historical-Type.

Israel experienced the Feast of Passover in Egypt and the mighty deliverance which resulted therefrom (*Exodus 12*). They also experienced the Feast of Unleavened Bread in their separation from the land by baptism into the Red Sea and the Cloud (*Exodus 13-14-15; I Corinthians 10:1-2*).

The 3 day journey brought them to the foot of Mt. Sinai (*Exodus 15-16-17-18-19*). Here at Mt. Sinai the nation experienced the Feast of Pentecost in the third month. God's intention was then to bring the Israel into Canaan land where they could enter into the third and final Feast and partake of the fruit of the land.

In Egypt they knew Passover. In the journeyings they knew Unleavened Bread. At Mt. Sinai they knew Pentecost. But only in Canaan land could they know and enjoy Tabernacles.

The great tragedy is seen when the nation came to Kadesh-Barnea. "Kadesh" means "Holy" or "Holiness", and "Barnea" means "An inconstant or fickle son".

It was at Kadesh 'Barnea that they rejected the land promised to Abraham, Isaac and Jacob. In rejecting the land of Canaan they also rejected the greatest Feast also, the Feast of Tabernacles (*Numbers 13-14*).

For 40 years God allowed them to wander in the Wilderness until all that generation died. Only Joshua and Caleb lived to enter into the land of Canaan with the new generation. The national sin was that of unbelief (*Numbers 13-14* with *Hebrews 3-4*).

It is evident that the new generation, after crossing the Jordan, kept the Feasts of the Lord. Read carefully *Joshua 5:10-12* with *Leviticus 23:9-14; Nehemiah 8:1-18; Ezra 6:19-22; 3:1-6*.

Thus the new generation experienced Passover, Pentecost and Tabernacles. Joshua and Caleb, as overcomers, also enjoyed the Feasts of the Lord in Canaan land at the end of the 40 years wanderings in the Wilderness. They had another spirit, and wholly followed the Lord.

B. Spiritual Israel — The Historical-Antitype

The Old Testament scene may be superimposed upon the history of the New Testament Church in remarkable comparison.

The Historical Books of the New Testament show the fulfilment of the first two Feasts. The four Gospels present Christ as the historical fulfilment of the Feast of Passover, Unleavened Bread and the Sheaf of Firstfruits. The Book of Acts shows remarkably the historical and anti-typical fulfilment of the Feast of Weeks, or Pentecost, in the church.

But where, in the history of the church, can one find the fulfilment of the third and final Feast, the Feast of Tabernacles? This is the one remaining Feast of Prophecy — the Feast unfulfilled in the church.

Alfred Edersheim, in his excellent book *"The Temple: Its Ministry and Services"* (p. 287) says concerning this Feast "... the fact remains that the Feast of Tabernacles is the one only type in the Old Testament which has not yet been fulfilled."

The New testament church follows the pattern of the Old Testament church. First the natural, then the spiritual; first the type, then the antitype; first the shadow, then the substance.

As natural Israel wandered for 40 years after Passover and Pentecost, and failed to enter into Tabernacles in Canaan rest through unbelief, so spiritual Israel — the church — has followed suit.

The church has been wandering, so to speak, through church History in so much unbelief of God's promises. Generation after generation has passed on, dying in the Wilderness, never experiencing the three Feasts of the Lord. However, there must be — there will be — a new generation that will arise to enter into the Covenant promises of God and experience all three Feasts of the Lord.

It is not that this third Feast is not dealt with in the New Testament for it is. Hebrews and Revelation especially deal with this Feast and its integral parts. However, the Lord has kept this Feast for the end-time generation who will fully believe Him and enter into His promises. The nation of Israel wandered for 40 years; the Church has been wandering for approximately 40 Jubilees (or, 40 x 50 = 2000 years).

But the Wilderness wanderings are coming to an end. A new generation is arising. They are experiencing Christ as their Passover. They are keeping the Feast of Pentecost in the Baptism of the Holy Spirit and the formation of the Church. They will not stop there but will move on and experience the Feast of Tabernacles and the truths symbolized therein.

The following simple diagram illustrates the truth of these things.

Natural Israel:
Historical-Type:

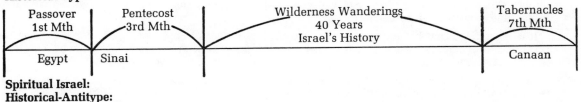

Passover 1st Mth	Pentecost 3rd Mth		Wilderness Wanderings 40 Years Israel's History	Tabernacles 7th Mth
Egypt	Sinai			Canaan

Spiritual Israel:
Historical-Antitype:

Passover 1st Mth	Pentecost 3rd Mth		Wilderness Wanderings 40x50 = 2000 years	Tabernacles 7th Mth
Gospels	Acts		Church History	Hebrews/ Revelation

III. THE FEAST POSTPONED AND SUBSTITUTED

In I Kings Chapter 12 we have an interesting account of the division of the united Kingdom of Israel into two Kingdoms; the Kingdom of the House of Judah and the Kingdom of the House of Israel.

Rehoboam, the son of Solomon, took the throne over the House of Judah, consisting of two tribes, plus the Priestly Tribe of Levi. Jeroboam, the son of Nebat and servant of Solomon, took the throne over the House of Israel, consisting of the remaining ten tribes. The Lord permitted this division to take place so that His sovereign purposes would be worked out in the nation (I Kings 12:1-24).

In the remainder of the chapter (verses 25-33), we see how Jeroboam set up a substitute Feast of Tabernacles, postponing it to another month. The salient points are noted here.

Jeroboam, fearing that the kingdom would return to Rehoboam, decided to set up a counterfeit religion. He had two golden calves made, setting them up as gods, even as Aaron had years before. One golden calf was set up in Bethel and the other in Dan. This became a sin unto the people, for the people began to worship these golden calves even as they had done under Aaron (Exodus 32).

Jeroboam also set up a house of high places and established his own priesthood which were not of the tribe of Levi. And then to add to his sin, he "ordained a Feast in the eighth month, like unto the Feast that was in Judah." He built an altar and sacrifices to these false gods, on the fifteenth day of the eighth month. The Scripture states that this was "the month which he had devised of his own heart." For his sins, God sent a prophet to bring judgment upon him. However, Jeroboam did not repent but went further into sin as I Kings Chapter 13 clearly shows.

The lesson which can be learned from this historical account is this. As Jeroboam set up a counterfeit religion and postponed and substituted the Feast of Tabernacles, so will other leaders do likewise.

The true Feast of Tabernacles was to be kept in Jerusalem in the place where the Lord recorded His Name. It was also to be kept in the seventh month (Leviticus 23:34-44). Evidently Jeroboam reasoned in his heart that the people of Judah would probably accept the postponed and substitute Feast rather than bothering to go up to Jerusalem. In this way he believed he would be able to keep the Kingdom of Israel from re-uniting with the Kingdom of Judah.

The tragedy today is that many leaders in Christendom would postpone this Feast to some other dispensation, or pass it on to other people, or even have a substitute Feast. By doing this the church is robbed of entering into this glorious Feast as God intended.

However, God will have a people that will indeed enter into all three Feasts of the Lord, rather than follow modern day Jeroboams and a counterfeit priesthood in an idolatrous system.

IV. THE FEAST OF TABERNACLES OUTLINED

Before proceeding in our study of this final Feast in detail we outline the three integral parts thereof. Passover had three integral parts to it. Pentecost stood alone. Tabernacles had three integral parts to it. All together the three Feasts comprehend seven Festival days in their respective months, times and seasons.

Leviticus sets out the three parts of this Feast of the seventh month
1. The Feast Day of Trumpets — Leviticus 23:23-25.
2. The Feast Day of Atonement — Leviticus 23:26-32.
3. The Feast of Tabernacles — Leviticus 23:33-44.

Other Scriptures dealing with the details of this Feast may be found in Numbers 29:1-40; 10:1-10; Leviticus 16 in the Old Testament, and the Book of Hebrews in the New Testament.

V. THE FEAST OF TABERNACLES — HISTORICALLY & PROPHETICALLY

The two major schools of interpretation of this Feast both recognize that this Feast is a Feast with prophetic import. Whether it is interpreted to be fulfilled in the nation of Israel or in the Church, both see that this Feast in its fulness has to find future fulfilment.

It is recognized that there has been an historical fulfilment of Passover. There has also been an historical fulfilment of Pentecost. There has not been an historical fulfillment of Tabernacles. Consistency of interpretation demands that this Feast, as the previous two, also find historical fulfilment.

Not only must there be an historical fulfilment, there must also be an experiential fulfilment. The historical-typical-symbolical fulfilment pointed to the historical-antitypical-experiential fulfilment.

As this Feast is studied it will be seen that certain elements in this Feast have been fulfilled historically in Christ and His redemptive work. The full truth typified has to find its fulfilment in the experience of the church. Hence, in studying the details of this final Feast, it is necessary to clearly understand and discern that which Christ has already fulfilled and that this has to be fulfilled in the church. Or, it is important to understand that which is historical and that which is prophetical. This twofold fulfilment should be distinguished, otherwise misunderstanding and misinterpretation will result. This will be noted by:

A. That which has been fulfilled by Christ historically, and judically, as to its temporal, and typical and symbolical elements.

B. That which has to be fulfilled in the church prophetically and experientially as to its eternal and spiritual elements.

This twofold fulfillment will be kept in view as we consider the details of this Feast as it involves Christ historically and the church, His Body, prophetically.

The following Diagram illustrates the truth of the Feasts as to their historical and prophetical significances in Israel's history and history of the church.

Three Feasts of Israel			
Historical Fulfilment Typical/Prophetical in Israel			
Passover	Pentecost		Tabernacles
Egypt	Sinai	Wilderness Wanderings	Canaan
1st Month	3rd Month	4th, 5th, 6th Months	7th Month
Passover 14th Unleavened Bread 15th Sheaf of First-Fruits 18th	The 50th from the Sheaf Waving		Trumpets 1st Atonement 10th Tabernacles 15th
Spring Rains Barley Harvest	Wheat Harvest Corn		Early/Latter Rains Wine & Oil Harvest Fruit
Historical Fulfilment Antitypical in Christ			
Passover	Pentecost		Tabernacles
Gospels	Acts	Epistles	Hebrews/Revelation
Crucifixion Burial Resurrection	Holy Spirit Outpoured Church Formed	Dark Ages	Ministry Voice Perfection of Church Ingathering souls Coming of Christ
Spiritual, Experiential Practical fulfilment in Church Salvation in Christ Separation to Christ	Baptism im Holy Spirit into Body of Christ		Perfection of the Church Coming of Christ
Early Church Outpouring			Latter Day Church Outpouring

The challenge comes to all believers as to which Feast they will stop at: Passover? . . . Pentecost? . . . Tabernacles? . . .

Church history shows how God's people have stopped at either the first Feast or the second Feast. God's people have built their denominations around the various truths of these two Feasts. And the sad history of the church shows that those who experienced Passover truths opposed those who experienced Pentecost truths. And, history repeating itself, shows that there are those who have experienced Pentecost truths who oppose those who seek to follow on to know God in Tabernacle truths!

Chapter Twelve
THE FEAST DAY OF THE BLOWING OF TRUMPETS

The Feast of Tabernacles is introduced on the first day of the seventh month by the day of blowing of trumpets. It was a festival of trumpets sounding throughout the land and calling the nation to prepare for the coming Day of Atonement, the Day of national cleansing.

Specially prepared offerings were presented to the Lord in this Day also, even as on every other Feast day, besides the regular daily offerings.

Psalm 89:15 (NAS, Marginal) "How blessed are the people who know the joyful sound! Or, **blast of the trumpet, shout of joy.**"

The specific scriptures dealing with this Feast are found in *Leviticus 23:23-25; Numbers 29:1-6*. Because this Feast Day is particularly called "The Day of blowing of the trumpets" the significance of trumpets in Israel should be understood.

I. TRUMPETS IN ISRAEL

There were basically two kinds of trumpets in Israel; trumpets made of ram's horns and trumpets of silver.

A. Trumpets of Ram's Horns

Exodus 19:16, 19; 20:18; Leviticus 25:9; Joshua 6:4-13, 20; I Samuel 2:1; I Chronicles 25:5. The horn here came from some sacrifice, from the bullock or the ram. The ram's horns were especially used to blast out the note of shouting at the fall of the walls of Jericho. It was the trumpet of Jubilee *(Leviticus 25:10-54)*.

B. Trumpets of Silver

Numbers 10:2, 8, 9; 29:1; II Chronicles 5:12-13; 7:6; Psalm 98:6. The trumpets here were made of silver. Silver was the symbol of the price of redemption of the soul. It was used as ransom or the atonement money *(Exodus 30:11-16)*.

It is possible that the two trumpets made from one piece of silver came from the atonement money after the numbering of the firstborn *(Numbers 3:40-51)*.

Two trumpets were made for the various callings in Israel. As noted already the number two is the number of testimony, the number of witness. "In the mouth of two or three witnesses shall ever word be established" *(Deuteronomy 17:6; 19:15; John 8:17-18; II Corinthians 13:1)*.

Here we have the silvery redemptive witness sounding forth in Israel in these two silver trumpets. The Jew and Gentile, two yet one in Christ are redeemed, not with corruptible things such as silver or gold but with the precious blood of Christ *(I Peter 1:18-20; Leviticus 17:11-14)*. Both speak with a united witness and testimony.

The trumpet in scripture is used to symbolize the prophetic voice, the spoken Word of the Lord coming to His people through the ministry. The prophets were told to lift up their "voice like a trumpet" *(Isaiah 58:1; Hosea 8:1)*.

The prophet Ezekiel was distinctly told to be a Watchman to Israel and blow the trumpet voice of warning to them, or call them unto the Lord *(Ezekiel 33:1-7)*.

The voice of the Lord Jesus is symbolized also by the sound of the trumpet *(Revelation 1:10; 4:1)*. Read also *Joel 2:1, 15; Amos 3:6-8; Isaiah 18:3; 27:13; Jeremiah 4:8; 19:21; 51:27)*.

For Israel, Aaron and his sons were responsible as priests to sound the trumpet message on the special occasions *(Exodus 28:1 with Numbers 10:3, 4, 10)*.

For the Church, the Body of Christ, the two silver trumpets may be likened to the Ministries. Christ and His Ministers sound the Word of the Lord to the spiritual Israel of God *(Ephesians 4:8-16)*.

It is important that the trumpeters make a clear and distinct sound so that the people of God may hear and understand the message *(I Corinthians 14:8; 13:1; Mark 4:23-25; Luke 8:18)*. The people of God need to take heed **"how"** and **"what"** they hear!

II. **USE OF TRUMPETS IN ISRAEL** — *Numbers 10:1-10.*

The scripture passage in Numbers gives nine specific occasions when the trumpets were to be blown in Israel. They find their historical fulfilment in Old Testament Israel and then their spiritual significance in New Testament Israel, the church.

A. **For the Calling of the Assemblies** — *Numbers 10:2*

Under this call the 12 Tribes gathered together as one nation. The trumpet was always used to call Israel, God's people together *(Isaiah 27:13)*.

So the church as the Israel of God gathers together as one in Christ *(Psalm 50:5; Matthew 18:20; Ephesians 4:10; John 17)*. At the coming of Christ the trumpet will sound and gather together all the elect from the four corners of the earth *(Matthew 24:30-31)*.

B. **For the Journeying of the Camps** — *Numbers 10:2*

When the Cloud moved, then the trumpets were to be blown and the people were to move on with God *(Numbers 9:15-23; 10:11-36; Hebrews 11:13)*.

So the church today must follow the Cloud of God's Holy Spirit as He leads the way.

C. **For the Calling of the Princes** — *Numbers 10:4*

When the leadership of the nation was to be gathered together, then only one trumpet was to be blown. Two trumpets would sound when the whole nation or the whole congregation was to be called *(Psalm 107:32; Ezekiel 34:1-7; Revelation 1:10)*.

So today God calls leadership together in special convocations so that He may speak to them and give them direction.

D. **For the Blowing of Alarms** — *Numbers 10:5-7*

At times they had to sound an alarm and warn the people of that which was coming *(Joel 2:1; Amos 3:6-7)*.

So today God sounds an alarm to His Church to warn her of coming events in the world and thus cause the church to seek His face.

E. **For War or Enemy Oppression** — *Numbers 10:9*

Trumpets were often blown in times of war and enemy oppression. When God heard the trumpet He would fight for His people and bring them deliverance *(Jeremiah 4:19, 21; Judges 3:27; 6:34; 7:4-22; Numbers 31:6-7)*.

So the New Testament church, in times of spiritual warfare and oppression can call on the Name of the Lord and experience great deliverance *(Acts 10:38; Ephesians 6:10-18)*.

F. **For Days of Gladness** — *Numbers 10:10*

There were time of great joy and gladness on the various Festival occasions. In these days the trumpets were blown as the people rejoiced together before the Lord their God. This is seen greatly in the Tabernacle of David order of worship. *(I Chronicles 13:8; 15:24-29; Psalm 47:4-5; 150:3; II Samuel 6:13)*.

So the church experiences days of gladness and joy as she gathers together to worship the Lord in Festival days as well as on the Lord's day *(Colossians 4:12; Ephesians 3:18)*.

G. **For Solemn Assemblies** — *Numbers 10:10*

There were other occasions when the people of Israel were called by the trumpets to days of Solemn Assemblies; in times of intercession, prayer and fasting *(Joel 2:1-17; Psalm 81:3; Zephaniah 3:14-20; II Kings 10:20)*.

So the church at times is called by the Lord to times and seasons of intercession and special prayer and fasting *(Isaiah 58:3-6; Joel 1:14; Mark 2:18-20; Matthew 17:21; Mark 9:29)*.

H. **For the Beginning of Months** — *Numbers 10:10*

All Feast Days and all the beginning of the months were announced by the sound of the blowing of trumpets. These trumpet sounds were to keep God's "times and seasons" in the people's mind *(Exodus 19:6, 13; Leviticus 23:24)*.

So the Spirit of God speaks to the church by the ministries so that God's people may remember the "times and seasons" of the Lord's calendar *(Ecclesiastes 3:1, 17; 8:6; Daniel 2:21; Leviticus 23:4; Acts 1:7; I Thessalonians 5:1; Acts 3:19-21)*.

I. **For the Offerings and Sacrifices** — *Numbers 10:10*

As the sacrifices were being offered upon the altar the trumpets were also blown. As the Lord heard the silvery note of redemption ascending over the ascending sacrifices, so He would remember His promise to accept His people through blood atonement *(Numbers 28:11-15; 29:1-6; II Chronicles 29:27-28).*

So the Lord accepts the church in her priestly ministrations through Christ. The believer offers spiritual sacrifices of joy and praise acceptable to God in Him *(Hebrews 13:15-16; Revelation 1:6; 5:9-10; I Peter 2:5-9).*

These were the major uses of trumpets in Israel. The Hebrew nation was familiar with the sound of the trumpet. All had to learn the distinctive messages that were being sounded in order to respond properly.

The Lord Jesus Christ, with trumpet voice called to the churches to "hear what the Spirit" way saying to them *(Revelation 2:7, 11, 17, 27; 3:6, 22; 1:10).*

We note briefly several other significant uses of trumpets in Israel as well as in the New Testament revelation.

A. Trumpets were used in the anointing of Kings *(II Kings 9:13; 11:14; II Samuel 15:10;II Chronicles 23:13).*

B. Trumpets were used at the Dedication of Solomon's Temple *(II Chronicles 5:11-14).*

C. Trumpets were used in the great year of Jubilee, which was every fiftieth year in Israel. It was a year of release, restoration and reunion *(Leviticus 25; Isaiah 61:1-3; Luke 4:18-19).*

D. Trumpets are associated with the final judgments of God and also at the second coming of Christ for His own *(Revelation 8:1-9; 11:15; I Thessalonians 4:16; I Corinthians 15:51-52; Matthew 24:31; Zephaniah 1::14-18; Zechariah 9:14).*

III. **THE FEAST DAY OF TRUMPETS** — *Leviticus 23:23-25; Numbers 29:1*

As seen previously, trumpets were blown at the beginning of the months, announcing each new month. The Feast of Tabernacles took place in the seventh month. This month was ushered in by the trumpets, but with special emphasis. So much so that this day was called "The Day of the Blowing of Trumpets." It was a different call and message that sounded forth on this Feast day.

Various expositors have interpreted this trumpet to be "the rapture trumpet." However, the Feast Day of Trumpets was distinctly the call to the great Day of Atonement, the Day of national cleansing. Daniel the prophet speaks of it as "the cleansing of the Sanctuary" *(Daniel 8:13-14).*

Right throughout the nation, regardless of which tribe a person belonged to, the call went to all Israelites to come to the Sanctuary of the Lord for this Solemn Day of Atonement.

This is what the Feast Day of Trumpets meant historically in and to the nation of Israel.

Several other important things relative to this day should be noted here.

A. **New Year's Day** — *Numbers 29:1*

The Feast Day of Trumpets was New Year's Day in Israel. It should be remembered that the Hebrews had a two-sided Calendar year, that is, the Sacred and the Civil.

The Sacred year began in Abib or Nisan, the first month, with the Feast of Passover and it concluded in Tishri or Ethanim, the seventh month, in the Feast of Tabernacles.

The Civil year began in the seventh month with the Day of Trumpets and finished twelve months later in the month Ebul. Hence the first month of the Sacred year became the seventh month of the Civil year while the first month of the Civil was also the seventh month of the Sacred year. Thus it was both an end and a new beginning; closing off the old and bringing in the new year. It is this which helps us to understand *Joel 2:23* concerning the former and latter rains coming down "in the first month." (The student is referred to the Hebrew Calendar in the text).

The spiritual truth conveyed here to the church is that God's endings are also new beginnings. He closes off the old to bring us into the new beginning. He Himself is "the First and the Last, the Beginning and the Ending" and the Finisher of our faith *(Revelation 1:8, 11; Isaiah 41:4; Hebrews 12:1-4).*

B. **A Sabbath Rest** — *Leviticus 23:23-25*

As were all other Feast Days, so the Day of Trumpets was a Sabbath Rest. No servile work was to be done. It was to be a day of rest—rest in the finished work of the High Priest in the atonement. *Leviticus 23* emphasizes the fact for each Feast that no servile work was to be done.

In the Feast of Unleavened Bread "no servile work" was to be done *(Vs. 7-8).* In the Feast day of Pentecost "no servile work" was to be done *(Vs. 21).* In the Feast day of Trumpets "no servile work" was to be done *(Vs. 25).*

In the Feast Day of Atonement no work was to be done and anyone doing work would be destroyed from the people of God (Vs. 28-31). **Rest** was to be entered into on these Feast days. Man was to cease from all his works.

The New Testament answers this for the believer, for the believer must "cease from his own works" and "enter into rest" (Hebrews 4:1-11; Matthew 11:28-30).

It is "in Christ" the believer finds true rest, ceasing from the works of the flesh (Galatians 5:19-21) and the works of the Law (Romans 3:27-28; 10:30-33). Christ is our Sabbath. The Old Testament Sabbath days pointed to the Person of Christ (Colossians 2:14-17).

C. The Seventh Month — Leviticus 23:24

Passover took place in the first month. Number one is the number of beginning, of commencement. Israel began their experience with the Lord in the **first** month (Matthew 6:33; Genesis 1:1; John 1:1-2). In this Feast the believer comes to the Lord Jesus and puts first the Kingdom of God and His righteousness.

Pentecost took place in the third month. Number three is the number of complete testimony, the number of Divine witness. Associated with the Pentecostal Feast in the Holy Spirit who is the **third** Person in the eternal Godhead. In this Feast the believer knows the blessedness of the indwelling and infilling Holy Spirit.

Tabernacles took place in the seventh month. Number seven is the number of perfection and fulness. In this Feast the believer is brought to the Fulness of the Godhead. Number seven is distinctly the number of the Book of Revelation. The number is used over 600 times in the Bible. Because the Feast of Tabernacles took place in the **seventh** month several important incidents in scripture will suffice to show its symbolic significance.

1. Seven priests with the Ark of God in the midst marched with seven trumpets around the wall of Jericho for 6 days. On the seventh day they marched around seven times. At the close of the march the trumpets were blown, the people shouted and God caused the walls of Jericho to collapse. The victory was complete (Joshua 5-6).

2. Seven priests blowing trumpets were also involved in the bringing up of the Ark of the Covenant into the Tabernacle of David (I Chronicles 15:24-28).

3. Seven messengers blow seven trumpets in the Book of Revelation, while at the blast of the seventh trump, the Ark of the Covenant is seen in the heavenly Sanctuary (Revelation 8-9-10-11). All has to do with the coming of the Lord Jesus Christ.

Thus the Day of blowing of the Trumpets began in the first day of the seventh month, introducing and calling Israel to the soon coming Day of Atonement, followed by the Feast of Tabernacles.

In application of this Feast Day to the Church we may consider the following remarks:

The church historically experienced Passover. The church historically experienced Pentecost. The church historically has experienced distinctive "Trumpet calls" as illustrated in Israel's history. Various men of God and revivals and awakenings may be viewed as "Trumpet calls" and messages to the church. Each Feast was introduced by a trumpet call.

In tracing church history we can see how the church entered into what has been called "The Dark Ages", when light and truth seemed almost extinguished. But God in His purpose and grace raised up Luther, Calvin and other Reformers. They proclaimed with trumpet voice the distinctive truths relative to the Feast of Passover; justification by faith in the blood of Jesus, sanctification unto the Lord. The Wesley revivals emphasized the truth of holiness and separation also. This may speak of the **Feast of** Unleavened Bread, the putting away of evil practices. Then followed subsequent awakenings, and more especially in the early years of the 20th Century (1900—), God poured out His Spirit and multitudes experienced the glorious Feast of Pentecost. Since then other ministries have proclaimed with trumpet-like voice the distinctive truths belonging to this Feast. The "Pentecostal" or "Charismatic" believers witness to this fact.

However, in the early 1950's God poured out His Spirit again revealing further truths which had been sealed in His Word. Many ministries were raised up by God about this period of time. It became a real "Feast of Trumpets" with the truths being proclaimed. The truth of the church coming to maturity and perfection; the great preparation for harvest ingathering; the coming of the Lord again to His church in glory. There was also a further call to cleansing, to holiness and separation unto the Lord. In other words, a call to the Day of Atonement.

In concluding then the Feast of Trumpets we see that this Feast finds its present fulfilment in the distinctive ministries with distinctive truths being spoken to the church, and then its ultimate fulfilment is in the judgments poured out in the Book of Revelation. All consummate at the **last** and **seventh** Trumpet at the second coming of Christ for His own and the establishment of His Kingdom (I Corinthians 15:51-57; I Thessalonians 4:15-18; Revelation 8-9-10-11; Matthew 25:30-31). God's people need to understand that the church must experience the Feast of Trumpets before experiencing "the last trumpet." "He that hath an ear to hear, let him hear what the Spirit saith unto the Churches" (Revelation 2:29; Mark 4:23-24; Luke 8:18; Isaiah 18:3).

FOR THE STUDENT:

Other prophetic and significant uses of the Trumpets may be considered for study.

A. There were 120 trumpets at the Dedication of Solomon's Temple in the Feast of Tabernacles (II Chronicles 5).

B. The Book of the Law was opened in the Feast of Trumpets (Deuteronomy 31:9-13; Ezra 3; Nehemiah 8; Revelation 4-5; Isaiah 29:11-12).

C. The 7 Priests with 7 trumpets brought about the collapse of Jericho (Joshua 5-6; Revelation 11:15).

D. Kings were anointed at the blowing of the Trumpets (I Kings 1:32-40; II Kings 9:11-13).

E. The Day of the Lord, or the second coming of Christ is heralded by the Trumpet (Zephaniah 1:14-18; Matthew 24:31; I Corinthians 15:52; I Thessalonians 4:16).

Chapter Thirteen
THE FEAST DAY OF ATONEMENT

We come now to the most solemn of all Feast Days, the Day of Atonement. The Day of Atonement was the Day of national and Sanctuary cleansing. On this Day special sacrifices were offered for atonement. The special and peculiar offerings were those of the two goats, one goat for Jehovah and the other goat for Azazel. One goat was slain, the other goat was taken into the wilderness by the hand of a fit man, bearing away the sins of the people.

On this day only, which took place but once a year, the High Priest entered into the Holiest of All, within the veil, with the blood of the Lord's goat, the sin offering. Here he sprinkled the blood on the Mercy seat. The blood of the sin offering on the great Day of Atonement brought about the cleansing of all sin, all iniquity, and all transgression. The Priesthood, the Sanctuary and Israel as a nation experienced blood atonement, thus being reconciled to their God.

The details of this Feast Day are provided for us in *Leviticus 23:26-32; Leviticus 16; Numbers 29:7-11* in the Old Testament, while the Book of Hebrews *(Chapters 8-9-10)* interprets this Feast Day for us in the New Testament.

Again the student needs to remember that, as for Passover and Pentecost, there is a twofold fulfilment relative to the Day of Atonement: that which finds its fulfilment in the Person and Ministry of Christ **historically,** and that which finds its fulfilment in the believers individually and in the church corporately both in the present and the future **experientially.**

It is important to keep this in view, so that there is a proper interpretation and understanding of this Day of Atonement relative to Christ and His Church. For, there are those who see an historical fulfilment in Christ but fail to see a future or experiential fulfilment in the church. And there are those, who, on the other hand, see a future fulfilment in the church but fail to see what Christ has fulfilled historically.

There is absolutely no doubt that full and complete **Atonement** has been made by Jesus Christ on Calvary's cross but there is also no doubt that the church has never fully and completely appropriated and received all that the Atonement has provided. It is the experiential appropriation of the Atonement that constitutes the Day of Atonement in the church.

Those who interpret this Feast Day to take place in the future in the Jewish nation, see it to be prophetic of a day of national cleansing for the Jew. And those who interpret this Feast Day to find its fulfilment in the church also see a futuristic fulfilment but founded on the work of Calvary.

In this section we consider both that which is Historical in Christ and that which is Prophetical in His Church.

I. THE DAY OF ATONEMENT — *Leviticus 23:26-28; 25:9*

The Day of Atonement was the most solemn of all days in Israel. As with Passover, Sheaf of Firstfruits, and Pentecost, so with the Day of Atonement. This day was a literal 24 hour day in Israel, in which significant events took place.

The Prophet Zechariah, in prophesying of this Day, said: "... and I will remove the iniquity of that land in **one day**" *(Zechariah 3:9).*

The scriptures often use the word "day" in both a literal 24 hour day meaning as well as an indefinite period of time, as the following references clearly show.

Proverbs 4:18. "Light that shines more and more unto the perfect day."
John 8:56. "Abraham rejoiced to see "My day."
Hebrews 10:25. The saints are to gather together and the much more as they see "the day" approaching.

II Peter 1:19. The believer is to watch as he sees "the day dawn" and "the day-star" arise in his heart.

Ephesians 4:30. The believer is sealed unto "the day of redemption."

Read also *Romans 12:13-14; II Thessalonians 2:2; Acts 13:41; Nahum 3:3; I Corinthians 13:10; Hebrews 9:28; Joel 2:1-11; Zephaniah 1:14-15; Malachi 4:1-6.*

Consistency of interpretation will show that as each of the Feast days were literal 24 hour days in Israel's history, so they are also in church history. But of course, once the initial day has been ushered in it remains open to all who will believe and enter into the Feast.

Thus Passover took place on a literal 24 hour day, yet this Feast has been open ever since to all who will believe. Pentecost took place on a literal 24 hour day and this Feast has been open ever since to all who will believe and enter into it. So it is the same with the Feast of Tabernacles, with the Day of Trumpets, Day of Atonement and Tabernacles proper. Several things should be noted about this Day.

A. **A Day of Holy Convocation** — *Leviticus 23:27-32; Numbers 29:7; Leviticus 16:31.*

Like every other Feast Day, the Day of Atonement was a holy convocation, and a sabbath rest. No servile work was to be done on this day. So serious was the command, that if any person did any work on this day he was to be cut off from the people of God.

The Day of Atonement was to be kept from "even to even." The same truth is applicable here as for other Feast Days and Sabbaths. Israel had to cease from their own works and rest in the work of the atonement, the work of the High Priest in Sanctuary service. For the believer, there is true rest in Christ's finished work. It is not by works of righteousness which we have done, but it is what Christ has done in His atoning work (*Ephesians 2:5-10; Romans 3:27-28; 10:30-33; Matthew 11:28-30; Hebrews 4:1-11; John 17:1-4; 19:30; Romans 11:32).*

B. **A Day of Fasting** — *Leviticus 23:26-32; Numbers 29:7; Leviticus 16:31.*

This day, although involved in the Feasts of Israel was really a **fast** day. In *Acts 27:9* (Marginal) this day is called "The Fast". It was the only day of the Feasts of the Lord specifically set aside as a day of national fasting.

Fasting has always been the affliction of the flesh. It is the discipline and subjugation of bodily appetites. Throughout Israel's history there were special occasions of fasting, days of national fasting and humiliation. The true and proper Fast is set forth in *Isaiah Chapter 58.*

As the Day of Atonement approaches for the church, there will be greater times of affliction of the flesh and subduing of bodily appetites. The days are at hand when the disciples of the Lord will fast, because the Bridegroom, Jesus Christ, is away. The student should read these scriptures on the importance and practice of fasting as in Israel and in the early church, *Ezra 8:23; Nehemiah 1:4; Matthew 4:2; Acts 13:1-4; Psalm 35:13; 69:10; 109:24; Daniel 9:3; Joel 2:12; Matthew 17:21; Acts 10:30; Luke 2:37; II Corinthians 6:5; 11:27; Matthew 9:14-15.*

C. **A Day of Affliction of Soul**

This day was also a time of "soul-affliction." Body and soul affliction were linked in this day of fasting and prayer. On this day the Israelites humbled themselves before the Lord in national repentance and humiliation as they sought the Lord.

God uses soul affliction to draw us to Himself (*Psalm 119:67, 71).* Any persons who refused to afflict their souls in Israel were cut off. All needed to accept the dealings of God. Soul affliction speaks of that judging of ourselves so that we be not judged of the Lord (*I Corinthians 11:28-32).*

As the church approaches the Day of Atonement "soul-affliction" will be manifested in the believers more and more.

D. **A Day of Solemn Assembly** — *Joel 2:15-17; Numbers 10:10*

The Day of Atonement was also the calling of a solemn assembly. There were days of gladness and rejoicing in other Festival occasions but this day was the most solemn day, a time of mourning and deep affliction. The Psalmist said: "Blow up the trumpet in the new moon, in the time appointed, on our solemn Feast Day . . . ." (*Psalm 81:3).*

The church also may expect times of solemn assembly, when the Lord calls by the trumpet voice to affliction of soul, to times and seasons of special prayer, intercession and fasting before Him so that His purposes may be fulfilled in and through the church.

E. **The Tenth Day of the Seventh Month** — *Leviticus 23:27; Numbers 29:7.*

The significance of numbers may be seen here in the fact that the Day of Atonement took place on the tenth day of the seventh month. This day brought all the nation together at the Tabernacle door, at the Sanctuary of the Lord for the great cleansing and reconciliation (*Leviticus 16:29-30).*

1. **Seven** is the number of fulness and completeness and perfection. Thus the seventh month completed the Feasts of the Lord and the Sacred year in Israel. Seven is also the number of rest, so this month brought Israel to fulness of rest through atonement.

2. **Ten** is the number of testing, trial, law and order, and also responsibility before the Lord (*Revelation 2:10; Daniel 1:12).* The 10 days between the day of blowing of Trumpets and the day of Atonement were days of preparation, and all were responsible to be ready for this great day.

II. **THE DAY OF ATONEMENT CEREMONIES** — *Leviticus 16.*

This chapter of Leviticus gives to us the intricate details of the ceremonies which were to be fulfilled on the great Day of Atonement. The symbolic significances all point to the work of Christ historically and then to His work prophetically in His church. We consider the Old Testament typical ceremonies of this day and what it meant to and in Israel and then see how Chirst fulfilled it in the New Testament and what it means in and to the church, which is His Body.

A. The Golden Censer Ministry — *Leviticus 16:1-2, 12-14; Hebrews 9:4.*

The Lord commanded that Aaron not come into the Holiest of All at all times but only on this one day during the year. Even then he was to take the golden censer, and with his hands full of sweet incense bring it within the veil.

As he entered within the veil, placing the incense on the fiery coals of the censer, a cloud of incense ascended, covering the Ark of Glory. Aaron dare not enter into the Most Holy Place of the Tabernacle without the rising cloud of incense.

The symbolism of the incense is clearly interpreted for us both in Old and New Testaments. Incense and its ingredients always speaks of prayer and its essential ingredients. Aaron the High Priest typifies the ministry of the Mediator and Intercessor. David said: "Let my prayer be set forth (directed) before Thee as incense . . ." *(Psalm 141:2).* Read also *Revelation 5:8; 8:1-5.* Rising incense speaks of the ascending prayers of the saints before God.

This finds its fulfilment in Christ and the church. Christ Jesus is our Mediator and Intercessor. He ever lives to make intercession for the saints according to the will of God *(Hebrews 7:24-25; Romans 8:34; I Timothy 2:5; I John 2:1).*

Since Christ's ascension to the throne of His Father, the prayers and intercessions in behalf of His own are presented continually before the Father God in the heavenly and true Sanctuary.

The prayers of the saints also ascend "within the veil", acceptable to God through Christ. It is in prayer and intercession that the believer approaches God.

At the first coming of Christ there was a revelation given to Zacharias at the golden altar of incense while the multitude were praying without. As the second coming of Christ approaches the spirit of prayer and supplication will again increase in the church. The book of *Revelation (8:1-5)* intimates this as it alludes to the Day of Atonement ceremony in this passage.

Thus, in fulfilment of the golden censer ministry, we see the prayers and intercessions of both Christ and the church. All will increase as the Day of Atonement approaches.

B. The Washing of Water — *Leviticus 16:4, 24*

On this day there was the special washing of water in preparation for the sacrificial offerings. Aaron washed before he entered the Sanctuary and then washed again in the Holy Place after the Sanctuary had been cleansed.

Again the scripture interprets the symbolic act here. The ceremonial washing of water in the Old Testament pointed to the "washing of water by the Word." It also involves the washing of regeneration *(Ephesians 5:26-27; Titus 3:5; John 3:1-5; 15:3; I Corinthians 6:11; Hebrews 10:22; Psalm 51:7).*

For Aaron it meant that he must be absolutely clean in order to make the atonement in behalf of the people of Israel. For Christ it meant that He was absolutely clean and sinlessly perfect when He made the atonement for His people. For the believer it means that he must be washed in the water of the Word in his approach into the Presence of the Lord.

C. The Linen Garments — *Leviticus 16:4, 23*

On this day Aaron laid aside the "garments of glory and beauty" *(Exodus 28:1-5)* and put on linen garments. He was wholly clothed in white linen as he made the atonement. He had on linen breeches, a linen coat, a linen girdle and a linen mitre. They were called "the holy garments."

After making the atonement for the Sanctuary and washing in the Holy Place, he was then to change back into his garments of glory and beauty.

How wonderfully Christ fulfilled the type in Himself. For He laid aside His reputation, emptying Himself of His glory and taking upon Himself the form of a servant, was made in the likeness of men. But He was a perfectly righteous man. The fine linen garments are interpreted as Divine righteousness, both of Christ and the righteousness with which the saints are clothed *(Revelation 3:4-5; 15:6; 19:7-8; Psalm 132:9; Isaiah 61:10; John 17:1-5).*

The linen garments symbolize the righteous and sinless humanity with which Christ clothed Himself, while the garments of glory and beauty speak of that glory which He had with the Father before the world began.

D. The Sacrifices of That Day — *Leviticus 16:3, 5-11, 14-28; Numbers 29:7-11.*

There were special sacrifices offered on this day, besides the daily sacrifice. These offerings were as follows:

1. A young bullock for a Sin Offering — for Aaron himself and his house.
2. A ram for a Burnt Offering — for Aaron himself.
3. Two kids of the goats for a Sin Offering — one goat for the Lord and the other goat for the people.
4. One ram for a Burnt Offering — for the people.

   Additional offerings as in *Numbers 29:7-11* were:

   a. Burnt Offering — young bullock, a ram, and seven lambs of the first year.
   b. Meal Offerings appropriate to each of the blood sacrifices.
   c. Sin Offering — a kid of the goats.
   d. The Daily Sacrifice of a Burnt, Meal and Drink Offering. The intricate details of these offerings is given in *Leviticus Chapters 1-7*.

All these sacrifices point to the **one perfect** and **once-for-all** sacrifice of Jesus Christ. No one offering was complete in itself to set forth all the intricate glories and perfections of Christ as to His Person and Work.

E. The Atoning Ministry.

The actual work of atonement falls into three main areas: that which pertains to Aaron and his household, that which pertains to the nation, and that which pertains to the Sanctuary.

1. Atonement for Aaron and his Household — *Leviticus 16:3-14*

Aaron, first of all, offered a bullock for a Sin Offering for himself and his own house, thus making atonement for his own household *(verses 3, 6)*.

After this he presented the two goats before the Lord, casting lots as to which goat was for the Lord in sacrifice and which goat would be taken into the wilderness and released *(verses 5, 7-10)*. After this Aaron was to take the blood of the bullock for his Sin Offering and enter within the veil, sprinkle the blood on the Mercy seat eastward and then 7 times before the Mercy seat. All of this was done amidst the rising cloud of incense from the golden censer *(verses 11-14)*. In this way Aaron made atonement for his own sins, and the sins of his household.

2. Atonement for the Nation — *Leviticus 16:15*

Aaron then killed the Lord's goat for a Sin Offering. This was the offering for the people of Israel. He did with the blood of this goat what he did with the blood of the bullock: he entered within the veil, into the Holiest of All, and sprinkled the blood on the Mercy seat of the Ark of the Covenant and then 7 times before the Mercy seat. In this way the Nation of Israel was atoned for.

3. Atonement for the Sanctuary — *Leviticus 16:16-20, 23*

After making atonement for himself and his household and then the nation, Aaron then made atonement for the Sanctuary and its furnishings.

This day is called by the Prophet Daniel "The Cleansing of the Sanctuary" *(Daniel 8:13-14)*.

The Holy Place or the Tabernacle of the Congregation was atoned for. The Most Holy Place or the Holy Sanctuary was atoned for. And then the golden altar of incense was atoned for *(Exodus 30:1-10)*. After the golden altar of incense was atoned for, Aaron sprinkled the blood of atonements 7 times on it, cleansing and hallowing it from Israel's uncleanness. The horns of the altar were also sprinkled with atoning blood.

The significance of this threefold work of atonement will be interpreted when we consider the New Testament fulfilment as set forth in the Book of Hebrews.

F. Aaron Alone makes the Atonement — *Leviticus 16:17*

When Aaron the High Priest fulfilled the atoning work, he was to enter alone, and no person was to be with him. He ministered alone in the supreme work of reconciliation. None could help him. So it pointed to the fact that Christ alone could reconcile man to God. Of the people, none could be with Him or help Him *(Hebrews 9:7)*. Even in His second coming there are areas of judgment that He alone will perform *(Isaiah 63:1-6)*.

G. Entrance within the Veil — *Leviticus 16:2, 12, 15*

It is to be seen that only on this day did Aaron enter "within the veil." The veil of the Tabernacle acted as a divider between the Holy Place and the Holiest of All. It signified a separation between God and Man that could only be bridged by the work of atonement *(Exodus 26:31-32)*. None dare presume to enter within the veil except on the appointed day, once a year.

It seems as if Aaron's two sons tried to presume within the veil on the day of dedication when the Glory of God fell. For this sin God judged them with death and then gave the details of the Day of Atonement and how Aaron should come within the veil (Compare *Leviticus 9:22-24; 10:1-11; 16:1-2*).

The Book of Hebrews takes this up for us and shows how Christ has entered "within the veil" and made it possible for the believer to do so too, because He is the Forerunner *(Hebrews 10:19-22; Matthew 27:51-52; Hebrews 6:18-20)*.

H. The Seven Times Sprinkling of Blood — *Leviticus 16:14*

The sprinkling of the blood 7 times on the Mercy seat was prophetic of perfect atonement that Christ would bring to His people. Throughout the scripture the theme of "The Seven Times" becomes prophetic of the end of the age and that which finds its ultimate in the seventh day of the Lord, the Kingdom Age.

The following are some of the examples of these "Seven Times" prophecies, the number seven speaking of fulness, perfection and the close of the present age as ushered in by Christ's coming.

1. Jacob bowed to Esau "Seven Times" *(Genesis 33:3)*.
2. Blood was sprinkled "Seven Times" in *Leviticus 4:6; 8:11; 14:7; 16:14-17*.
3. Israel was to be punished "Seven Times" for her sins *(Leviticus 26:18, 21, 24, 28)*.
4. The walls of Jericho were compassed about "Seven Times" before its collapse *(Joshua 6:4-15)*.
5. Elijah prayed and then after "Seven Times" great rain fell *(I Kings 18:43)*.
6. The furnace of persecution was heated "Seven Times" when the Hebrew believers were cast in and preserved *(Daniel 13:19)*.
7. Naaman immersed himself "Seven Times" before his healing took place *(II Kings 5:10)*.
8. Oil was sprinkled "Seven Times" in the cleansing of the leper *(Leviticus 14:16-18)*.
9. Forgiveness is to be beyond "Seven Times" *(Matthew 18:21-22)*.

Thus the "Seven Times" sprinkling of blood becomes symbolic and prophetic of the perfections that the blood of Jesus will bring to His church in the end times and at His coming.

In Passover Feast the blood was sprinkled upon the door. In Pentecost Feast the blood was sprinkled on the people and the Covenant Book. In Tabernacles the blood was sprinkled seven times on the Mercy Seat.

The Day of Atonement in the church will be the fullest manifestation of the power of the blood of Jesus. It will bring the church to perfection, making an end of all sin, all iniquity, all transgressions and all sins of ignorance and all uncleanness.

I. The Scapegoat — *Leviticus 16:8, 10, 20-22, 26*

When the atonement was completed as to his household, the nation and the Sanctuary, then the live goat fulfilled its function in the ceremony.

After Aaron had come out from the Tabernacle of the Congregation, he then laid his hands on the head of the live goat. As he did this symbolic act, he confessed over the goat all the sins, iniquities, transgressions and uncleannesses of Israel. When this was completed, the Scapegoat (or "goat for sending away") was taken by the hand of a fit man into the Wilderness. The goat was to bear away all the iniquities of the people into a land uninhabited, or a land of separation. There the fit man was to release the goat of the Wilderness. Upon his return to the camp he was to bathe himself wholly in water and then take his place in the camp of the Lord and of Israel.

The symbolic truth concerning the Scapegoat will be dealt with in due time under the antitypical fulfilment in Christ and His church.

J. The Bodies without the Camp — *Leviticus 16:23-28*

After the Scapegoat had been sent into the Wilderness by the hand of the fit man, Aaron entered into the Holy Place, washed himself and changed his garments.

Then he took the fat of the Sin Offering, burnt it on the Altar in the Outer Court, for the fat belonged exclusively to the Lord for His altar *(Leviticus 4:9-10; I Samuel 2:16)*.

However, the **bodies** of the Sin Offering, both the bullock and the goat, were taken by a fit man outside the camp where all was burnt. The skins, the flesh and dung were wholly burnt. The person who did this was then to return to the camp, wash his clothes, bathe his flesh in water and then enter again into the fellowship of the Israel nation.

The writer to the Hebrews takes this up and clearly shows how Christ fulfilled the Sin Offering. For He went "outside the camp" of Jerusalem, outside of Judaism, after His rejection. Here on Golgotha He was crucified. His body was indeed outside the camp. It was not burnt physically, as it was incorruptible, but it did suffer the consuming fires of God's holiness and righteousness against sin *(Hebrews 12:29; 13:10-13)*.

III. The Anointed High Priest — *Leviticus 16:29-34*

Only the High Priest who was anointed and consecrated to minister in his father's stead could make the atonement. This anointed High Priest made the atonement for all other priests, for all the congregation of Israel and the Sanctuary of the Lord.

The Lord Jesus Christ is our great High Priest, anointed in His Father's stead to make the reconciliation for the church, the New Testament priestly Body *(I Peter 2:5-9; Revelation 1:6; 5:9-10)*.

The difference between Aaron and Christ is this. Aaron and his animal sacrifices were two separate identities, sinful and inferior. Christ is both Priest and Sacrifice in His two natures, yet one undivided Person, sinless and superior. In His Divine nature He is the Priest; in His human nature He is the Sacrifice. Thus Christ (the Priest) offered Himself (the Sacrifice) for us *(Galatians 2:20; Ephesians 5:25-27; Hebrews 8:1-4; 9:11-15)*.

IV. AN EVERLASTING STATUTE — *Leviticus 16:29, 34*

The Day of Atonement ceremony was to be "an everlasting statute" in Israel on the appointed day of the year.

Anything under the Old Covenant that was "everlasting" can only find its true fulfilment in and through the New Covenant, and "everlasting life" as found in Christ.

All of the things pertaining to the Old Covenant were temporal and typical, but the things under the New Covenant are spiritual and eternal. Christ lives in the "power of an **endless life**" *(Hebrews 7:16)* and it is only in this way can the atonement be an "everlasting statute".

The redeemed will eternally remember the atoning work of Christ, thus fulfilling the "everlasting statute" of the Day of Atonement *(Revelation 4:8-11; 5:1-14)*.

V. THE ATONEMENT FOR SINS, TRANSGRESSIONS, INIQUITIES AND UNCLEANNESS — *Leviticus 16:16, 21; Daniel 9:24-27.*

In the ceremony of the Day of Atonement **"all iniqutieis"** and **"all sins"** and **"all transgressions"** as well as **"all uncleanness"** were fully atoned for.

The ministry of reconciliation took care of all these evil things in the nature of fallen man. Each of these words show some facet of the fallen nature of man and that which needs the atonement, or the reconciliation.

A. **Iniquity** — Vanity, perverseness of spirit *(Matthew 23:38; Titus 2:14; Isaiah 53:5, 6, 10; 59:12)*.

B. **Sin** — To err, to miss the mark, go astray, to fall *(I John 5:17; James 4:17; Romans 14:23; I John 3:4)*.

C. **Transgression** — Rebellion, lawlessness, deceive, trespass *(Isaiah 58:1; I John 3:4; Daniel 8:23)*.

D. **Uncleanness** — Foulness, defiled, pollution (moral and physical), *Leviticus 14:57; Numbers 19:7-22; II Corinthians 12:21)*.

The Lord Jesus Christ, by His own sinless and atoning blood, has provided cleansing and reconciliation to God for His people. By the power of His redeeming blood, all sin, iniquity, transgressions and uncleanness shall be fully cleansed from the church in the great Day of Atonement, and at the coming of Christ.

THE NEW TESTAMENT INTERPRETATION IN HEBREWS

There is no mistaking the interpretation of the ceremony of the Day of Atonement. The New Testament, especially the Epistle to the Hebrews is basically given over to the symbolic significance of this day.

We take the major points of the ceremony which have not been interpreted in the course of following the Old Testament outline and see how the Book of Hebrews interprets such for us.

I. THE SACRIFICES

All sacrifices and oblations pointed to the perfect and supreme sacrifice of Jesus Christ. As noted earlier, the animal sacrifices were brought in as a substitute for man's sin until **the** sacrifice and oblation came Himself to put away sin. Thus the sacrifices of all Feast Days, Sabbaths as well as the Daily Sacrifice were all fulfilled and abolished by the one sacrifice of Christ. His body and blood caused the sacrifice and oblation to cease. This fulfilled the prophetic word that Messiah would come and "cause the sacrifice and oblation to cease" (Daniel 9:27 with Hebrews 10:1-10).

Again, it is to be noted that there were **many** sacrifices, untold thousands, offered upon the altars. In contrast to the many is the **one** sacrifice of Christ offered on Calvary's altar. Those priests stood daily offering oftentimes the same sacrifices which could never take away sins, but Christ Jesus offered one sacrifice for sin **once-for-all** (Hebrews 10:11-14).

Above all this is the fact that no **animal** sacrifice can cleanse the sin of **man.** Thus when Jesus died, He was presented as a **human** sacrifice for the sin of man. Therefore His sacrifice is totally, absolutely and supremely seen to be above all animal sacrifices and offerings.

Calvary is the altar of God upon which His Son was offered. There is no further sacrifice for sin to be made. None can add up to take away from this finished work, as far as Christ's sacrifice is concerned. It is perfect, full and complete (John 17:4; 19:30). This is an historical and doctrinal fact never ever to be repeated. Christ dieth for sin no more, death has no more dominion over Him. The Atonement has been made.

However, as far as the believer is concerned, and the church as a whole, we have yet to enter into and receive the full benefits of the atonement of Christ. There is no believer living upon the face of the earth that can claim to have experienced fully the **complete Atonement!**

It is the understanding between that which is referred to as "judicial truth" and "experiential truth" that shows the twofold aspect of the work of Christ. The walk of faith is that which bridges both aspects. It is this which is to be understood in the work of the Day of Atonement as pertaining to the church.

II. THE MINISTRY OF ATONEMENT

Under the historical and typical Day of Atonement, Aaron had to make atonement for himself, then his household, then the nation and finally the Sanctuary. In contrast and comparison we note the following relative to Christ, our Great High Priest.

A. No Atonement for Christ

As far as Christ was concerned He did not need the atonement. He was God incarnate. He was born of the virgin. He was sinless and perfect in thought, word and deed and needed no redemption from sin. If He had sin then He could not be our Saviour and Redeemer. Aaron needed atonement as he was a sinful and imperfect priest. Christ needed no atonement for He was a righteous and perfect Priest (Hebrews 5:1-6; 7:22-28). Thus the antitype far surpasses the type.

B. Atonement for His House and the Nation

Here we have further comparison. As Aaron atoned for his priestly household and then the nation of Israel, so Christ made atonement for His household, the church, and all believers, who, since the cross, constitute the Israel of God, "the holy nation and royal priesthood" after the order of Melchisedek (Hebrews 5:1-6; I Peter 2:5-9; Hebrews 3:1-6; 7:11-28; 8:1-4; 9:11-15; Revelation 1:6; 5:9-10; Ephesians 2:11-13; Galatians 6:16).

C. Atonement for the Sanctuary

The third area involved in the Day of Atonement ceremonies was "the cleansing of the Sanctuary" (Daniel 8:13-14).

The Book of Hebrews deals much with this area of Christ's ministry. It deals with the cleansing of the true and heavenly Sanctuary. This is a truth that is not always perceived by believers. The scriptures show two aspects of God's Sanctuary. Let us note the truth of the things under their respective sub-headings.

1. The Heavenly Sanctuary

    a. There is a heavenly Tabernacle, or heavenly Temple. This is the **true** Sanctuary, the original (Hebrews 8:1-2; Revelation 11:19; 13:6; 15:5-8).

    b. This heavenly Sanctuary is the dwelling place of God, of Christ and the elect angels.

    c. This heavenly Sanctuary, as the original, cast its shadow on earth. The earthly Tabernacle of Moses and the Temple of Solomon were the material expressions of such. They were the earthly types of the heavenly prototype (Hebrews 8:1-5; 9:1-10).

    d. The heavenly Sanctuary consists of three heavens, even as the Tabernacle and Temple had three "holy places." The words "heaven" or "heavens", and "place" and "places" used in Hebrews 9:12, 23-24 confirm this thought.

        The first heaven (to man) is the atmospheric heaven; the second heaven is the planetary heaven, and the third heaven is the immediate Presence of God, the Paradise of God. This is the heaven of heavens where Paul saw and heard unspeakable things (II Corinthians 12:1-4; Revelation 2:7; 22:14). Solomon recognized that the Temple as God's earthly house could not contain God, let alone heaven and the heavens, God's real dwelling place (I Kings 8:27-30; Isaiah 66:1; Acts 7:49; 17:24).

e. As Aaron had to cleanse the Sanctuary on the Day of Atonement in its three places, so the heavens have to be cleansed. The reason why the heavenly Sanctuary, God's dwelling place, needed cleansing was because of sin.

As the earthly Sanctuary had to be cleansed because of Israel's sins, transgressions, iniquities and uncleanness, so the heavenly Sanctuary has to be cleansed. Sin originated in heaven. It was at the very throne of God that the "mystery of iniquity" began in Satan and the fallen angels.

The heavens have been defiled by sinning angels. Job himself said "the heavens are not clean in Thy sight" (Job 15:15; 4:18; 25:5).

It is not that the angels will be redeemed, for they sinned as spirit beings in the blazing white light of God's holiness and Christ did not die to redeem them. However, heaven has been defiled by their sinful presence and thus has to be cleansed. The power of the atoning blood of Jesus will do this. This is seen to be the teaching of the Book of Hebrews (Hebrews 8:1-5; 9:1-28).

The Book of Revelation also shows a time when the Devil and all his angels are cast out of the heavens to the earth. At this time the heavens are told to rejoice because the accuser of the brethren is cast down. The believers are overcomers through the blood of the Lamb and the word of their testimony (Revelation 12:1-12). It is here that the atonement manifests its supreme power in the cleansing of the heavenly Sanctuary of the presence of the originator of sin in the universe.

Thus this is the first aspect of the "cleansing of the Sanctuary."

2. The Church His Sanctuary

There is another aspect of the truth of the Sanctuary. This pertains to the church. The church also is God's Sanctuary, His earthly Sanctuary, His dwelling place by the Spirit (I Corinthians 3:16; II Corinthians 6:16; Ephesians 2:20-22; I Peter 2:5-9).

The church has yet to come into the full power of the atoning work of Christ which was accomplished on Calvary.

As far as God is concerned all was finished at Calvary. God saw a "finished work" (John 17:4; 19:30). This is spoken of as judicial truth. But as far as the believer is concerned individually, and the church corporately, we have yet to enter by faith into that finished work. This is spoken of as experiential truth.

As the church experienced Passover truths, and Pentecost truths, so she will experience Tabernacle truths. All will be upon the basis of Christ's finished work on Calvary.

Such experience will be the Day of Atonement for the church. What Christ has done for us historically will be fulfilled in us experientially. Hence there has been two aspects of God's Sanctuary; the heavenly and the earthly. This was true in the Old Testament Israel. It is true in the New Testament Israel, the church.

III. ENTRANCE WITHIN THE VEIL

As with each of the Feasts there is that which is historical which Christ has fulfilled in Himself, and there is that which is spiritual and finds fulfilment in the church, so it is with the truth of entrance "within the veil."

There is that which relates to Christ and that which relates to the church. On the great Day of Atonement Aaron entered within the veil. Hebrews show the fulfilment of this in the ministry of Christ.

As long as the veil of the Tabernacle or Temple stood, the Holy Spirit was signifying that "the way into the Holiest of All was not yet made manifest while the first tabernacle was yet standing: which was a figure for the time present . . ." (Hebrews 9:7-9).

When Jesus died on the cross, the veil of the Temple was miraculously rent from top to the bottom by God Himself (Matthew 27:51-52). It signified that the way into God's Presence was now open to all who believe in God through Christ. Believers can come to God through the veil of Christ's flesh and blood (Hebrews 10:19-22). The rending of the veil of the Temple was connected with the rending of the veil of Christ's flesh, the Christ's temple (John 2:18-22).

We consider here also the twofold aspect of "entrance within the veil" as pertaining to Christ and His church.

A. Christ within the Veil

When Christ ascended up on high to heaven, presented His blood and then took His place at the Father's right hand, this fulfilled the type of entrance within the veil.

The Lord Jesus ascended on high and entered within the veil of the heavenly Sanctuary. He is now there and remains within the veil, hidden from human view during this church period. At His second advent He will come forth from the heavenly Sanctuary in flaming fire and glory to receive His own unto Himself and judge all outside Himself (John 20:17; 16:27-28; Ephesians 1:17; 4:8-10; Proverbs 30:1-4; Psalm 68:18; Mark 16:19-20; Luke 24:50-53; Acts 1:9-11; Hebrews 4:14; 8:1-2; 9:11-14, 24-28).

Christ risen, ascended and glorified is the Forerunner into the heavenly Sanctuary, within the veil (Hebrews 6:17-20). This is the Order of Melchisedek. Others will follow Him who is the Forerunner. This was Christ fulfilling "the Day of Atonement" in the heavenly Sanctuary.

B. The Believer within the Veil

There is also within this aspect a dual aspect concerning the believer entering within the veil. This pertains to the living believer as well as the believer who dies and goes to be with the Lord.

1. The Living Believer

All believers have the privilege in prayer and in spirit to enter "into the Holiest of All" by the blood of Jesus, the new and living way (Hebrews 6:17-20; 9:8-10; 10:19-22). All believers have access into the Presence of God by the Spirit (Ephesians 2:11-18) and in this way enter within the veil. However, there is a fulness in this experience that the church has yet to enter into and this is what is typified in the Day of Atonement.

The student will be able to read and sing many of the great Hymns and Songs of the church which speak of this experience of entrance "within the veil."

2. The Dead in Christ Believer

When a believer dies and goes to be with the Lord, his redeemed spirit goes to heaven and certainly experiences entrance within the veil, into heaven's Sanctuary.

It is here that the spirit of just men made perfect are awaiting the coming of the Lord and their immortalized bodies (Hebrews 12:22-24; Philippians 3:20-21; Luke 16:20-22; Philippians 1:23).

IV. THE GLORY OF THE LORD

Entrance within the veil, by the power of incense and the atoning blood brought Aaron into the very Presence and Glory of the Lord. The Hebrews refer to this visible manifestation of God's Presence as "The Shekinah".

It was only on this Day of Atonement that Aaron entered into that Glory of the Lord. In fulfilment of this we see the Lord Jesus Christ in His ascension was "received up into glory" (I Timothy 3:16), and He was glorified with "the glory which He had with the Father before the world began" (John 17:1-5, 24-26).

It is also significant of the fact that as the church enters the experience of the Day of Atonement there will be an entrance into the glory of the Lord. His glory shall be seen upon the church. The church will be changed "from glory to glory" (II Corinthians 3:15-18). Even on this earth various saints have experienced measures of the glory of God.

A. The Glory of God appeared to Abraham (Acts 7:2).

B. The Glory of the Lord appeared to Israel (Exodus 16:7, 10; 24:16-17).

C. The Glory of the Lord filled both Tabernacle and Temple in the day of dedication (Exodus 40:34-35; I Kings 8:11; II Chronicles 5:14).

D. Moses beheld the Glory of the Lord and had that same glory seen upon his face (Exodus 33 with II Corinthians 3).

E. Jesus also shone with the Glory of God on the Mt. of Transfiguration (Matthew 17:1-8; II Peter 1:17-18; Mark 9:1).

F. Stephen's face shone with the Glory of God also (Acts 7:55).

G. The church is to shine with the glory of God also (Isaiah 60:1-3; Revelation 12:1; Romans 8:18; Colossians 1:27; Ephesians 5:27).

The Glory of the New Covenant is far greater than Glory of the Old Covenant (II Corinthians 3-4). It is in this way that the glory of the Lord will fill all the earth also (Numbers 14:21; Isaiah 6:3; Habakkuk 2:14; Isaiah 40:5).

V. THE TWO GOATS

As seen in the historical-typical ceremony two goats were involved in the Day of Atonement, in the ministry of reconciliation. The student is referred to the dual offerings as noted under the comments on the Feast of Pentecost.

Here again in the dual offering of the goats there seems to be a "double type" to find fulfilment in Christ and the church.

A. Fulfilment in Christ

1. The Goat for Jehovah

The goat chosen by lot for Jehovah was killed. This goat **died** to reconcile. Its blood was sprinkled within the veil on the Mercy seat.

This pointed to the **death** of Jesus, who was "the Lord's goat" and our Sin Offering. He died to reconcile us to God. His blood was brought into the heavenly Sanctuary, within the veil. The writer to the Hebrews shows how this was fulfilled in Christ's sacrifice (*Hebrews 13:11-13; 9:1-14*).

2. The Goat for Azazel

Many expositors see that the Scapegoat or the goat for Azazel was also symbolic of Christ's ministry. The Lord's goat symbolized **Christ in His death** — He died to reconcile. The Scapegoat symbolized **Christ in His resurrection** — He lives to reconcile.

The Scapegoat after the laying on of hands was sent by the hand of a fit man into the Wilderness bearing away the sins, transgressions, iniquities and uncleanness of Israel.

The word "forgiveness" conveys the truth of the Scapegoat ministry. The word "forgiveness" means "to send away, to bear or carry away."

Thus Christ in His death and resurrection died for our sins, and carried them right away, never to be remembered any more (*Luke 7:21; Acts 3:14; 25:11, 16; Ephesians 4:32; Colossians 2:13; 3:13; I John 1:9; 2:12; Psalm 103:3; Jeremiah 31:31-34*).

There is also difference of opinion as to the exact meaning of the word "Scapegoat." It is spoken of as the Scapegoat or Azazel. The Hebrew word "Azazel" (S.C.5799), translated "Scapegoat" means "the goat for departure"; the goat for going away. It signifies entire removal.

It has also been suggested that Azazel means "the evil one." That is to say that the goat for Azazel was the goat to subdue the evil one, that is, Satan.

If this is so, then it is certainly fulfilled in the ministry of Christ. In His death, burial, resurrection and ascension He conquered Satan and all his hosts.

The ultimate victory of Calvary over Satan will be manifested when Satan is cast into the Lake of Fire, when all his hosts are eternally subdued. The basis of the victory is the atonement.

B. Fulfilment in the Church

The other aspect of truth concerning the Scapegoat finds its fulfilment in the church. The dual sacrifices in the previous Feast pointed to Christ in His church.

The two birds offered in the cleansing of the leper pointed to Christ and His Church, the only two agents involved in cleansing of the lepers (*Leviticus 14*).

The two trumpets used on special occasions pointed to Christ and His ministries (*Numbers 10:1-10*).

And here the two goats point to both Christ and His church involved in the ministry of reconciliation.

Of course, it is to be understood that any sacrifice offered for sin can only and ever typify Christ the sinless sacrificed One. But when there is association of another with that one then it can also symbolize the church, for Christ and His Body are really inseparable.

Many times what is said of Christ is also said of the church, His Body (Note — *John 8:12; Matthew 5:14; John 6:48-51; I Corinthians 10:15-17*).

We ask: In whay way then may the church be identified with the Scapegoat ministry? The following number of ways answer such.

1. The Scapegoat was presented before Jehovah along with the Lord's goat. So the church is presented before God with Christ.

2. The Scapegoat was also to be without spot or blemish with the Lord's goat. So Christ and His church are both without spot or blemish (*I Peter 1:18-2; Ephesians 5:26-27*).

3. The Scapegoat shared with the Lord's goat in the ministry of reconciliation. Only Christ and His church have been given the ministry of reconciliation (*Hebrews 2:17; II Corinthians 5:17-21*).

4. The Scapegoat **lived** to reconcile while the Lord's goat **died** to reconcile. So the church lives to reconcile man to God while Christ died to bring reconciliation.

5. The Scapegoat was used to subdue Azazel, the evil spirit. Christ and His church are the only agents associated in the ministry of subduing Satan and his wicked hosts (*Mark 16:15-20; Revelation 12:1-12*).

6. The Scapegoat was involved in the sending away of sin, in the ministry of forgiveness. Christ and His church are involved in the forgiveness of sins (*James 5:15-17; Acts 7:60; Mark 16:19-20; II Corinthians 5:18-21; Luke 24:49; John 20:22-23*).

7. The Scapegoat was taken outside the camp bearing the reproaches of Israel upon it. So the church is called to go outside the camp bearing the reproaches of Christ (*Hebrews 13:10-13*). People in society often refer to somebody who takes someone elses reproach as being "the scapegoat." The church certainly bears the reproach of Christ in this world (*Romans 15:3; Hebrews 11:26; Luke 6:22; I Peter 4:14; Zephaniah 2:8*).

8. The Scapegoat was eventually taken into the Wilderness by the hand of a fit man. It was then let go alive in a land uninhabited, a land of separation (*Leviticus 16:22*, Margin). So the church is taken into a Wilderness, a place prepared of God, and preserved alive in the last days of this age (*Revelation 12:1-6, 13-16; Song of Solomon 3:6; 8:6; Luke 21:34-36*).

VI. THE ATONEMENT OR RECONCILIATION

The key word in the great chapter in *Leviticus 16* is the word "atonement." This word is used at least **14** times in this chapter, generally in the singular and yet sometimes the word is used in the plural (Note — *Exodus 30:10; Leviticus 17:11-14; Romans 5:11*).

The basic meaning of the word "Atonement" is "reconciliation". Where it is translated "atonement" in *Romans 5:11* it should be translated "the reconciliation.

There are various words relative to the full meaning of the atonement yet no one word on its own supplies the full significance, yet all together give us the thoughts of God on the matter.

These theological words are noted briefly here in order to help us understand and appreciate more fully the work accomplished on the Day of Atonement, both historically and prophetically.

A. Redemption — to buy back again with a price out of the hands of another.

B. Ransom — the price paid in the transaction of redemption.

C. Propitiation — the sacrifice offered to God to avert wrath and secure mercy.

D. Reconciliation — to make enemies friends after being at variance. It is the effect of the sinner being made one with God.

E. Atonement — the atonement was the official presentation to God of the blood on the Mercy seat.

Thus on the great Day of Atonement the truth of these words was seen in operation and all together they effected **the reconciliation!**

The Sin Offerings became the ransom, the price of Israel's redemption. They were the propitiation to avert God's wrath and secure mercy. When Aaron entered within the veil and officially presented the **blood** to God on the Mercyseat, this was the atonement. And the effect of all was the reconciliation of Israel as a nation to God!

All of this was fulfilled in the sacrifice of Christ on Calvary. At Calvary we see ransom, redemption and propitiation taking place, as He presented His body and blood on Calvary's altar and suffered for our sins.

In His ascension to the Father's throne, into the heavenly Sanctuary, within the veil, we see the actual atonement and the effect of the atonement. The Atonement then was the official presentation of **the blood of Jesus** at the throne of God in heaven. The effect of this in the church and upon all who believe is **the reconciliation!**

The ultimate of the Day of Atonement will bring about full reconciliation of man with His God, both Creator and Redeemer!

The Cross was the brazen altar where the sacrifice of Christ took place. The Throne was the Ark of the Covenant where the sacrifice of Christ, His body and blood, were presented. It is this which comprehends the Day of Atonement.

Read — *Romans 5:11; John 17:21; II Corinthians 5:20; Colossians 1:10-21; Daniel 9:24-27; Hebrews 2:17-18*.

XII. THE POWER OF THE BLOOD OF JESUS

On the Day of Atonement the blood of the Sin Offering was sprinkled "Seven Times". As seen already, seven is the number of fulness, completeness and perfection.

The ultimate truth concerning the sprinkling of the blood seven times is that the blood of Jesus will bring the church to perfection. This perfection will be a sinless perfection. There is enough power in the blood of Jesus to do this for every believer. Every genuine Christian believes that the work of the cross will finally bring about the eradication of sin. Or in other words, sinless perfection. It is this state of perfection that every believer longs for and will experience throughout eternity. Many Scriptures could be listed on the benefits of the blood of Jesus. We list just a few. Hebrews the ninth chapter makes much of the blood of Jesus in heaven for us and the cleansing that it will bring to the church. If the blood of animals brought ceremonial cleansing, how much more perfect cleansing shall the blood of God, the blood of Jesus bring to us?

A. Justified by His blood *(Romans 5:9)*.

B. Communion in His blood *(I Corinthians 10:16; 11:25-27)*.

C. Redemption through His blood *(Ephesians 1:7)*.

D. Access to God's Presence by the blood *(Ephesians 2:13)*.

E. Reconciliation through the blood *(Colossians 1:14, 20)*.

F. Remission of sins through His blood *(Hebrews 9:22)*.

G. Covenantal relationship through the blood *(Hebrews 10:29)*.

H. Sanctification by the blood *(Hebrews 13:20)*.

I. Conscience purged by the blood *(Hebrews 9:14)*.

J. Cleansing through the blood *(I John 1:7)*.

K. Entrance within the veil by the blood *(Hebrews 10:4, 19-20)*.

L. Admission to heaven because the blood is there *(Hebrews 9:7-25)*.

M. Propitiation by the blood *(Romans 3:25)*.

N. Perfection by the blood *(Hebrews 6:1; 7:11, 17-19; 10:1)*.

O. Overcome Satan by the blood of the Lamb *(Revelation 12:11)*.

VIII. THE DAY OF ATONEMENT AND THE JUBILEE YEAR — *Leviticus 25:8-55; Psalm 89:15*

In concluding our chapter on the Day of Atonement we consider the laws pertaining to the Jubilee year.

The Jubilee years were vitally connected with the Day of Atonement. Every seventh year was a Sabbath year, while every fiftieth year in Israel was a Jubilee year. Seven Sabbaths of years passed (or, 7x7=49), and the following year, the fiftieth, was the Jubilee.

Jubilee year was literally "the time of shouting." The Hebrew word **"Yobel"** (S.C.3104) coming from S.C. 2986 means "the blast of a horn" (from its continuous sound); specifically the signal of the silver trumpets; hence the instrument itself and the Festival thus introduced. It is translated "jubilee, ram's horn, trumpet."

Thus on the year of Jubilee the trumpet proclaiming liberty was to sound throughout the land. This **trumpet** was to sound on the great **Day of Atonement** of this fiftieth year.

With the cleansing of the nation, the priesthood and the Sanctuary, liberty could now sound throughout all Israel.

Several significant things took place in this year of Jubilee, all of which Christ came to fulfil in His atoning work.

A. **Liberty** was to be claimed throughout the land unto all the inhabitants.

The Lord Jesus began His ministry "proclaiming liberty to the captives" in the acceptable year of the Lord *(Isaiah 61:1-13; Luke 4:18-21)*.

Pentecost, the fiftieth day was also a day of liberty and rejoicing. So the fiftieth year was one liberty and shouting. Christ came to bring liberty from all enslavement *(Galatians 5:1; Romans 6:18)*.

B. The **fiftieth** year was a hallowed year, a sabbath year also for the land. No sowing or reaping was to be done. The land was to rest.

The Lord promised that the land would be blessed that it would bring forth fruit in the sixth year to carry them over the seventh, the eighth and into the ninth year. That is to say, God's blessing would be so great, Israel would have enough fruit to carry them through the sabbaths and the Jubilee years *(Leviticus 25:18-22, 11-12)*.

C. Every man was to return to his **possession.** If he was poor and had lost or forfeited or sold his possession, his inheritance, then in the year of Jubilee he was able to possess it again. This was especially so if he was not able to redeem it or have it redeemed by a kinsman Redeemer *(Leviticus 25:13-17, 23-34; Numbers 36:4).*

D. All slaves were set free in this year. If a brother became poor and had to borrow money to live, or sell himself as a slave for service, then in the year of Jubilee he was set free unless some kinsman could redeem him between the Jubilee years *(Leviticus 25:35-55).*

The sound of the trumpet of Jubilee was "the joyful sound" that blessed the people of God *(Psalm 85:15).* The Jubilee years were "the times of restitution" which the prophets also spoke about in the latter times *(Acts 3:19-21).*

What a time of rejoicing in Israel as liberty was proclaimed by the sound of the silver trumpet in the land. Debts were cancelled, slaves were set free, families were reunited, lost and forfeited inheritances were restored. It was indeed a year of shouting.

Every Jubilee was prophetic of the ministry of Christ. The Jubilee was proclaimed on the basis of the work of the High Priest on the Day of Atonement. So Christ's liberating ministry is founded on His atoning work.

When Jesus began His ministry He spoke of His six-fold "Jubilee" ministry in *Luke 4:17-19* with *Isaiah 61:1-3; 63:4.*

1. To preach good tidings to the poor and meek.

2. To heal and bind up the broken hearted.

3. To preach deliverance to the captives and open prison doors.

4. To recover sight to the blind.

5. To set at liberty them that were bruised.

6. To preach the acceptable year of the Lord (i.e., Year of Release, or Year of Jubilee).

The year of Jubilee was the year of liberty, the year of redemption. Christ in the reconciliation became our Redeemer and all the liberties of the Jubilee year are available through His work.

The church also is joined with Christ in the "Jubilee" ministry in the preaching of the Gospel of redemption, proclaiming the atonement.

It is significant that **time** from Adam until now has almost been 6000 years; that is, 120 Jubilees approximately (120x50=6000). The 6000 years speak of the 6 Days of the Lord *(Psalm 90:4; II Peter 3:8; Job 24:1; Genesis 2:17).*

The seventh day is a day of rest *(Revelation 20:1-6; Hebrews 3-4).* The number 120 points to the end of the age of flesh also and the reign of the Spirit *(Genesis 6:3; II Chronicles 5:12-14; Acts 1:15; 2:4).*

The ultimate fulfilment of all that took place under the Jubilee year will take place at the second coming of Christ.

The earth will be redeemed and come into full and complete rest from the curse brought upon it by Adam's sin. Complete restoration of man's lost inheritance will take place. God's people will be totally set free, set at liberty, from all sin, sickness and disease, death and the curse. Satan, the source of all these things, will be bound and true rest will be realized.

An end will be made of sin, transgression will be finished, reconciliation for iniquity will be realized in fulness and everlasting righteousness brought in. There will be no more need of vision and prophecy for He who is in the burden and sum of such will be dwelling with His people. The Tabernacle of God shall be with men and He shall dwell with them. He shall be their God and they shall be His people *(Daniel 19:24-27; Revelation 21:1-8).*

This will be the completion of the Jubilee ordinances because of the work of atonement of our God and His Christ. This will complete the "Times of restitution" of all things which the prophets have spoken of since the world began *(Acts 3:19-21; Romans 8:17-25).*

Several significant scriptures concerning **"the year"** of release and liberty may be seen in these references.

The prophet spoke of **"the acceptable year of the Lord"** *(Isaiah 61:1-3* and *Luke 4:18-19).* He also spoke of **"the year of My redeemed is come"** *(Isaiah 63:1-4).* The sabbath year or every seventh year in Israel was **"the year of release"** *(Leviticus 25:1-7; Deuteronomy 31:9-11).* And then we have **"the year of Jubilee"** *(Leviticus 25:8-17).*

All point to the end of the age and the coming of the Lord Jesus Christ which brings in the eternal ages to come when the fulness of redemption's plan will be experienced by the redeemed.

Chapter Fourteen
THE FEAST OF TABERNACLES

The final part of the Feast of the seventh month is the Feast of Tabernacles proper. The instructions for the keeping of this Feast are found especially in *Leviticus 23:33-34*. We consider the story in brief before looking at symbolic truths therein.

THE STORY IN BRIEF:

With the closing harvest of the year — the fruit harvest — gathered in, the people of Israel were to set aside seven days into the Lord. From the fifteenth day unto the twenty-first day there were to be seven days of rejoicing before the Lord. They were to leave their houses and dwell in booths made of various trees and rejoice before the Lord their God.

On the first and on the eighth day there were to be extra sabbath days or holy convocations. The whole Feast pointed back to the first Feast, Passover, because the Feast of Tabernacles was the consummation of that which began in the Feast of Passover.

The symbolic details show the truths therein for Israel under the Old Covenant and for the church under the New Covenant.

I. TITLES FOR THE FEAST

There were several significant titles or names for this Feast.

A. The Feast of Tabernacles — *Leviticus 23:34; Deuteronomy 16:13; Zechariah 14:16; Ezra 3:4.*

Or, more literally, "The Feast of Booths." The Hebrew word for "Booth" is **"Succoth"**. The Feast of Tabernacles, or Booths pointed back to Israel's first encampment after their Exodus from Egypt, as they encamped on the edge of the Wilderness (*Exodus 12:37; Numbers 33:1-6)*.

The booths spoke of a temporary dwelling place, enroute to the promised land and permant dwelling places.

B. The Feast of Ingathering — *Exodus 23:16.*

This title pointed to the final harvest, the fruit harvest, which was the final ingathering at the end of the year.

C. The Solemn Feast — *Deuteronomy 16:15; Hosea 12:9; 9:5; Psalm 81:1-3.*

The Feast of Tabernacles was the most joyful yet also the most solemn Feast of Israel's sacred year. It involved the solemnity of the Day of Atonement, yet the rejoicing of the Feast of Tabernacles.

D. The Feast of the Seventh Month — *Nehemiah 8:14.*

The number seven again points to the Feast of fulness and completion.

E. The Feast of Booths — *Nehemiah 8:14-15.*

Refer to notes above.

II. INTERPRETATION OF THE FEAST

The most outstanding truths in the Feast of Tabernacles proper involve the seasonal rains, the final harvest of the year, and then the special days of sacrifice and finally the rejoicing in booths. These things had special significance to the Israelites and will find their spiritual fulfilment in the church in the last days.

A. The Seasonal Rains

The student is referred again to the comments on the Feast of Pentecost. There it will be remembered that Israel, as in any agricultural nation, had two periods of harvest involving two periods of rain, to prepare and ripen the harvest.

According to the Hebrew calendar, having both Civil and Sacred years in the same year, Passover and Pentecost had "latter" or Spring rains, while the Feast of Tabernacles had "Former" or "early rains."

Some expositors suggest that Passover and Pentecost had "the former and early rain" while Tabernacles had the "latter rain." This is because of the dual calendar Israel had. The first month of the Sacred year was the seventh month of the Civil year while the seventh of the Sacred was the first of the Civil year.

The Prophet Joel speaks of the "former rain and the latter rain in the **first** month" *(Joel 2:23)*. The student is referred again to the Hebrew Calendar as used in this text. Regardless of the designation used, whether "former" or "latter" rain, the truth of the matter is that the three Feasts involved great outpourings of rain.

For the purpose of simpliciation the writer uses "early rain" to identify with the "early church" and "latter rain" to connect with the "latter day church."

The Lord promised Israel that, upon their obedience to His Covenant, He would give them the rains in their due season, "the first rain and the latter rain" that they would gather in their corn, wine and oil *(Deuteronomy 11:10-17)*. He also promised that He would also withhold the rains and allow the land to be blighted if they failed to obey His laws. The rains were always the seal of the Palestinian Covenant, the token of God's blessing. No rain was judgment and the curse of God on the land as well as on the people *(Deuteronomy 11:16-17; I Kings 8:35-43; 17:1-7; 18:41-46; Proverbs 16:15; Amos 4:6-13; Joel 1:10-12)*.

The outpoured rains and showers of blessing were symbolical of the outpouring of the Holy Spirit and the revelation of the Word of God.

The Word of God is likened to rain *(Deuteronomy 32:1-3; Isaiah 55:8-12)*. **The Holy Spirit** is also likened to rain, to living waters of blessing, to rivers flowing forth from the throne of God and the Lamb *(Joel 2:21-32; Hosea 10:12; James 5:7; Hosea 6:3; John 7:37-39; Revelation 22:1-3)*. Rain speaks of revival, refreshing and restoration.

The outpouring of the Holy Spirit and the revelation to the Apostles of the doctrine of Christ in the early church may be likened to "the first rain" or "the former rains." It was the Spring of church history. The Spirit and the Word flowed copiously.

When Joel speaks of "the former rain moderately" being poured out it is likened to "the teacher rain — the teacher of righteousness" *(Joel 2:23, Marginal)*.

The last 70 years or so have seen a tremendous outpouring of the Holy Spirit in the nations of the earth. Along with this has come an increased illumination of the Word of God. There is a great return to the doctrine of the Apostles and "the faith once delivered to the saints" *(Hebrews 6:1-2; Jude 3)*.

Untold thousands have come into the Baptism or infilling of the Holy Spirit and further truths in the Word of God. It is indeed the time of "latter rain" outpouring, when the Spirit is being poured upon all flesh. This is the rain that the Husbandman has long patience for as spoken of by the Apostle James *(James 5:7)*.

The remarkable prophecy of *Joel 2:23* promises the former and the latter rain in the first month (i.e., first of the Civil yet seventh of the sacred year, or visa-versa). That is, **a double portion** of rain!

However, the rain of the Spirit and the Word so far has been but "showers of blessing" *(Ezekiel 34:26)*. The Feast of Tabernacles is to see a mighty deluge of the Spirit, a universal outpouring of the Spirit. This will be accompanied by signs and wonders and gifts of the Holy Spirit, as well as revelation and illumination in the Word of God beyond all that has ever been in church history.

This is prophetic significance of the rains in the Feast of Tabernacles. It will touch every nation, both Jewish and Gentile.

"The early and latter rain" is a Bible expression and in spiritual sense speaks of the two great outpourings of the Holy Spirit in the earth, in the beginning and ending of church history.

The believer who is living in the time of the latter rain is called to seek the Lord and ask Him to send rain on His people *(Zechariah 10:1; Hosea 6:3; 10:12; James 5:7; Joel 2:23-32; Psalm 65:9-10; 46:4; Jeremiah 5:24; 31:10-14)*.

All that the early rain meant to the early church, the latter rain will mean to the church in the last days, but in double portion and blessing and power.

The rain which came at the "seven times" praying of Elijah typifies the great rain that will be manifest in the seventh Feast *(I Kings 18:41-46)*.

B. The Harvest Time

Associated with rains and actually the purpose of such were the great harvest times. As there were two great seasonal rains so there were two great harvest seasons. Rains and harvests were really inseparable. One was the precursor of the other; the harvest was the result of the rain. No rain, no harvest.

The first great harvest was the **corn** harvest as seen under the Feasts of Passover and Pentecost. There the barley and the wheat were gathered in *(Ruth 1:22; 2:23; Exodus 34:32-22; Judges 6:11)*. Then between the harvest months of Passover and Pentecost came the fourth, fifth and sixth months, the dry season, when generally no rain fell. Then came the rains of the Feast of Tabernacles, the Feast of the seventh month. All were intended to ripen the harvest as well as prepare for the new seasons sowing.

The last great harvest was the **fruit** harvest and this came in the Feast of Tabernacles.

Tabernacles is spoken of as the Feast of Ingathering which took place in the **end** of the year *(Exodus 23:16; 34:22)*. In this harvest was gathered in all the fruits of the land; wine and oil. The corn harvest was the harvest of the firstfruits for it pointed to the final harvest in the end of the year *(Deuteronomy 11:10-15)*.

Many references link the rains and especially the two harvests together as the Lord promised to send His people "the corn, wine and oil" *(Deuteronomy 11:14; Hosea 2:8-9, 21-22; Joel 1:10; 2:23-24; Revelation 6:6; Deuteronomy 12:17; 14:23; Nehemiah 5:10-11; 10:39)*.

A number of expositors see symbolic significance and national significance in these harvest.

Barley harvest has been used to symbolize the Jewish converts; wheat harvest to symbolize the first Gentile converts. This is seen in the Book of Acts and the history of the early church under the historical fulfilment of Passover and Pentecost. Jesus and the Apostles went to the Jews first (barley), then the cities of the Gentiles (wheat).

Then the fruit harvest has been used to symbolize the vast variety and multitude of converts out of every kindred, tongue, tribe and nation in the four corners of the earth. This final harvest comes under the historical and spiritual fulfilment of the Feast of Tabernacles in the church.

The symbolic truth of the harvest ingathering is the major thing and the scripture speaks of converts and believers as being the fruits of the harvest seasons *(James 5:7; James 1:18; I Corinthians 15:20,23; 16:15; Revelation 14:4)*.

The Father God as the Divine Husbandman has long patience as He waits for the precious fruit of the earth and the early and latter rains *(James 5:7-8)*.

"Corn, wine and oil" is used in scripture to symbolize the Word of God, the joy of the Lord and the anointing of the Holy Spirit.

The "fruits" and the "rains" are certainly not speaking of the natural but the spiritual. The Father wants the final harvest of souls, the greatest ingathering ever in church history.

The Feast of Ingathering took place in the **end** of the year *(Exodus 23:16)*. There is no mistaking the symbolism here. Jesus spoke of the harvest of the wheat and the tares, the good and the bad, as taking place in the **end** of the age *(Matthew 13:29-30, 36-43)*.

Thus under the closing days of grace, in the end of this age, the harvest will take place. The same rain that ripens the wheat also ripens the tares. The same rain that matures the righteous will also mature the wicked.

The Apostle John saw both of these harvests in *Revelation 14:13-16, 17-20*. One is the harvest of the righteous and the other is the harvest of the wicked which are cast into the winepress of God's wrath.

The Prophet Joel in prophesying of a double portion of rain also spoke of **a double portion harvest** ingathering. The end of the age shows an outpouring of former and latter rains; that is, the rains of Passover, Pentecost and Tabernacles. The double portion of rain will result in a double portion of harvest.

Joel says that the floor shall be full of wheat and the vats shall overflow with wine and oil. The rain will restore the lost and wasted years. Thus wheat, wine and oil speaks of the **corn** harvest and the **fruit** harvests together *(Joel 2:21-32)*. It is here that the plowman shall overtake the reaper, and the treader of grapes him that soweth seed *(Amos 9:13-15)*. The Lord has promised to do a quick work and cut it short in righteousness in these days. It will be God's strange work and act *(Romans 9:28; Isaiah 28:22)*.

Pentecost was the harvest of firstfruits. Tabernacles is the harvest of the final fruits. The first pointed to the final. The end of the age will result in the greatest ingathering of souls ever seen. Thus the symbolic and prophetic significance of the Feast of Tabernacles relative to the harvest ingathering in the end of the year points to that harvest ingathering in the church.

The Lord Jesus is concerned about the bringing in of the final harvest by the church before He returns the second time *(Matthew 9:37-38; 13:30,39; Mark 4:29; Luke 10:2; John 4:35; Revelation 14:15)*.

Type:

Passover 1st month	Pentecost 3rd month	4th, 5th, 6th months	Tabernacles 7th month
Former & Spring Rains Barley & Wheat		No rain	Latter Rains Wine & Oil
Corn Harvest			**Fruit** Harvest

Antitype:

Passover 1st month	Pentecost 3rd month	4th, 5th, 6th months	Tabernacles 7th month
First Outpouring of Spirit Jews & Gentiles Harvest of Souls		Dry Season Dark Ages	Last Day of Outpouring of Spirit Worldwide Harvest of Souls.

C. The Feast of Tabernacles/Booths

This Feast was also called the Feast of Tabernacles or the Feast of Booths.

1. Hebrew Word & Thought

The Hebrew word "Tabernacle" as used here is **"Sook-kaw"**, and means "a hut (as of entwined boughs) or lair." It is translated "booth, cottage, covert, den, pavilion, tabernacle" *(Leviticus 23:34; Deuteronomy 16:13,16; 31:10; II Chronicles 8:13; Ezra 3:4; Zechariah 14:16-18)*.

The custom took place when all of the harvest was gathered in. The Israelites were to take booths of goodly trees, the palm, the willow, the olive, the pine, the myrtle as well as other trees and make booths out of them. They were to leave their houses,or else build them on the roofs of their houses, and rejoice in these booths for seven days before the Lord *(Leviticus 23:39-44; Nehemiah 8:13-18)*.

The palm tree was symbolic of victory; the willow of weeping; the myrtle of joy; the olive of anointing *(Nehemiah 8:15; Psalm 137:1-5)*. The other branches also had symbolic meaning in Israel.

The Israelites were also to bless their families, their servants, and the Levites, the strangers, the fatherless and the widow in their gates. They were commanded to rejoice before the Lord.

With the harvest gathered in, they could look back over the labours of the year, all because of the blessing of the Lord in sending the rains. All this was sufficient grounds for rejoicing together. The Feast of Tabernacles was the most joyous season of the year. Pentecost was joyous. Tabernacles was the most joyous. In both Feasts, the Levites, the widows, strangers and fatherless were ministered to and blessed *(Deuteronomy 16:9-12, 13-16; Acts 5:41; 8:8,39; Luke 14:15-24; Joel 2:21)*.

Another reason for the Feast of Booths was in order that the Israelites would remember how the Lord caused them to dwell in booths when He brought them out of Egypt *(Leviticus 23:42-43)*. In other words, the Feast of the seventh month reminded them of the first month; the end reminded them of their beginning; Tabernacles reminded them of Passover.

Allusions to this Feast may be found in *Matthew 21:1-11* and *Revelation 7:9-12*. There we see the waving of palm trees amidst loud Hosannas to the Son of David, amidst great rejoicing.

2. Greek Word & Thought

The Greek word for "Tabernacle" is **"Skene"** and means "a tent or cloth hut (literally or figuratively), and it is translated "habitation, tabernacle" *(Luke 16:9; Acts 7:43)*. This and other relative words are used in the following manner.

a. It is used of the body of Christ in His incarnation when "the Word was made flesh and dwelt (Tabernacles) among us" *(John 1:14)*.

b. Peter used it of his own physical body when he was about to die and spoke of it as the putting off of his tabernacle *(II Peter 1:13-14)*.

c. The Apostle Paul also spoke of our physical body as being an earthly house, a tabernacle in which we groan, waiting for our house from heaven *(II Corinthians 5:1-5)*.

d. The Tabernacle of Moses was also spoken of as a tent or habitation of God *(Acts 7:44; Hebrews 9:2-8; 13:10)*.

e. Abraham, Isaac and Jacob lived in tabernacles also as pilgrims and strangers in earth *(Hebrews 11:9)*.

f. The Tabernacle of David was a tent or dwelling place of God *(Acts 15:16)*.

g. The scriptures speak of the Jews Feast of Tabernacles (lit., the tabernacle fixing) when Jesus entered the Temple *(John 7:2,27-29)*.

h. The New Testament also speaks of the heavenly Tabernacle and Temple, God's true dwelling place *(Hebrews 8:2; Revelation 13:6; 15:5)*.

Eventually the Tabernacle of God, the heavenly Jerusalem, will be with men *(Revelation 21:3)*.

    i. On the Mount of Transfiguration Peter suggested to Jesus that they make "three tabernacles"; one for Him, one for Moses and the other for Elijah *(Matthew 17:4; Mark 9:5; Luke 9:33)*. Perhaps this was an allusion to the Feast of Booths as far as Peter was concerned.

Thus the word is used in a variety of ways. The basic meaning of both the Hebrew and Greek is that of a temporary dwelling place; a tent or a habitation.

We note two of the major truths which may be discovered upon a consideration of the Hebrew and Greek thought.

1. **Dwelling in Booths** for 7 days reminded the Israelites of their exodus from Egypt and that they were but pilgrims and strangers in the earth.

So the believer is but a pilgrim and stranger in this word, looking for a city whose builder and maker is God, even as Abraham, Isaac and Jacob looked for *(Hebrews 11:10-16; 13:10;13; I Peter 1:17; 2:11)*.

2. **Dwelling in Booths** also reminded Israel that these "tabernacles" were only temporary dwelling places, not eternal. The eternal dwelling place was yet to come.

So the believer in Christ is reminded that the earthly physical body is only a temporary tabernacle. He will one day have to put it off, either in death or by the change-over to immortality. At the coming of Christ he will receive a new and heavenly house, his eternal dwelling place, which is an immortalized and glorified body *(II Corinthians 5:1-5; I Corinthians 15:51-57; I Thessalonians 4:15-18; Philippians 3:20-21)*.

The fulness of this Feast of the seventh month will be experienced at the coming of Christ and the resurrection and glorification of the saints of all ages. The Kingdom age will be an age of glory. There the believer will look back over his earthly pilgrimage of this life and remember the goodness of the Lord and rejoice in the glory of God.

Then the Tabernacle of God shall be with men and He will be to them a God and they shall be His people *(Revelation 21:1-8)*. This will be the completeness of the Feast of Tabernacles indeed.

D. **The Feast of the Seventh Month** — *Nehemiah 8:14*

The significance of the number seven has already been discussed, under the Feast of Trumpets and Day of Atonement.

The number seven is especially stamped on this Feast more than any of the previous Feasts and more particularly under the sacrifices which were offered during these festival days.

The number seven points to the end of this age, to its completion, and then it overflows into the Kingdom Age, which is the seventh Day of the Lord.

Remember that Hebrew time was from "even to even" or sunset to sunset, and therefore the evening of the fourteenth day was the beginning of the fifteenth day, we see, what may be called, **'the overlap'** of time. So it is with the number seven. The number seven is seen in the end of the age in many of its uses, yet it **overlaps** into the seventh Day of the Lord, i.e., the Millenniel Kingdom. So it is with the Feast of the Seventh month. It finds fulfilment in the close of this present age, yet overflows or overlaps on into the next age.

We note the special days marked out in this Feast.

1. The fifteenth day was the first day of this Feast *(Leviticus 23:33-35)*.

2. Then the Feast was to last for seven days, during which special sacrifices were offered, as the people rejoiced in booths. Thus from the fifteenth to the twenty-first day the Feast lasted *(Leviticus 23:36-44)*.

3. Then the eighth day (or the twenty-second day of the month) was to be a special day also, a holy convocation. It was a solemn assembly *(Leviticus 23:36; Numbers 29:35)*.

As seen previously, all Feast days were extra sabbaths, or holy convocations in Israel, besides the weekly sabbaths *(Leviticus 23:37-38)*. All speak of **rest** in the finished work of the Atonement.

The truth is set forth in the use of these symbolic numbers, which can only be dealt with in brief.

The number **fifteen** is seen by these several scriptures to be the number of **rest** *(Leviticus 23:5-7, 34-35; Esther 9:18)*. In Christ Jesus only is there true rest *(Matthew 11:28-30)*.

The number **seven** is the number of perfection, fulness and completion. It is the number of the Book of Revelation *(Genesis 2:1-3; Exodus 34:18; Leviticus 23:34; Exodus 20:9-11; Revelation 1:4,6,12,20; 4:5)*. In Christ there is perfection, fulness and completion.

The number **eight** is the number of resurrection and new beginning. It is seen that it relates to the "morrow after the sabbath" as in the Sheaf of Firstfruits and Pentecost. Those days were also an eighth day, as also is this eighth day solemn assembly *(Leviticus 23:36; Numbers 29:35; Exodus 22:30; Acts 20:7; I Corinthians 16:2)*. In Christ alone is there resurrection and life and a new beginning.

E. The Sacrifices — *Leviticus 23:33-38; Numbers 29:12-40*

Undoubtedly the most peculiar thing associated with this Feast were the specified offerings which were to be offered from the first day unto the eighth day, the day of the solemn assembly.

The seven days of the Feast were stamped with the number seven, as in the sacrifices offered. The student is encouraged to study the scriptures carefully. Only the basic facts can be noted here. No other Feast had as many sacrifices offered therein as in this Feast, as seen here.

1. Passover Feast had it particular sacrifice in the offering of the Passover Lamb *(Numbers 28:16)*.

2. Unleavened Bread had its particular number of sacrifices. These totalled 14 bullocks, 7 rams, 14 lambs, as well as their associated Meal and Drink offerings, plus 7 goats for the Sin offerings *(Numbers 28:17-25)*. Thus there were sweet-savour and non-sweet savour offerings here.

3. Pentecost had its specified offerings also. These totalled 2 bullocks, one ram, 7 lambs and their associated Meal and Drink offerings, plus the goat for the Sin offering *(Numbers 28:26-31)*.

4. Trumpets had its specified number of sacrifices too. These consisted of one bullock, one ram and 7 lambs with their Meat and Drink offerings, plus the goat for the Sin offering *(Numbers 29:1-6)*.

5. The Day of Atonement also followed a similar pattern. There was one bullock, one ram and 7 lambs with their Meat and Drink offerings, then the goat for the Sin offering. Then there were the two special goats chosen, the goat for Jehovah and the Scapegoat for the Day of Atonement ceremonies *(Numbers 29:7-11)*.

6. The Feast of Tabernacles had its specified number of sacrifices, as seen in the following outline. All these sacrifices on the Feast days were beside the regular "daily sacrifices" of the morning and evening.

In the 7 days of this Feast there were:

a. 70 bullocks offered, beginning the first day with 13 bullocks and offering one less bullock per day unto the seventh day. The Jews believed these 70 bullocks were offered in symbolism of the 70 nations of earth to which the Gospel would go. On the eighth day there was one bullock offered, thus altogether making 70 plus 1 = 71 total. It also symbolized the Sanhedrin consisting of 70 Elders plus the Chief Priest as President.

b. There were 14 rams offered for the 7 days, then 2 on the eighth day.

c. Then there were 98 lambs offered for the 7 days, then 14 on the eighth day.

d. Then along with each of the above bullocks, rams and lambs there was offered the attendant Meal and Drink offerings, in their respective tenths deal of flour and wine. In all there were 182 tenths deals of fine flour offered for the 7 days, then on the eighth day there were 9/10ths deals offered.

e. Then the non-sweet offerings were 8 goats offered for a Sin offering to the Lord; 7 goats for each of the 7 days of the Feast, and one goat on the eighth day.

f. For the Daily sacrifices there was a total of 14 lambs, then 2 for the eighth day Solemn assembly. These were the morning and evening sacrifices *(Exodus 29:38-41)*. Along with these were the Meat and Drink offerings of fine flour and wine; 8/10ths in all for the 8 days and 8/4ths of a hin of wine for the Drink offering.

The numbers which stand forth especially in their multiples are the numbers **seven, eight** and **ten!**

Seven brings us to the number of completion and perfection. It points to the perfections and completeness of Christ's sacrifice. This was the Feast of the Seventh month. The Feast lasted for seven days. The sacrifices are stamped with multiples of seven in the seven days.

Eight is the number of resurrection and new beginning. The eighth day of the Feast of this seventh month being set aside pointed to the day after the seventh day. This was fulfilled in Christ's resurrection after the seventh day, at the close of the sabbath, on the first day of the new week, the new beginning. Dispensationally it points to the New Heavens and New Earth, the New Jerusalem, which comes after the seventh day of the Lord, as in the Millenniel Kingdom.

Ten is the number of law and order. On the eighth day of this Feast a total of ten sacrifices were offered besides their attendant Meat and Drink offerings. It points to the fact that the atoning work of Christ in the perfections of His death (7), and resurrection (8) bring the believer into God's eternal law and order (10) from which man fell through sin.

3. **The Relationship of Passover, Pentecost and Tabernacles**

It has already been drawn to our attention that Passover was the first month of the Sacred year as well as being the seventh month of the Civil year.

Tabernacles was the seventh month of the Sacred and the first of the Civil year. This arrangement of the Lord immediately shows us that there is a connection and vital relationship between Passover, and Tabernacles, or the First and Seventh months.

This is especially seen in the days and dates specified in these months, which may be seen in sharper focus as set out here.

Passover/Beginning (The First-Seventh Month)	Tabernacles/Ending (The Seventh-First Month)
The first day of Passover the beginning of months	— The first day—blowing of Trumpets the beginning of seventh month
The tenth day — Lamb set aside to die	— The tenth Day of Atonement The Lord's goat dies
The fourteenth day—Lamb slain at even which was then the fifteenth day	— The fifteenth day—The Feast of Tabernacles
Unleavened bread kept for 7 days—15th-21st	— Feast of Tabernacles kept for 7 days — 15th-21st
The Sheaf of Firstfruits waved on the eighth day	— The eighth day — The solemn Feast day.

Here we see the principle of the Kingdom of heaven parable as in *Mark 4:28* fulfilled in the Feasts. First the blade (Passover), then the ear (Pentecost), then the full corn in the ear (Tabernacles).

Passover looked forward to Tabernacles, while Tabernacles looks backward to Passover, yet consummates that which began in Passover. The end was in the beginning, as the fruit is in the root, and the tree is in the seed!

In summary of our study of the Feasts and their intricate details we note the major truths therein.

Passover, Unleavened Bread and the Sheaf of Firstfruits set forth the work of Christ in His first coming, in His death, burial and resurrection.

Pentecost with its two wave loaves presented before the Lord on the fiftieth day after the waving of the Sheaf of Firstfruits set forth the work of the Holy Spirit in the church composed of Jew and Gentile. It shadows forth also the Pentecostal age between the first and second advents of Christ.

Tabernacles, with its trumpets, Day of Atonement and Ingathering sets forth the final operations of the Lord God in the earth prior to and at the second coming of Christ. It sets forth the gathering of the saints unto the Lord, the perfection of the church by the power of blood atonement and the final harvest of souls before Christ comes. The fulness of this Feast of the seventh month overflows into the seventh Day of the Lord, the Kingdom age, and will be enjoyed for all eternity.

Chapter Fifteen
HEAVEN AND EARTH CONNECTIONS

A very important truth is that which shows the connection and relationship of heaven and earth in the Feasts of the Lord. It is usually impossible to separate them. For, when a Feast took place on earth, there was something which took place in heaven.

Heaven worked with earth in the Festival occasions. This is to be expected because apart from heaven there would be no Feasts on earth. Earth is dependent on heaven.

In the fulfilment of the Feasts it is Jesus Christ who brings heaven and earth together, bridging the communication gap that was brought about by sin. In His perfect sacrifice for sin He links earth and heaven together in the great reconciliation.

He Himself said: "All power is given unto Me in **Heaven and Earth**" (*Matthew 28:18*). He is our Melchisedek, Priest of the Most High God, Possessor of heaven and earth (*Genesis 14:18-20*). He is our "Jacob's Ladder" who connects heaven and earth, and angels as ministering spirits ascend and descend upon Him ministering to the heirs of salvation (*Genesis 28:12* with *John 1:51; Hebrews 1:13-14*).

When He ascended on high and sat down at the right hand of the Majesty on high, He continued to work with His disciples as they preached the Word of the Gospel on earth (*Mark 16:15-20*).

So it is in the Feasts of the Lord. As the shadow moved on earth, the substance in heaven attested to the same. In Passover, as Jesus died on earth, the sun in heaven was darkened by the Father God. In Unleavened Bread and the Sheaf of Firstfruits, Christ was resurrected from the grave on earth and ascended to heaven, presenting Himself as the Surety for all believers. In Pentecost, Jesus had ascended to heaven 10 days previously, and then the Holy Spirit was sent from heaven to earth to the waiting disciples, who formed the church, the Body of Christ in its conception. In Tabernacles, Jesus, in fulfilment of the Day of Atonement, entered within the heavenly vail of the heavenly Sanctuary, and the believer on earth has access in the Spirit to that Holiest of All.

When the final and last trumpet blows, then Jesus descends from heaven to earth and receives His own unto Himself. Finally "The Tabernacle of God" will be with men and He will dwell with them. It will indeed be "heaven on earth".

Thus "heaven and earth" connections are seen in each of the Feasts. It is Jesus Christ who unites heaven and earth, through His Person and His atoning Work. The "great gulf" brought about by sin has been bridged in the cross and now all believers may come and feast with their Lord and Saviour, Jesus Christ.

Chapter Sixteen
THE REDEMPTIVE WEEKS IN ISRAEL

The prophet Jeremiah, in referring to the Feasts of the Lord complained about the rebellious heart of the people of Judah. He lamented the fact that they did not say "Let us now fear the Lord our God, that giveth **rain**, both the former and the latter, in his season: He reserveth unto us the **appointed weeks of the harvest**" *(Jeremiah 5:24)*.

In this verse we note the connection between the former and latter rains and the harvest time, the appointed weeks of the harvest.

The Hebrew word for **"week"** simply means **"seven"**. Hence "the appointed weeks" were "the appointed sevens" of the harvest.

The Hebrew mind was saturated with the concept of the "Weeks of the Lord" and the whole context of Scripture shows indeed that God was shadowing forth the "redemptive week" in the patterns of the sevens in Israel.

In the whole of scripture we see a seven-fold revelation of these Weeks, the ultimate being manifested in the Week of Redemption.

I. THE WEEK OF CREATION — *Genesis 1:1, 2:3*

In Genesis we have the account of creation. Here we see how God worked for six days, then the seventh day He rested. He sanctified the seventh day as the crowning glory on the work of the previous six days. This is the first "week" or the first "seven" to be revealed in the scripture. It sets the pattern for all the following "weeks" or "sevens". It is thus called "the Week of Creation."

II. THE WEEK OF DAYS — *Exodus 31:12-17*

In this passage we see the Lord calling His chosen nation, Israel, to work for six days and then to rest the seventh day. The seventh day was the holy sabbath and no manner of work was to be done in it. Man's days were 24 hour days. But God, in commanding Israel concerning this "week" pointed back to the Week of Creation. He Himself had worked six days, then rested on the seventh day, hence Israel was to follow a similar pattern. They were to work for 6 days, then rest the seventh. For Israel it was "the Week of Days."

III. THE WEEK OF WEEKS OF DAYS — *Leviticus 23:15-22*

Remembering that the word "week" simply means "seven" we see here in the Feast of Pentecost the pattern of a week of weeks, or a seven of sevens.

The Israelites were to count from the day of the waving of the Sheaf of Firstfruits 49 days, or 7 x 7 days; that is, 7 weeks. Seven sabbaths were to elapse. Then the day following, which was "the morrow after the seventh sabbath", or the 50th day, they were to keep the Feast of Pentecost. Thus the Feast of Pentecost was founded on "the Week of Weeks." Pentecost was really called "the Feast of Weeks" because of this.

So for Israel this pattern was "the Week of Weeks of Days."

IV. THE WEEK OF MONTHS — *Leviticus 23:1-44*

The next order of number seven relative to the weeks of the Lord is that which is seen in the Feasts of the Lord as dealt with in this text.

Passover, Pentecost and Tabernacles were encompassed within "a week", that is, "a Week of Months." Passover took place in the first month, Pentecost in the third month and Tabernacles in the seventh month. Thus there was the cycle of the seven or the week again. The seventh month, as seen, was the most sacred month. It was sanctified or set apart from the previous six months. Because the Feasts of the Lord took place within the cycle of seven months it is called "the Week of Months."

V. THE WEEK OF YEARS — *Leviticus 25:1-7; Exodus 21:1-6*

The Week of Years has to do with the rest of the land and the liberation of slaves in Israel.

The Lord commanded Israel to work the land for 6 years, but the seventh year was to be a year of rest, a sabbath, for the land. No sowing or reaping was to be done. The land was to rest. Failure to keep the sabbath years of rest for the land brought about the Babylonian captivity for 70 years, or 70 sabbaths *(II Chronicles 36:21; Daniel 9:1-2)*.

Thus we have again "the Weeks of Years." Work the land for six years, then rest it the seventh year.

Relative to this same period of time, this "week" or "seven" we have the Lord's word concerning the slaves. If an Israelite bought a slave then the slave was to work for his master six years, but in the seventh year he was to be set free, unless he desired to be a love-slave forever. The slave therefore understood "the Week of Years." This was called the year of release *(Deuteronomy 31:10)*. Once again we have God's pattern of the Week, impressed here on the years, even as the previous were on days and months.

VI. THE WEEK OF WEEKS OF YEARS — *Leviticus 25:8-17.*

The Week of Weeks of Years follows a similar pattern to that which was seen in the Feast of Weeks and Pentecost. There it was 7 x 7 = 49 days, then the 50th day was Pentecost.

In this pattern we have 7 x 7 = 49 years, then the 50th year was the Jubilee year, another sabbath year and year of release for Israel. Thus we have 7 "weeks of years" or seven sevens of years making 49 years in all. The following year was the year of Jubilee, which began on the Day of Atonement.

Here again we have God's pattern of "weeks" or "sevens." This is called "the Week of Weeks of Years."

VII. THE WEEK OF MILLENNIUMS — The Bible

Each of the previous patterns of "weeks" or "sevens" shadow forth the total purpose of God relative to earth. God has been at work in the week which we call "the Week of Redemption." Since the Fall of Adam, God has been working almost six days, that is, 6000 years, for "A day unto the Lord is a thousand years and a thousand years as one day" *(Genesis 2:17; Psalm 90:4; II Peter 3:8; Job 24:1)*.

Sin broke God's rest as well as man's rest. Hence God began to work again. This time in redemption's plan *(John 5:17; 19:30)*. Jesus came to bring us rest *(Matthew 11:28-30)*. The believer enters into rest now by the spiritual Feasts of the Lord, but the full rest is yet to come.

The writer to the Hebrews speaks of the fact that "there remaineth **a rest** (Lit., a sabbath) unto the people of God *(Hebrews 4:9)*.

The Millenniel Day will be this seventh day rest. The New Heavens and New Earth will bring the redeemed to the eighth day, or that which is symbolized in "the morrow after the Sabbath." This will be eternal rest.

All of the sevenths pointed to the seventh day of the Lord. The seventh day, the seventh month, the seventh year, etc., all pointed to God's seventh **day,** the Millenniel Age.

Each of these "weeks" or "sevens" pointed to the Week of the Lord, the Week of Redemption. All were shadows and prophetic of the eternal rest *(Leviticus 23:3; Colossians 2:17)*. All the weekly sabbaths pointed to the Millenniel sabbath and each of "the morrow after the Sabbath" pointed to the Eternal Rest.

True and complete rest will only come when all sin is made to end, transgression is finished, reconciliation for iniquity has been realized and Satan and his evil hordes are cast into the Lake of Fire for all eternity. This will be rest indeed! Read *Daniel 9:24-27.*

In the light of these "Weeks" we see how the Week of Creation shadowed forth the Week of Redemption, and the Weeks of the Lord in Israel were typical of both. They pointed back to the Week of Creation yet also pointed forward to the Week of Redemption. The seventh day of the Lord is revealed to be 1000 years *(Revelation 20:1-10)*. The previous six days have proved to be approximately 6000 years from Adam to Christ's second coming. Hence from Adam to Christ's first coming, we have four Days of the Lord (4000 years), then two days of the Lord (2000 years of this present Age of the Holy Spirit), making 6 days or 6000 years in all. In these six days **God,** as Father, Son and Holy Spirit, is at work. The seventh day will be **rest** — the sabbath of the Lord!

We close this chapter off by showing the relationship between the seventh day sabbath and the Morrow after the sabbath, and their typical import.

The Sabbath		The Morrow after the Sabbath
The seventh day	—	The eighth day
The Natural Creation	—	The Spiritual & New Creation
The First Man	—	The Second Man
The First Adam	—	The Last Adam
The Sabbath	—	The Rest of God & Man
Physical work	—	Spiritual work
For Israel	—	For the Church
Sign of the Mosaic Covenant	—	Sign of the New Covenant
Command of Law	—	Willingly of Grace
Works	—	Grace

The Millenniel Kingdom consummates God's plan relative to the work of redemption in the earth, and fulfills the seventh day, the holy sabbath of the Lord and the redeemed.

The New Heavens and New Earth fulfills the morrow after the sabbath and ushers in the fulness of eternity, being the eighth day, the day of new beginnings. In this all things are made new. There is the New Heavens and New Earth, the New Jerusalem and the New Creation. Read *Revelation 20-22-22* chapters in connection with these remarks.

Chapter Seventeen
THE FEASTS OF THE LORD IN RELATION TO THE TABERNACLE OF MOSES

The Feasts of the Lord are inseparable from the Tabernacle of Moses or the Temple of Solomon. Once Israel was brought out of Egypt in the exodus and the Sanctuary of the Lord was established, then all the festival occasions were centered in the Tabernacle of the Lord, or the Temple of the Lord.

The Lord clearly told His people that they were not to sacrifice in any and every place but only in the place where His Name was recorded (*Deuteronomy 12 and 16 chapters*).

In **Passover** the lamb was slain and presented to the Lord on the altar in the Outer Court of the Tabernacle in behalf of the whole nation.

The **Sheaf** of **Firstfruits** was also brought to the door of the Tabernacle and presented by the Lord there.

In **Pentecost** the two Wave Loaves were waved before the Lord in the Tabernacle, in the Holy Place and there accepted for Israel.

In **Tabernacles** the Sanctuary service was greatly involved. At the blowing of the **trumpets** all Israel had to gather themselves to the Lord at the door of the Tabernacle on the great **Day** of **Atonement.**

As they stood there, all waited in silent prayer as the High Priest entered within the veil making the atonement for himself, his house and the whole nation. There they waited until the Sanctuary had also been cleansed. At the close of the Day of Atonement ceremonies they received the blessing of their High Priest.

The Day of Atonement involved entrance within the Holiest of All, or the Most Holy Place. This was only entered once a year and that with the blood of atonement.

The Feast of **Tabernacles** itself also symbolized that God Himself was tabernacled amongst His own people as they also with Him. It pointed to the final dwelling place of God with His redeemed as seen by John in the eternal city of God, the New Jerusalem.

In each Feast the believer was linked with a place of the Tabernacle, proceeding in truth from the Outer Court to the Holy Place and finally to the Most Holy Place where the Lord Himself dwelt. So this is the approach of all unto God through Christ, as set forth in the Tabernacle of Moses or the Temple of Solomon.

The diagram illustrates the basic truths above.

The Tabernacle

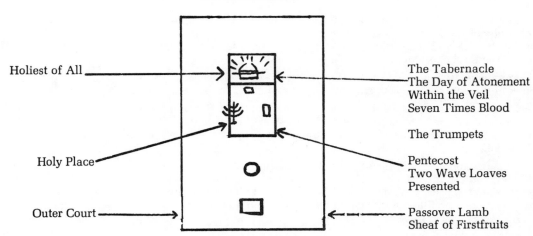

Holiest of All —————→

The Tabernacle
The Day of Atonement
Within the Veil
Seven Times Blood

The Trumpets

Holy Place

Pentecost
Two Wave Loaves
Presented

Outer Court —————→

Passover Lamb
Sheaf of Firstfruits

Chapter Eighteen
HISTORICAL AND PROPHETICAL SIGNIFICANCES OF THE FEAST OF TABERNACLES

There are several remarkable historical and prophetical events which took place in Israel's history relative to the Feast of Tabernacles. This Feast being the greatest of all Feasts is spoken of more than the previous Feasts. It is the burden of the Books of Restoration; Ezra and Nehemiah and Haggai and Zechariah in particular.

A consideration of these things provide examples and spiritual truth and lessons for the church of New Testament times. For as we see the things which took place in Israel under this glorious Feast we can anticipate more fully and clearly what the church can expect under this same Feast. The things which happened in Israel relative to the Feasts were also types and ensamples to us and are written for our admonition (*I Corinthians 10:6,11*).

I. THE FEAST OF TABERNACLES AND THE OPEN BOOK — *Deuteronomy 31:9-13, 16-30*

When Moses was 120 years of age and about to pass from the scene of life's responsibilities, the Lord commanded him to renew the Covenant with the new generation in Israel. The former generation had died in the wilderness because of unbelief. Now the second generation were to arise and enter into the land of promise.

The Lord told Moses to write the "second law" in a Book and deliver it to the Levites, the priests of the Lord.

They were to take this Book of the Law, or the Book of the Covenant, and place it in the side of the Ark of the Covenant. It was to be a witness to them and a warning against Israel's rebellion.

This Book of the Law was especially the Pentateuch, the first five books of the Bible as written by Moses under the inspiration of the Holy Spirit. It contained the revelation of the beginnings of the human race, the chosen Hebrew nation and the dispersion of the Gentile nations.

It contained the account of Israel's miraculous deliverance from Egypt and the failure of that first generation to enter into Canaan land. The Book declared all the words of the Mosaic Covenant with its moral, civil and ceremonial laws. The ordinances of the Lord were written therein and the ground of Israel's approach to the Lord as well as the grounds on which His Presence could dwell with them.

In this Book were the blessings of obedience and the curses of disobedience to the Law of the Lord. It also declared God's purpose for the chosen nation which was to bless all other nations. Ultimately the Messiah would come of this race and make redemption available for all mankind. The priests, the Levites were to teach the tribes of Israel the Law of the Lord.

Now the significant thing about the Book of the Law was this. At the end of every seven years, **in the solemnity of the year of release, in the Feast of Tabernacles,** the Levites were to take the Book of the Covenant out of the Ark and read it to the people. This was to take place in the land of Israel, in the appointed place where the Lord chose to place His Name.

How the Book was placed in the side of the Ark is not specifically stated. But the significant thing is that the Book of the Law was to be opened, read and explained to the people in the Feast of Tabernacles.

Not in Passover, not in Pentecost but in Tabernacles the Book was to be read. It was the responsibility of the Levites and priests to teach the people God's Word (*II Chronicles 17:7-9; Malachi 2:1-10*). Thus although there was the general teaching of the Law there was a special emphasis in the year of release, in the Feast of Tabernacles.

In connection with all this may be added the instruction given for kings as written in *Deuteronomy 17:14-20*. When the king sat on his throne, he was to write for himself a copy of the Book of the Law out of that which was before the priests, the Levites. This Book was to be in the throne of his kingdom and he was commanded to read it, and meditate in it day and night, and then do it.

Thus there was the Book of the Law in the side of the Ark of Covenant, the throne of God in the earth. Then there was a Book of the Law in the throne of Israel's earthly king. The king was to read his copy of the Book continually. The Levites were to read the copy of the Book which was in the side of the Ark every seven years in a special convocation to all Israel in the Feast of Tabernacles.

An historical illustration of this is found in the Books of Ezra and Nehemiah (Ezra 3 and Nehemiah 8). This will be dealt with under their historical setting.

In applying this to the New Testament Church we have the account of John's vision in the Book of Revelation (*Revelation 4-5*). John was caught up in the Spirit and saw a throne set in heaven. One was seated upon the throne and in His hand there was a seven-sealed Book. John wept much because none was found worthy to open the Book, and loose the seven seals thereof.

However, the Lion of the Tribe of Judah, the Lamb of God, was found worthy. He took the Book out of the hand of Him who sat on the throne and broke the seals thereof. This Book is the Book of redemption, the Book that only the Kinsman Redeemer can open. In it we behold the consummation of God's purposes in the earth. In the consummation of the ages, the Book of the Lord will be opened to the saints of God and they will come into their full inheritance with Christ and God.

This Book which John saw was in the throne of the King of the universe. He who is the King of Kings and Lord of Lords brings revelation and illumination to John, who typifies the ministry to the people of God.

Thus we may say that, as the church experiences the Feast of Tabernacles, increased light and understanding will be her portion. Thank God for the truths of Passover, and Pentecost. But in the Feast of Tabernacles full and complete and full truth will break forth on the church.

The Feast of Tabernacles is the Feast of the Open Book! It is the responsibility of the ministry to teach the Word of God to the people of God. And although there is that general teaching of the Word of God, it is evident that the Feast of Tabernacles will bring a special emphasis and illumination in the opened Book (*Luke 24:27, 44-46; Acts 17:1-3; Revelation 4-5*).

II. THE FEAST OF TABERNACLES AND SOLOMON'S TEMPLE — *I Kings 8:1-11*

The Scripture provides the details of the building of Solomon's Temple in *I Kings Chapters 5-8 and II Chronicles 3-7.*

The Temple of the Lord is a subject in itself and needs a text-book to deal with this magnificent structure. Basically it followed the same pattern as the Tabernacle of Moses, only on a much larger scale.

The pattern of the Temple and its furnishings, priestly courses, and ordinances was first given to David by the Spirit which he then committed to writing and delivered it to his son, Solomon (*I Chronicles 28-29*).

In the Outer Court there was the one great altar of sacrifice. Then there were 10 additional smaller lavers for the washing of sacrifices, plus the one great molten sea for the priests to wash the rest.

In the Holy Place there were 10 golden candlesticks in contrast to the one golden candlestick in the Tabernacle of Moses. Also there were 10 golden tables of shewbread in contrast to the one in the Tabernacle of Moses. However, there was but one golden altar of incense in the Holy Place, as in the Tabernacle of Moses.

In the Holiest of All was the ark of the covenant — not a new ark but the same one as had been in the Tabernacle of Moses and the Tabernacle of David.

The significance of these things can but briefly be commented upon. The **one** ark, the **one** altar of sacrifice and the **one** altar of incense strictly pertain to Christ. He is the **one** and **only** Mediator between God and man. He is the **one** and once-for-all sacrifice for sin. There can be no other (*I Timothy 2:5-6; Hebrews 8:6*). His atoning work was done once and for all.

The ten lavers, ten golden candlesticks and ten golden tables of shewbread point to the works of Christ in the church, the royal priesthood. The church needs to offer spiritual sacrifices, receive much spiritual illumination and spiritual nourishment, as symbolized in these articles of furniture.

Now the significant thing relative to the present text is that which involves the Feast of the Lord with Solomon's Temple. By comparing *I Kings 8:1-11* and *I Chronicles 5:1-14* we see the details of the dedication of the Temple or House of the Lord.

The Temple took seven years to complete and now with the finishing of the work, the dedication service was needed before it could be indwelt by God and ministered in by the priests of the Lord.

Some of the most prominent things about this dedication are outlined here.

A. The Temple of the Lord was built in Jerusalem, the city of God.

B. The Temple was built in Mt. Moriah where Abraham had offered Isaac typically years before (*Genesis 22*). Thus the Temple arose out of the foundation of a typically sacrificed and resurrected only begotten son (*Hebrews 11:17-19*).

C. The Temple was built on the threshing floor of Ornan the Jebusite (*II Chronicles 3:1 with I Chronicles 21 and II Samuel 24*).

D. The Temple was built out of stones prepared in the quarry and then brought to the Temple site *(I Kings 6:7)*.

E. The Temple was built of cedar, overlaid with gold and studded with precious stones, beautifying the whole house.

F. The Temple had its particular furniture following the same pattern as that of the Tabernacle which Moses built.

G. The Temple was completed after seven years *(I Kings 6:37)*.

H. The Temple was built to the Name of the Lord, even as was the Tabernacle of Moses.

I. The Temple was dedicated to the Lord by blood sacrifice.

J. The Temple was sanctified by the Presence and Glory of God.

Now the significant thing about the dedication service was this. The Ark of the Covenant which had been in the Tabernacle of Moses for years. and then was, in due time, transferred to the Tabernacle of David, was now brought from there to the Temple of Solomon. It was placed in the Holy Oracle beneath the two great olive Cherubim. The staves were taken out, for the pilgrim journey was over. The only content of the Ark was the Law of God as in the two Tables of Stone *(II Chronicles 5:7-10)*.

The priests came out of the Holiest of All and the Levitical singers and trumpeters began to sing and praise the Lord. As all the musicians and singers of the order of David's Tabernacle were of one accord and making one sound, the Glory of the Lord filled the Temple so that none could minister. There were 120 trumpets at the dedication of Solomon's Temple. The Glory-Cloud filled the House of God as it came and stood over and upon the blood-stained Mercyseat of the Ark of the Covenant.

All of this took place in **the Feast of the Seventh Month, Ethanim,** which was **the Feast of Tabernacles** *(II Chronicles 5:3; I Kings 8:1-2)*.

In contrast to this the Tabernacle of Moses was dedicated in **the first month, the Feast of Passover Month,** at which the Glory-Cloud filled the tent and no man could minister by reason of the Glory *(Exodus 40:1-38)*.

The Tabernacle of Moses pointed more particularly to Christ who fulfills in Himself all that which was typified there. The Temple of Solomon points, not only to Christ, but more especially to the church, the fulness of Him who filleth all in all.

The New Testament recognize that, since the Cross, the church is now God's holy Temple *(I Corinthians 3:16; II Corinthians 6:16; Ephesians 2:19-22; John 2:18-22)*.

There is some correspondence to and a measure of fulfilment in the early church as pertaining to Solomon's Temple.

In Solomon's Temple we see the 120 trumpeters and singers of one accord, making one sound. There we see the Glory-fire of the Lord falling and filling the Temple.

In the early church, the New Covenant Temple, we also see 120 trumpets or 120 disciples, praising the Lord, in one accord and one place. Then the Holy Spirit came as rushing wind and tongues of fire, and filled them all with Himself. The flesh was subdued and the Spirit was supreme.

But there was this difference. The dedication of the Temple of Solomon took place in the Feast of Tabernacles, the Feast of the Seventh Month. The dedication of the early church took place in the Feast of Pentecost, the Feast of the third month. Thus the Tabernacle of Moses was dedicated in Passover Feast, the early church was dedicated in Pentecost Feast and the Temple of Solomon was dedicated in the Feast of Tabernacles.

Believing that the scriptures were inspired by the Holy Spirit we perceive that there is Divine reason for this difference.

The whole scene points prophetically to the fact that **the true dedication** of the church, God's Temple, is yet to take place. This will be as the church enters into the fulness of the final Feast, the Feast of Tabernacles. The fact that it took place in the seventh month points to the end-times when it takes place in the church. At this dedication the church will experience **the glory** of the **Lord** as never before. Jesus Christ, as the Ark of God, will take His place in His church.

The church, God's holy Temple, is in preparation in these days. God is preparing the believers as His lively stones. At the set time the Temple of God will come together. All will find their place as living stones in His House. The dedication will take place in the Feast of Tabernacles and the church shall be full of the Glory of God *(John 17:21-26; Isaiah 60:1-3; Ephesians 5:25-27)*, thus making it a glorious church indeed and a fit habitation for God by the Spirit *(Ephesians 2:11-22)*.

III. THE FEAST OF TABERNACLES AND THE BOOKS OF RESTORATION

There were four Old Testament Books which especially deal with the restoration of Israel and its relation to the Feast of Tabernacles. These Books are the Books of Ezra and Nehemiah and Haggai and Zechariah. Each deal with the restoration of the House of Judah from Babylon, both from the historical and prophetical point of view. They provide instructive material historically for the Jews and prophetically for the church. Our consideration includes that which took place historically and the spiritual and moral lessons we may learn and which may be applied to the history of the church.

A. The Books of Ezra and Nehemiah — Historical

Ezra and Nehemiah, as Books of Restoration, center around the return of the Jews from Babylon and the restoration of the city of Jerusalem, the walls thereof, and the Temple and Feasts of the Lord *(Ezra 8-9-10-11; Nehemiah 8)*.

A careful study of the above chapters provide further insight as to how Judah kept the Feasts. They also provide spiritual lessons showing what it will mean for the church. We parallel the historical in Israel and the typical in the church in order to glean these lessons of restoration.

1. Under Solomon Israel built the Temple of the Lord and saw the Glory of the Lord fill the same, as seen previously. There the 120 trumpeters and singers were of one accord, making one sound in the time of dedication.

   So in the early church, The Book of Acts shows the 120 disciples in one place, of one accord, as the Glory of the Lord filled the New Covenant Temple, the church.

2. During Israel's history and the successive leadership, the Temple of the Lord became defiled by sin and idolatry. In due time the Glory of the Lord departed *(Ezekiel 8-9-10-11)*.

   So in the history of the church as the Temple of the Lord. Over the years, sin, backsliding and apostasy crept into the church under its successive leadership. Finally the Glory of the Lord departed.

3. Once the Glory of the Lord departed from Solomon's Temple, it came under judgment. If any defile the Temple of God they would be destroyed. Thus God permitted His Temple to be destroyed under Nebuchadnezzar, the King of Babylon. He allowed His people to be carried captive to Babylon for 70 years.

   The church in the period known as "The Dark Ages" was also in its "Babylonian Captivity". The Glory of the early church was gone. The Temple was defiled and thus destroyed *(I Corinthians 3:16-17)*.

4. In due time, the captivity ended and God sent a message to Babylon that He wanted His people to come out of Babylon and return to the city of God. It was a message of restoration. Not everyone responded but there was a remnant that believed the message of restoration.

   So the call has come to the people of God, to come out of Babylon (i.e., Religious Confusion), and accept the message of restoration. God wants to restore His House, His Temple, His Church. Not all believe the message but there are those who do and respond to it.

5. When the remnant returned to Jerusalem, they began the work of restoration. They restored the altar of the Lord, the foundation of the Temple, as well as the city and its walls. Much opposition was experienced but in due time the work was completed.

   So from the period of the Reformation, as far as the church is concerned, the work of restoration has been progressing in the church. The foundation principles have been recovered to the church. God's Temple is being restored amidst opposition from foes within and without.

6. Vitally connected with the restoration of the Temple was the keeping of the Feasts of the Lord again; in particular the Feast of Tabernacles *(Ezra 3; Nehemiah 8)*. These chapters deal with this keeping of this Feast.

   The main points worthy of attention in these chapters are:

   a. All those of the returned remnant came out of their cities and gathered as "one man" *(Ezra 3:1; Nehemiah 7:73; 8:1)* to Jerusalem. There was great unity amongst the people.

   b. They all gathered as one before "the water gate" *(Nehemiah 8:1)*. Water speaks of the washing of water by the Word *(Ephesians 5:23-27)*. The water gate was the gate where they brought the water from the pool of Siloam in the outpouring of water at the altar in the Feast of Tabernacles.

   c. The first thing established was the altar of God for sacrifice *(Ezra 3:1-6)*. This symbolized the foundation of blood-atonement, which is the first and fundamental step in the restoration of the Lord's House.

   d. From the first day of the seventh month and onwards, Ezra the Scribe and teaching Priest opened the Book of the Law and taught the people. He read in the Book of the Law of God distinctly and gave the sense and counselled the people as he caused them to understand the reading *(Ezra 8:1-12, 18)*.

The first day of the seventh month was the Feast day of the Trumpets (*Leviticus 23:23-25*). The opening of the Book illustrates the reading of the Law in "the year of release, in the Feast of Tabernacles" as commanded by Moses (*Deuteronomy 31:9-11, 24-26*).

So in the church, the Feast of Trumpets brings an opening of the Word and great understanding to the people of God, as an introduction to this final Feast (*Luke 24:27, 44-46*).

e. As they studied the Law and the Word was expounded unto them they found that they should have been keeping the Feast of Tabernacles. They obeyed the Word. They built booths and kept the Feast of Tabernacles in the seventh month with great joy and rejoicing. The scripture says that they had not kept as great a Feast since the days of Joshua (*Nehemiah 8:13-18; Ezra 3:4*).

They kept all the "set Feasts of the Lord" also (*Ezra 3:5*).

It typifies the fact that the church, after coming out of its "Babylonian Captivity" must enter in and keep the Feasts of the Lord also.

f. However, even though the Jews kept the Feasts here, the foundation of the Lord's House was not yet completed. In due time it would be, as the work of restoration progressed (*Ezra 3:6-7, 10-13*).

Hence these chapters in the Historical Books provide great lessons for the church. The restoration is not yet complete. The foundation principles of Christ's doctrine are being re-discovered and laid properly as the work of restoration progresses. At the same time the people of God can enjoy the Feasts of the Lord; Passover, Pentecost and Tabernacles. In God's appointed time the Temple will be complete and shall be filled with the Glory of the Lord.

It is at this period of time under Ezra and Nehemiah that we see the ministry of the Prophets, Haggai and Zechariah. They also work with the people in the restoration of the Temple and in connection with the Feasts of the Lord, especially the Feast of Tabernacles.

B. **The Books of Haggai and Zechariah — Prophetical**

Because of the opposition to the restoration and the rebuilding of the Temple of God, the work had ceased (*Ezra 4:23-24*).

God raised up two prophets by the name of Haggai and Zechariah, who began to call the people in the Word of the Lord to continue the work. These prophets helped the people both practically and spiritually (*Ezra 5:1-2*)

Under their ministry the Temple was finished. They also kept the Feasts of Passover and Unleavened Bread at this time (*Ezra 6:14-15*).

However, these prophets of restoration had something special to say to the people relative to the Feast of Tabernacles.

1. **The Prophet Haggai**

Haggai's very name has great significance. It means "Feast" or "Festival of Jehovah" or "Born at the time of a Festival."

With the opposition that the returned exiles experienced, the building of the Temple ceased for several years. About the year 520 B.C., the Word of the Lord came to Haggai and he began to challenge the people about the completion of the House of God. They had become so busy in the building of their own ceiled houses while God's House lay waste. They felt, because of the opposition, that it was not time to build the House of the Lord. Because they were more interested in building their own houses, God allowed drought to come. The early and latter rains were withheld and the corn, wine and oil harvests suffered accordingly (*Haggai 1:1-11; 2:16-19*).

The people responded to the prophetic challenge and were stirred in spirit to continue restoring the Temple of God (*Haggai 1:12-15*). These prophecies were given in the sixth month, beginning on the first day and continuing to the twenty-fourth day (*Haggai 1:1,15*).

Now the next dated prophecy of Haggai is found in *Chapter 2:1-9*. The time element is remarkable and links Haggai with the Feast of Tabernacles, as well as with the significance in his name.

Haggai in his prophecy told the remnant that the Lord was going to shake all things; the heavens, the earth, the sea, the dry land and all nations. He also said that "the Desire of all nations" would come and fill the restored House with the Glory of the Lord.

The great prophecy was that "the Glory of the latter house shall be greater than the former" (*Haggai 2:9*).

As we read *Haggai 2:1* we discover that this prophecy was given on the twenty-first day of the seventh month. That is, **the last day** of the Feast of Tabernacles proper. Remembering that the Feast of Booths lasted from the 15th to the 21st day of the seventh month we see how the 21st day was the final day of this Feast. The 22nd or the day following was to be the Solemn Assembly.

Thus the Glory of the latter house is associated with the Feast of the seventh month, the Feast of Tabernacles. The Jews would remember the glory of "the former house", Solomon's Temple, and how the Glory of the Lord filled that house in the Feast of Tabernacles, the Feast of the seventh month. So the Glory of "the latter house" would come in this seventh month. Thus both Solomon's Temple and the restored Temple are linked with the Glory of the Lord in the Feast of Tabernacles.

A most remarkable link up is seen in the New Testament in John Chapter 7 when Jesus ministered in Herod's Temple at the Feast of Tabernacles. On **the last day of the Feast** Jesus spoke of rivers of living water which were to flow from the innermost being of all who believed on Him. This was about the same day that Haggai had ministered in the restored Temple years before! *(John 7:37-39)*.

The application to the church should be evident. The church is God's House. It is still under restoration as yet. God's people are not to be concerned about building their own "ceiled houses" or organizations but to be concerned about the building of God's House.

As we look at the early church — the former house — we see the early glory, but the last day church — the latter house — is to have the greater glory. This Glory will be revealed in the Feast of Tabernacles.

As Solomon's Temple was filled with Glory in this Feast and as Haggai spoke of the Glory of the latter house in this Feast, so both become typical and prophetical of the Glory of the church, the New Covenant Temple and the Feast of Tabernacles.

2. The Prophet Zechariah

Zechariah began his ministry about two months after Haggai. Both prophets were involved in the work of restoration, historically and prophetically *(Ezra 5:1-2)*.

We have seen how Haggai ministered in conjunction with the Feast of Tabernacles. The prophet Zechariah also speaks of this same Feast. The passage under consideration is found in *Zechariah 14: 16-21*. This passage is undoubtedly one of the more difficult passages to understand and to interpret, as to its content and time element, unless proper hermeneutical principles are applied to it.

For natural Israel under the Old Covenant times there was the literal fulfilment, having a literal Temple, Priesthood, animal sacrifices, and altars in the literal city of Jerusalem.

Since the Cross the Old Covenant literalness is swallowed up in New Covenant spirituality and reality. Old Covenant language is now interpreted through the Cross by New Covenant language. Therefore, we draw some of the main spiritual lessons from this passage in Zechariah, looking at, first the natural, then the spiritual.

a. All nations were called upon to go up to Jerusalem to worship the Lord from year to year. The Lord was King in Jerusalem, the city of righteousness and peace *(Zechariah 14:9, 16)*.

The believers out of every kindred, tongue, tribe and nation now go up to the spiritual and heavenly Jerusalem. It is here that true worship takes place; worship in spirit and in truth. Jesus Himself repudiated worship at the earthly Jerusalem. He repudiated external and formal worship. The only worship that is acceptable to God now is that which is in spirit and in truth. Jesus Christ is the King in heavenly Zion, heavenly Jerusalem *(John 4:20-24; Acts 8:7; 24:11; Hebrews 12:22-24)*.

Earthly Jerusalem where our Lord was crucified is spiritually Sodom and Egypt and is in bondage with her children *(Revelation 11:8; Galatians 4:24-26)*.

b. All nations are called to keep the Feast of Tabernacles at Jerusalem as they worship the King *(Zechariah 14:16, 18, 19)*. In order to keep the Feast of Tabernacles, Israel had to follow God's order. They had to keep Passover first, then Pentecost and then Tabernacles in the first, third and seventh months.

Since the Cross the Feasts are spiritual and can only be experienced and enjoyed "in Christ". There are no Feasts outside of Him, even though orthodox Jewry keeps a form of the Feasts today. Thus it is in Christ the believers out of all nations keep the Feast of Tabernacles, even as the other Feasts.

c. The nations who failed to respond and keep the Feast of Tabernacles have the rains of blessing withheld from their land. The former and latter rains were the seal of God's blessings as they kept the Feasts. This has been considered under the Feast of Passover, Pentecost and Tabernacles relative to rain and the harvest times *(Zechariah 14:17-18)*.

The spiritual truth of this can be seen in the fact that the believers who fail to keep the Feasts of the Lord do not receive the early and latter rains of blessing. It is true that God rains His spiritual blessing on one city and not another, even as He did in Israel (Amos 4:6-12).

The Feast of Tabernacles shows the latter rain outpouring of the Holy Spirit on all flesh in these last days. God's people who are not entering into this Feast are not being rained upon. There is spiritual dryness, barrenness and lack or loss of harvest. The Lord will come to His people as the former and latter rain as they follow on to know Him in the glorious Feast (Hosea 6:1-3; Zechariah 10:1; James 5:7; Joel 3:9-16; 2:18-32).

d. All nations and all the heathen were to smitten with the plague if they refused to keep the Feast of Tabernacles. This plague was to be the punishment of God on all nations, according to Zechariah. Plagues were the result of the broken law. Plagues came when there was no atonement to cover the people. When ever Israel was to be numbered before the Lord, all had to bring the ransom money of ½ shekel. This atonement money was to prevent the plague. No atonement money opened the way to the plagues of judgment (Exodus 30:11-16; Proverbs 26:2; Numbers 16:48-50).

The true atonement or ransom, since the Cross, is not in silver or gold, but in the precious blood of Christ (I Peter 1:18-20). Christ is the One who alone can prevent the plague of Divine judgment on both sinner and saint. Outside of Christ all mankind will come under the judgments of God. They will suffer eternal punishment (II Thessalonians 1:7-10).

As the believer keeps the Feasts of the Lord, Passover, Pentecost and Tabernacles, no plague shall come nigh their dwelling (Psalm 91:1-10).

e. The distinguishing characteristic upon the bells of the horses was to be "Holiness unto the Lord" (Zechariah 14:20). This was the engraving upon the golden mitre of the High Priests (Exodus 28:36-38). Those who sacrificed to the Lord at His altar would do so out of the pots or bowls. All would be stamped with this inscription "Holiness unto the Lord." No Canaanite would be there in God's House. The language here would be very meaningful to the Israelites under the Old Covenant economy. What spiritual lessons can the believer learn from these things under the Old Covenant economy? Chiefly, these lessons can be learned here.

The church is now the Lord's House (Hebrews 3:6; I Timothy 3:15; Isaiah 2:1-5; I Peter 2:5-9).

The only sacrifices which God accepts now are spiritual sacrifices acceptable to God by Jesus Christ, our great High Priest (I Peter 2:5-9; Hebrews 13:15-16). Animal sacrifices will never again be acceptable to God. The Cross is now our altar (Hebrews 13:10-16). The vessels in the Lord's House are the people of the Lord also. There are vessels of honour and vessels of dishonour (II Timothy 2:19-21). The priesthood is that of the royal priesthood of all believers. As the High Priest had the engraving on his mitre "Holiness unto the Lord", so the believer is to have the mind of Christ and be holy in thought, word and deed.

The characteristic of those who experience the Feasts of the Lord should indeed be holiness unto the Lord. At the second coming of Christ with His armies, all are clothed with fine white linen, which is the righteousness of saints (Revelation 19:8-14).

The name "Canaanite" means "trafficker" and it signifies that all unholy traffic will cease in the House of the Lord as the Feast of Tabernacles is kept in spirit and in truth.

Hence that which was literal under the Old Testament Israel now finds blessed fulfilment in the spiritual under the New Covenant Church.

The Feast of Tabernacles is the Feast of the Open Book.
The Feast of Tabernacles is the Feast of the Glory in the Temple.
The Feast of Tabernacles is the Feast of the Restoration of the Temple.
The Feast of Tabernacles is the Feast of Holiness unto the Lord.

Chapter Nineteen
THE FEASTS OF THE LORD IN THE NEW TESTAMENT

Coming to the New Testament revelation we see how the Lord Jesus Christ ministered in conjunction with the Feasts of Jehovah. And rightly so, for they pointed to Him in all their intricate details, and He is the fulfilment of them (*Matthew 5:17-18; 11:13*).

We consider in this Chapter several of the New Testament chapters which deal specifically with the Feasts.

I. THE FEASTS IN THE GOSPEL OF JOHN

A study of the Gospels, especially John's Gospel, shows how the Lord Jesus worked in conjunction with the Feasts of the Lord. Sad to say they are called "feasts of the Jews."

The things which Jesus did at these Feasts are certainly demonstrations of what He becomes to the believer as that particular Feast is experienced.

A. The Feast of Passover

There are four recorded Passovers in the Gospel of John; three being the historical and typical, the fourth being the historical and antitypical. The fourth Passover was Christ Himself and He fulfilled and abolished in Himself the Old Testament type.

The first Passover Feast Jesus attended at Jerusalem is recorded for us in *John 2:13-17*. He did attend the Passover Feasts with His parents from year to year (*Luke 2:41-42*), but when He began His ministry we have the account of His deeds and teachings at the three Passovers recorded in John's Gospel. However, it is significant that Jesus, as a boy of twelve years of age, did confound the doctors at this Passover Feast He attended with His wisdom.

Now, at the Passover Feast Christ attended as recorded in John 2 we see Him coming to the Temple of God. He found it defiled with the money-changers. Instead of the Temple being His Father's House and a House of Prayer, it had became a den of thieves. So Jesus drove them out, upsetting the tables, and driving out of the Temple the sacrifices and those that sold them. The disciples remembered the zeal for the House of God that the Messiah was to have.

Thus Christ at the Passover revealed Himself as the cleanser of the Temple. He came suddenly to His Temple and none could stand the time of His appearing or His minsitry (*Malachi 3:1-6*).

The church is now God's Temple and must be kept clean for the keeping of the Feasts of the Lord. It is to be a House of Prayer. Christ will come to His church as the cleanser in the Feast of Passover. Every believer is God's Temple also and must keep the Temple clean. In Passover Christ cleansed the believer's life of all that would defile (*I Corinthians 3:16-17; II Corinthians 6:14-18*).

The next recorded Feast in John's Gospel is found in *Chapter 5:1-47*. Which Feast is not stated and cannot be settled definitely. Some have suggested the Feast of Purim, some the Feast of Pentecost, but the weight of opinion suggests that it was the Feast of Passover. Assuming this to be so we see what the Lord Jesus did at this Feast.

At Jerusalem there was by the sheep gate a pool called Bethesda, which means "House of Mercy" and it had five porches. In these porches lay a great multitude of impotent folk waiting for the moving of the waters which took place at a certain season when an angel troubled them. The first into the water was healed of whatever disease they had.

A certain man had been there for 38 years but was unable to get in first into the troubled pool. Jesus, by the word of His Father, went to the pool and ministered life and healing to Him. This took place on the sabbath day. He warned him against going back to a life of sin lest something worse came upon him.

Christ in this Passover Feast is revealed as the healer of men, in body and soul. He is the forgiver of sin, and the healer of disease.

Old Testament Passover Feasts also had healing associated with them. In the original Passover, as Israel fed upon the body of the lamb, they were healed (*Exodus 12* with *Psalm 105:37*).

Under godly King Hezekiah's reign he prayed that the Lord would heal the people as they kept the Passover, which the Lord did (*II Chronicles 30:15-20*). Thus healing is associated with Passover. And here

Christ, at this Passover, healed the impotent man.

The third account of the Feast of Passover in John's Gospel is found in Chapter 6. In this chapter we see Christ feeding the multitudes with the miracle bread and fish. As He fed them, He also taught them. The distinctive truth of the miracle was that Christ Himself is the Bread of Life. All must eat of Him or perish. He is the true Manna which came down from heaven. He told His disciples that they must eat of His flesh and drink His blood or else they have no life in them.

The fact that Christ did this miracle and teaching at the Feast of Passover causes all to be linked with the first and original Passover. There the body and blood of the lamb took its God ordained place. The Israelites fed on the flesh of the lamb. The blood was sprinkled on the door. There they also ate of the unleavened bread. Thus bread and flesh were fed upon by all at Passover. Now all is fulfilled in Christ. He is the Bread of Life, the Unleavened Bread, the heavenly Manna. His body would be broken, His blood would be shed for us as the true Passover Lamb. Only in Him would any find life.

The fourth Passover is when Christ Himself is slain at Calvary. All the intricate details of this Passover Feast of Old Covenant times now find fulfilment in Him (John 11:55-57; 12:1-8; 13:1-17; 18:1-40; 19:1-42).

Thus in John's Gospel, Christ ministered at the Feasts, and here at the Passover festivals.

In tne first Passover He is the Temple-cleanser. In the second Passover, He is the Healer of body and soul. In the third Passover He is revealed as the Bread of Life. In the fourth Passover, He is the Lamb of God which taketh away the sin of the world (John 1:29,36). He is the fulfiller and abolisher of all typical Passover sacrifices and ceremony.

B. The Feast of Tabernacles

The Feast of Tabernacles was commanded by the Lord under the Law of Moses. However, in the times of Jesus there were some Post-Mosaic Festivals added. With regards to the Feast of Tabernacles there were certain additions. The fact that Jesus identified Himself as the fulfilment of such shows that the Lord permitted such and that such had spiritual significance which Christ fulfills. We consider here the Mosaic and Post-Mosaic ceremonies of the Feast of Tabernacles. Two of the most significant things associated with the Feast of Tabernacles were the Outpouring of the Waters and the Illumination of the Temple.

1. The Feast of the Outpouring of the Waters

The events of John's Gospel, as set out in Chapters 7-8-9 center around the Feast of the Seventh Month, Tabernacles.

The behaviour of the Lord Jesus at this Feast surely has some great significance for the church. We note some of the specific verses in these chapters relative to this great Feast.

Opposition was rising against Jesus in Jerusalem and in Jewry and they sought to kill Him. This opposition had been increasing over the several years of His ministry, especially since the act of cleansing the Temple at Passover and the healing of the impotent man on the sabbath at Passover time (John 7:23).

As the Jews Feast of Tabernacles drew nigh Jesus' brethren after the flesh suggested to Him that He do His miraculous works in Judea and show Himself to the world instead of being so secretive about His mission (John 7:1-5). This suggestion arose out of their own unbelief about His mission. Jesus replied that His time was not yet come and He told them to go up to the Feast by themselves (John 7:6-8).

After waiting in Galilee a little while longer Jesus went up to the Feast **"not openly, but as it were in secret"** (John 7:9-10). The Jews sought Him at the Feast but there was much division over Him. Some said He was a deceiver, others said He was a good man but were fearful to confess Him openly (John 7:11-13).

Now about the midst of the Feast Jesus went up to the Temple and taught the people. The "midst of the Feast" could have been about the 18th day of the seventh month, as the Feast lasted from the 15th to the 21st day, or seven days.

Jesus taught the people His Father's doctrine. He challenged them in this Feast that if they did the will of God they would know of the doctrine, whether it was of God or man (John 7:14-31). As He continued teaching the Pharisees opposed Him and the chief priests sent officers to take Him, but they feared to do so when they heard His teaching (John 7:32-36, 40-53).

The most significant prophetic word which Jesus spoke at this Feast are found in Verses 37-39.

Alfred Edersheim in **"The Temple —** It's Ministry and Services as they were in the Time of Christ" (pp. 269-289) gives what seemed to be the custom and order of the Feast of Tabernacles in the times of Messiah, which we adapt here.

The Feast of Tabernacles fell on the 15th day of the seventh month, Tishri, after the harvest fruits had been gathered in and the land now awaited the coming of the latter rains. The Feast was therefore called "the Feast of ingathering", or "the Feast" *(Exodus 23:16; 34:22; Leviticus 23:34, 43; Deuteronomy 16:13, 16; 31:10; II Chronicles 8:13; Ezra 3:4; I Kings 8:2; II Chronicles 5:3; 7:8-9).*

It lasted for 7 days from the 15th to the 21st day, and then was followed by an eighth day on the 22nd of Tishri, as a holy convocation. The first and the eighth days were holy convocations and sabbath besides the regular weekly sabbath when no servile work was to be done.

The Feast followed five days after the great Day of Atonement when the sin of the nation had been removed and covenant relationship with God had been restored.

The Feast was specifically marked by three things; joyous festivities; dwelling in booths, hence the Feast of Booths *(Leviticus 23:39, 42, 43)*; and peculiar rites and sacrifices after the week of seven days *(Numbers 29:12-40).*

On the first day of the Feast of Tabernacles, according to the Law of Moses, the people were to take branches of trees and rejoice before the Lord. Then they were to build booths out of them and dwell in them for the seven days of the Feast. This was in commemoration of the time when they dwelt in booths after the exodus of the nation from Egypt *(Leviticus 23:40-44; Nehemiah 8:15,18).* They were not to live in houses during this period of time. On the 14th day of Tishri, the pilgrims had arrived at Jerusalem. The booths had been made on roofs, in the courtyards, in the streets and in public squares, as well as along the roads and in the gardens. All this was done within a sabbath day's journey. Now all were prepared to commence the week of festivities.

It seems as if the branches cut down at the entry of Christ into Jerusalem alludes to this Feast also *(Matthew 21:8-9; John 12:12-13).*

Now we come to one of the most exciting parts of the Feast as far as the Jews were concerned. Although not commanded under the Law of Moses, the Jews had other ceremonials added to the Feast. On the **first day** of the Feast there was the custom of "The Drawing out of the Water."

The custom was that the altar was cleansed in the night-watches. Then the gates of the Temple were thrown open at midnight. Edersheim says (pp. 268-281) "While the morning sacrifice was being prepared, a priest, accompanied by a joyous procession with music, went down to the Pool of Siloam where he drew water into a golden pitcher..." At the same time that the procession started for Siloam, another went to a place at the Kedron valley... where they brought branches, which amidst the blasts of the priests trumpets, were stuck in either side of the altar of the burnt offering, bending them over towards it, so as to form a canopy."

The rest of the ceremony involved the outpouring of wine, and the outpouring of the waters of Siloam. The Temple music began and *Psalms 113-118* (Hallel) were sung. In the course of the singing the worshippers shook their branches towards the altar. This apparently was done over the seven days of the Feast.

Then on the seventh day or the last day of the Feast, the Priests circuited the altar seven times, remembering the fall of the walls of Jericho after the seven times march amidst trumpet blasts and poured out the waters from Siloam for the last time.

It is at this significant moment, as the people were watching the outpouring of the waters and all it symbolized in the Jewish mind, that Jesus stood and cried out the word of *John 7:37-39.* **"In the last day, that great day of the Feast"** Jesus stood and cried. This day was the 21st day, "The Day of the great Hosannah" or "The Day of the Willows."

He spoke of the rivers of the Spirit that would flow from the innermost being of those who would believe on Him. The symbol is interpreted for us by Jesus Himself. The rivers of water symbolized the Holy Spirit which was to be poured out when Jesus was glorified.

The Jews counted the outpouring of the wine and the outpouring of the waters of Siloam as symbolic of the coming outpouring of the Spirit when Messiah came. The Feast of Tabernacles was also the outpouring of rain. The Jews counted this as symbolic of the Holy Spirit being outpoured under Messiah upon Israel and the Gentile nations.

It may be asked: How many Jews saw that the Feast of Tabernacles with its ceremonies, sacrifices, festivities, and outpouring was all to be fulfilled in and by Christ Himself who stood in their midst? He was the true Siloam — "The Sent One" *(John 9:7).* He was the sacrifice for sin and the cross of Calvary would be His altar. Upon the basis of His shed blood, the waters of the Spirit would be poured out, even as it was upon the basis of a smitten rock that the waters flowed forth for Israel to drink. The believing and the thirsting would come to Him and drink.

Ordinarily Jesus should have been arrested by the Temple officers for breaking into the service like this but "never man spake like this" and the officers feared to do so.

It is worthy to note that Jesus spoke these things concerning the rivers of the Spirit during the Feast of Tabernacles, **not** the Feast of Passover, and **not** the Feast of Pentecost! Although the passage is often used relative to the Pentecostal effusion, it finds its fulness in the Tabernacles outpouring of the Spirit, or the "rain" of God, on all nations.

In summary we see:

—Jesus going to the Feast of Tabernacles in secret, not openly. It speaks of the secret coming of Christ to His Temple in this Feast (verses 2, 10).

—Jesus going into the Temple about the midst of the Feast and teaching His Father's doctrine. Those that do the Father's will shall know the doctrine whether it is of God or man (verses 14-17).

—Jesus prophesying of the rivers of the Spirit to be outpoured as He taught on the last day of the Feast (verses 37-39). It should be remembered that this was the very same day which Haggai had spoken his prophecy concerning the "glory of the latter house" being greater than the former, as he also stood in the Temple (Haggai 2:1-9).

Thus as the believer individually and the church corporately experiences this Feast, Christ will come to His people in a new visitation, there will be increased insight into His doctrine and there will be a mighty flow of the river of the Spirit of God from the church, His Temple (John 14:15-23; Hosea 6:1-3; Hebrews 5:12-14; 6:1-2; Deuteronomy 32:1-2; Isaiah 55:8-11; Zechariah 10:1; Ezekiel 47:1-12; Psalm 46:4; Revelation 22:1-3).

2. The Feast of Illumination

A further symbolical ceremony associated with the Feast of Tabernacles was the Illumination of the Temple.

Again it is to be noted that this was a Post-Mosaic addition to the Feast of Tabernacles. However, the very fact that Jesus ministered in connection with this Feast and its additional ceremonies shows us that He used such to show them the real truth is their symbolic rites.

While the outpouring of the waters took place in the morning, the lighting of the lamps took place in the evening of the first day of the Feast.

Edersheim in **"The Temple"** (pp. 282-287) deals with this custom as in the time of Christ, which we adapt here for the purpose of this text.

In the Feast of Tabernacles, the daily sacrifice was first offered and then the additional sacrifices and freewill offerings. Then there came the festival meal and the study of the Law. After this the evening sacrifice was offered and then the people went with joy to the pouring out of the water.

Edersheim says (p. 283), "At the close of the first day of the Feast, the worshippers descended to the Court of the Women where great preparations had been made. Four golden candelabras were there, each with four golden bowls, and against them rested four ladders; and four youths of priestly descent held, each a pitcher of oil, capable of holding 120 log, from which they filled each bowl. The old, worn breeches and girdles of the priests served for wicks to these lamps. There was not a court in Jerusalem that was not lit up by the light of 'the house of waterpouring.' The 'Chasidim' and 'the men of Deed' danced before the people with flaming torches in their hands and sang before them hymns and songs of praise; and the Levites, with harp, and lutes and cymbals, and trumpets, and instruments of music without number . . . and sang hymns."

According to the custom they stood on the 15 steps of the Court of the Women in fulfilment of the 15 Songs of Degrees in the Psalms, and all this amidst trumpet blasts of the priests as they went on the steps.

For the Jews, the illumination of the Temple symbolized the coming of the Shekinah-Glory-Light into the Temple of Solomon at the dedication in the Feast of Tabernacles (I Kings 8:1-11). It also symbolized "the great light" that would come to the people who dwelt in darkness and in the land of the shadow of death (Isaiah 9:2). According to Jewish tradition, the Cloudy Pillar of Fire first appeared to Israel on the 15th day of the seventh month, Tishri, in the Feast of Tabernacles. It is certain that the Shekinah Glory came to Solomon's Temple in that Feast (I Kings 8; II Chronicles 7), in the dedication.

The 24 courses of the Priests were involved in this Festive occasion. Undoubtedly "the palms" and "the four and twenty elders" seen in Revelation 7:9-10; 4:4; 5:8-10 are allusions to this Feast also.

Thus in this Feast, Jerusalem, as a city set on a hill, by the lighting of the lamps, the golden candlesticks (Matthew 5:14-16) became ablaze with light bringing joy to the hearts of all who witnessed it. The city became a city of **light!**

The outpouring of the Water and the Illumination of the Temple were each a part of the Post-Mosaic ceremonies of the Feast of Tabernacles. Jesus therefore ministered in connection with each of these parts. In the Outpouring of the Water He spoke of the rivers of living water to flow forth by the Spirit. But in the Illumination of the Temple and the city, He spoke of the coming of the light.

The significant acts and teaching that Jesus did in connection with this part of the Feast was the forgiving of a sinner and the healing of the blind man, and the revelation that He was **the light** of the world in connection with both of these acts.

After the teaching in the Temple on the last day of the Feast, Jesus went to the Mt. of Olives (John 8:1). Early in the morning, He came again to the Temple and continued teaching. In the course of His teaching, the Scribes and Pharisees brought to Him a woman taken in the very act of adultery. By a word of wisdom Jesus upheld the Law of God, eliminated the Scribes and Pharisees by Law of Conscience and then ministered both **grace** and **truth** to the condemned woman (John 8:3-11; 1:17). Jesus then spoke of Himself saying "**I am** the light of the world; he that followeth Me shall not walk in darkness, but shall have the light of life" (John 8:12). Following further teaching, the Pharisees sought to stone Him but He escaped from their hands (John 8:13-59).

Thus sin and darkness are synonymous. The forgiveness of sin is the coming of the light to the human heart. Only Christ who is the light of the world can cause darkness to flee away. The Jews may light the Temple and the city of Jerusalem, but only Christ can light the human temple, the human heart.

Closely connected with this act of forgiveness of sin is Christ's declaration of being the light of the world in connection with the healing of the blind man as recorded in John 9.

As Jesus passed by He saw a man who had been born blind. His disciples questioned Him as to the cause, whether it was the result of sin in him or his parents. Jesus said that the blindness was there in order that the works of God would be manifest in him. Again He spoke of Himself as being "the light of the world" (John 8:1-5). Jesus then made clay of His spittle on the ground and anointed the eyes of the blind man. He told him to go and wash in the Pool of Siloam, which by interpretation means "Sent." As the man obeyed in faith, he washed and came seeing.

The tragic result was that the man was excommunicated from the Synagogue for his confession of Christ. Jesus used this whole occasion to show the Pharisees that, although they could see physically, they were blind spiritually. They were in darkness while professing to be in the light. They believed they had the illumination but were in spiritual and religious darkness and confusion (John 9:6-41).

The significance of these acts of forgiveness and healing of blindness is that both took place relative to the Feast of Tabernacles, the Feast of Illumination. In both acts Jesus reveals Himself to be "the light of the world" — not merely the light of the Jewish nation, which light they rejected.

The lighting of the lamps and the outpouring of the waters of Siloam pointed to Messiah. He would bring light and illumination. He would bring the outpouring of the Holy Spirit. The opening of the eyes of the blind man by washing in the pool of Siloam pointed to Christ's ministry. He would open the eyes of those in spiritual darkness, by the anointing and washing of water bv the Word. For He Himself was **the** Anointed One, the true Siloam, "the Sent One."

As the church in these last days experiences the Feast of Tabernacles, there will also come great light and illumination, forgiveness and healing. What the Lord Jesus did back there in connection with the Feast of Tabernacles becomes prophetic of what He will do at the close of the age.

Paul prayed that the spirit of wisdom and revelation, or illumination, in the knowledge of Christ would come upon the believers (Ephesians 1:17-18). He prayed that the eyes of our understanding would be enlightened.

So in the Feast of Tabernacles, the Feast of Illumination, eyes will be opened, blindness and darkness will be removed and men will see the light of the world. At the same time the religious and the Pharisaical who believe they see will really be blind to their own need and thus miss the significance and experience of this Feast. Truly Christ is the One who brings the outpouring of the water, and Christ is the One who brings light and illumination. It is all fulfilled **in Him!**

II. THE FEAST IN THE BOOK OF ACTS

Not much needs to be said concerning the Feast in the Book of Acts as this has been dealt with earlier.

As the Gospels deal especially with the Feast of Passover and Christ fulfilling its intricate details, so the Book of Acts deals with Christ fulfilling the Feast of Pentecost.

The original Pentecost took place in Acts 2 but it is evident from other references that the early church commemorated this Feast each year, and especially until the Temple was destroyed in A.D. 70.

The first Pentecost took place 50 days after the resurrection of Christ and it fell as rain upon the 120 waiting and believing disciples. The Holy Spirit came from heaven as a rushing mighty wind and filled the house where they were sitting. Tongues of fire sat upon the head of the men and the women and all began to speak in tongues as the Spirit gave them utterance (Acts 2:1-4).

Once noised abroad, Jews out of every nation gathered together, amazed at the things which they heard in "other tongues." Under the preaching of Peter and the convicting power of the Holy Spirit 3000 souls were converted to Christ and added to the church. These Jewish converts became the "firstfruits" of the Pentecostal harvest, the Feast of Weeks (Acts 2:5-47).

Although the initial Day of Pentecost can never be repeated again, yet there is a continual Pentecostal Feast available for all who believe in Christ our Passover.

It should be remembered that once the Feast of Passover was fulfilled, its experience is open for all who believe. Every time a person is born again, he experiences the Passover Feast.

The same is true concerning Pentecost. Once Pentecost was inaugurated, the experience of Pentecost is available for all believers for this is "the Pentecostal age."

Thus we say the Samaritans experienced "Pentecost" in Acts 8:5-24 under Peter and John.

The Apostle Paul experienced his "Pentecost" in Acts 9:17-19. The Gentiles in the house of Cornelius experiencied their "Pentecost" in Acts 10:44-48; 11:15-17 under the ministry of Peter. The Ephesian believers, years later, experienced their "Pentecost" under the Apostle Paul in Acts 19:1-7.

Then about the year 60 A.D., Paul hastened to be at Jerusalem for "the Day of Pentecost" (Acts 20:16; I Corinthians 16:8), when the Jews would celebrate the old ritual of the Feast. For the Jews, Pentecost was a Mosaic Festival; celebrating the giving of the Law on tables of stone on the 50th day. For the Christians, Pentecost was the giving of the Holy Spirit to the disciples, and the writing of the Law of God on the tables of the heart. The general day of celebration in the church is called Whitsunday — the Day of the Holy Spirit.

With the Pentecostal effusion of the Spirit on both Jews and Gentiles in such a sovereign way, we see the purpose of the Lord to make of two ethnic divisions one body. Hence Paul writes: "For by one Spirit are we baptized into one body, whether we be Jews or Greeks, bond or free, and have all been made to drink into one Spirit" (I Corinthians 12:13).

In the making of the two Pentecostal wave loaves, many grains of wheat, crushed into fine flour, baken in the oven, were united together. All symbolized the union of the Jew and Gentile as the bread of God, for "we being many are one body and one bread" (I Corinthians 10:16-17).

The emphasis in the Book of Acts is on the Feast of Pentecost, the coming together of the Jew and Gentile in one body, and the great harvest of firstfruits of the saved ones.

III. THE FEASTS IN THE CORINTHIANS EPISTLES

The Corinthians Epistles speak especially of two Feasts, Passover and Pentecost.

First Corinthians deals with the Feast of Passover, and Second Corinthians deals with that which points back to the original Feast of Pentecost. Because most of the details of these Feasts have already been considered, it will suffice to simply bring the main points into focus and a few details not previously covered.

A. First Corinthians — The Feast of Passover.

—Christ our Passover has been sacrificed for us (I Corinthians 5:7).

—The believers are to purge out the old leaven, that they may be a new lump, and keep the Feast of Unleavened Bread (I Corinthians 5:6-8).
—Christ the Sheaf of Firstfruits has been raised from the dead (I Corinthians 15:20, 23).

The Corinthian Church was founded by the Apostle Paul in Acts 18:1-17. After ministering in the Synagogue and being rejected of the Jews, Paul commenced a Christian Synagogue in the house of Justus. The Lord appeared to Paul in a vision and told him that He had much people in the city of Corinth. Paul stayed there for 18 months establishing the church in the Apostle's doctrine.

Several years after Paul had moved from Corinth, reports came to him of many problems in the church and thus the Corinthian Epistles are Paul's correctives and exhortations to the saints there. Although dominantly a Gentile church, we see some of the things which Paul had taught them. Among the foundational doctrines which Paul taught was the foundational Feast — the Feast of Passover, with its integral parts.

It is the Corinthian Epistle which provides for us such specific "keys of interpretation for the three parts of the Old Testament Feast of Passover.

B. Second Corinthians — The Feast of Pentecost

As First Corinthians gives us interpretive keys for the Feast of Passover, so Second Corinthians gives interpretive keys for us relative to the Feast of Pentecost, especially as it pertains to the giving of the Law.

The student should read and study II Corinthians 3 in conjunction with Exodus 20; 31:12-18; 32-32;

34:1-7; Acts 2:41; Matthew 12:28; Luke 11:20; Hebrews 10:16-17; 8:8-13).

For brevity and clarity we use the comparative mention principle of interpretation as we compare and contrast the Old Testament and New Testament Feast of Pentecost and the giving of the Law of God.

Old Testament Pentecost	—	**New Testament Pentecost**
Moses the Mediator	—	Jesus the Mediator
The Old Covenant	—	The New Covenant
Ministration of Death	—	Ministration of Life
3000 people slain	—	3000 people live
Written and engraven on tables of stone	—	Written and engraven on tables of the heart
Written by the Finger of God	—	Written by the Spirit of God
Glorious	—	More glorious
Glory to be done away	—	Glory remaineth
Ministration of Condemnation	—	Ministration of Righteousness
Glory in the face of Moses	—	Glory in the face of Jesus
Vail over Moses' face	—	Open face of Jesus
Israel not able to look thereon	—	Believer beholds His face
To be abolished	—	Glory remains and excells
The Letter which killeth	—	The Spirit which gives life

The Jews celebrate the 50th day as the Day of the Giving of the Law. The details of this Feast became prophetic of the New Covenant laws of Jesus which were to be written on the tables of the heart. The commandments of God were to be internalized by the Spirit of God, who is the Finger of God. The Old Covenant commandments were externalized, telling Israel what to do but giving no power to perform. The weakness of the flesh brought about failure and condemnation. The New Covenant commandments would be on the heart, commandments of love to God and love to man. These would fulfil the 10 Commandments of the Old Covenant *(Romans 7:6-25; Matthew 22:34-40; Romans 13:8-10).*

This is the glory of the New Testament. The believer is an able minister of the New Covenant, not of the letter, but of the spirit. The letter kills, but the Spirit gives life. As he gazes into the face of Jesus Christ he sees the glory of God and is changed from glory to glory even as by the Spirit of the Lord. The keeping of the New Covenant commandments conform him to the image and glory of God *(II Corinthians 3:18).* It is this that is the real purpose of the Feast of Pentecost.

IV. THE FEAST IN THE EPISTLE TO THE HEBREWS

The Gospels have dealt with Passover, and Paul has dealt with it also in I Corinthians. The Book of Acts has dealt with Pentecostal Feast and again Paul deal with it in II Corinthians. Thus the Gospels and I Corinthians relate and Acts and II Corinthians relate.

But it is in the Epistle of Hebrews that we deal with the most solemn Feast of Tabernacles, that is, especially the Day of Atonement.

Because the ceremonies of this great Day of Atonement have already been considered we draw from this Epistle only the major comparisons and contrasts of the Old Testament and New Testament Day of Atonement as set forth in *Hebrews 9-10* chapters.

Old Testament Day of Atonement	—	**New Testament Day of Atonement**
The First or the Old Covenant	—	The Second or New Covenant
Ordinances of Divine service	—	Realities of Divine service
The Worldly Sanctuary	—	The Heavenly Sanctuary
The Holy Places made with hands	—	The Holy Places made by God
Aaron the High Priest	—	Christ the King-Priest
Enters within the veil on the Day of Atonement	—	Enters within the veil of heaven's Sanctuary on a Day
Once a year	—	Once for all
Way into the Holiest not yet open	—	Way of access now opened for all believer priests
The body and blood of animals	—	The body and blood of Jesus
Cleansing of the Sanctuary	—	Cleansing of heaven's Sanctuary
Many sacrifices offered	—	One sacrifice offered
Never to take away sins	—	Take away sins forever
Priests ministering daily and always standing	—	Christ sat down after a finished work
Aaron represented Israel in the earthly Sanctuary	—	Christ represents the Church in heaven's Sanctuary
The type and shadow	—	The antitype and substance

Without the Epistle of Hebrews we would miss the interpretive keys for the Feast Day of Atonement, as well as that which pertains to the Tabernacle service, the sacrificial system and the Levitical Priesthood. Hebrews becomes the New Testament interpretation of much of Exodus, the Book of Leviticus and various chapters in the Book of Numbers.

Truly the New Testament fulfilment of the Day of Atonement far surpasses all that was shadowed forth under the Old Testament Day.

V. THE FEASTS IN THE BOOK OF REVELATION

In surveying the Book of Revelation we discover much that has to do with the Sanctuary services, both of the Tabernacles of Moses and David and the Temple of Solomon. This is to be expected as Revelation is the Book of Ultimates, consummating in itself all the previous Books of the Bible and their streams of truth.

We list out briefly those references and allusions that are to be found in this Book relative to the Tabernacle ministrations and the Feasts, especially the Feast of Tabernacles.

A. In *Revelation 1:12-20* we have the vision of the risen Christ as our great High Priest clothed in the garments of glory and beauty.

B. In *Revelation Chapters 2-3* we see Christ standing in the Holy Place ministering to the church, symbolized by the golden candlesticks, even as Aaron ministered to this article morning and evening.

C. Allusion to the use of trumpets, and the Feast of Trumpets are found in *Revelation 1:10; 4:1; 8:1-2, 6; 11:15*. The Feast of Trumpets is consumated in the trumpets as blown in Revelation.

D. Allusion to the Manna and the Rod of Aaron are given in the promises to the overcomer in *Revelation 2:17, 27*. Both of these articles were in the Ark of the Covenant, within the veil, in the Holiest of All in the Tabernacle.

E. The Brazen Altar is spoken of in *Revelation 6:9-11*. This article was in the Outer Court of the Tabernacle.

F. Allusion to the palm trees of the Feast of Booths is given in *Revelation 7:9, 15*, where the Lamb of God "tabernacles" with His people.

G. In *Revelation 8:1-5* there is distinct allusions to the ceremonies of the great Day of Atonement. On this Day the golden censer was taken off the golden altar before the veil as Aaron entered within the veil with the blood of atonement to sprinkle on the Mercy seat of the Ark of the Lord. Incense symbolized the prayers of Israel, and in the New Testament, of the church.

H. The opening of the Book in the Feast of Tabernacles is alluded to in the opening of the Seven-sealed Book in *Revelation 5:1-9* and the opened little book in *Revelation 10:1-11*. The Book is God's Word, the Holy Bible, the Book of Redemption.

I. The Ark of the Covenant is referred in *Revelation 11:19*. This was only seen on the great Day of Atonement when Aaron entered within the veil. The Ark is always associated with atonement and then judgment.

J. The Firstfruits as seen in the Feasts is alluded to in *Revelation 14:4*, while the Harvests of corn and fruit of spoken on in *Revelation 14:14-20*.

K. The Sea of Glass is an allusion to the brazen laver of the Tabernacle of Moses and the molten sea of the Temple of Solomon. Read *Revelation 4:6; 15:2*.

L. The ultimate picture is that of the foursquare city of God, for it is the Tabernacle of God with men. He will dwell with His people, and be their God and they shall be His people *(Revelation 21-22)*. This will be the eternal Feast of Tabernacles and the city is seen to be filled with the Glory and Presence of God. Thus it fulfills all that was typified in the foursquare Holiest of All in both Tabernacle and Temple.

On the great Day of Atonement, every article of furniture was touched with sacrificial blood. The Book of Revelation shows Christ our great High Priest after the Order of Melchisedek ministering in the heavenly Sanctuary, within the veil of the heavenly Temple. There He ministers to the saints, to the church, in the spiritual Feasts as typified in Passover, Pentecost and Tabernacles.

It is Revelation which brings to ultimate fulfilment the prophecies of *Daniel 8:13-14* and *9:24-27*, when transgression shall be finished, sin will be sealed up, and iniquity will be fully covered. And all this will be upon the basis of the blood of atonement, the blood of the Lord Jesus Christ *(Revelation 1:5; 5:9-10; 12:11)*. This is why the prominent revelation of Christ in this Book is "the Lamb" — the Lamb of God which taketh away the sin of the world. *(John 1:29, 36)*.

Chapter Twenty
POST-MOSAIC FESTIVALS

Besides the Post-Mosaic Festivals added to the Mosaic Feast of Tabernacles, there are two other Jewish Feast worthy of note. These Feasts are the Feast of Dedication which took place on the 25th of the 12th month, Adar, and the Feast of Purim which also took place in the same month. These we consider here.

I. THE FEAST OF DEDICATION

This Post-Mosaic Festival called the Feast of Dedication was also kept in the time of Christ. John's Gospel is the only Gospel which speaks of it particuary and records what Jesus taught at this time.

"And it was at Jerusalem the Feast of Dedication . . . And Jesus walked in the Temple in Solomon's porch" *(John 10:22-23).*

The Feast of Dedication of the Temple is called "The Dedication of the Altar" in I Maccabees 4:52-59. Josephus (Antiquities XII.7,7) called it "The Feast of Lights."

Under the period of the Syrian rule over Palestine, the Jews suffered great persecution. Antiochus Epiphanes, ruler of Syria, a wicked and godless man led a victorious campaign against Egypt, but had to withdraw at the command of Rome. He vented his wrath against the Jews as Palestine was under the Syrian Kingdom at this time. He entered Jerusalem, destroyed a large part of it, and slaughtered men, women and children. The crowning act was to enter the Temple of the Lord, take away the golden altar, the golden candlesticks and its vessels as well as other treasures. He set an idol statue of Jupiter in the Holiest of All and commanded Jews to worship it. He also sacrificed swine to the Greek god Jupiter, sprinkling its blood around the Temple. The Laws of Moses were forbidden to be practiced. The rite of circumcision, the keeping of the sabbath and the laws concerning clean and unclean meats were forbidden on pain of death. Only swine were allowed to be offered on the altar. Syrian officials enforced the laws of Antiochus.

In time a godly faithful company of Jews resisted these laws and revolted against the desecration of the Temple. Notable among these was the priestly family of the Maccabees. A revolt took place under the Maccabees and eventually the Syrians were driven from Jerusalem. This took place about B.C. 164.

Judas Maccabees solemnly cleansed the Temple from the profanations to which it had been subjected under Antiochus. He removed the old polluted altar, and put the stones in a separate place on the Temple mount, and restored the worship of the Lord (I Maccabees 4:52, 56, 59). This "cleansing of the Sanctuary" *(Daniel 8:13-14)* took place on the 25th day of Chisleu (December the 25th), and the joyous celebration lasted for eight days.

On each of these days the 'Hallel' was sung, the people carried palms and branches of other trees. The Temple was illuminated as well as the private houses about Jerusalem. Tradition says that they found a jar of consecrated oil which miraculously lasted for eight days and thus the Temple was lighted again. Jews today light candles at this Feast, generally a candlestick with nine candles thereon.

The Temple was the central power of unity, binding the Jews together as one. According to the prophetic word of the last prophet, Malachi, the Messiah would "suddenly come to His Temple" *(Malachi 3:1).*

The very fact that the Lord Jesus attended this Post-Mosaic Festival at Jerusalem shows that He used it to set forth some significance in relation to Himself.

The Feast took place two months later than the Feast of Tabernacles. The distinctive teaching of the Lord Jesus was given in the parable or dark saying of "the shepherd and the sheep" *(John 10:1-18).*

The Jews were divided over these sayings of Jesus, even saying that He had a devil and was mad and it was a waste of time even to listen to Him *(John 10:19-21).*

Because of the winter cold, Jesus walked in Solomon's porch during the Feast of Dedication. The Jews challenged Him to clearly and plainly tell them if He was the Messiah. Jesus reminded them that if they were His sheep they would have heard His voice as the Shepherd. The very fact they did not hear His voice proved that they were not of His fold. The works of Jesus spake loud enough for all to hear, if they had ears to hear.

The result was that the Jews took up stones to stone Him because He said He was one with the Father God. However, He escaped out of their hand *(John 10:22-38).*

If Judas Maccabees was the one they celebrated and remembered as "the Temple-cleanser and illuminator" then much more could Jewry have seen this in the Lord Jesus. He had come suddenly to His Temple, His Father's house, as the Messenger of the Covenant, but they failed to recognize Him. He had cleansed the

Temple twice in His ministry, but they rejected such cleansing. They were more interested in the Temple than in the One who would cleanse the Temple from their religious abominations. Instead of being as clean sheep, they had become as unclean swine, unfit for the Temple of God and God's altar. They had become worshippers of the Temple but failed to worship the Lord of the Temple (Matthew 23:16-39). They kept the Feast of Dedication but sought to stone the One to whom the Temple was dedicated. Thus they missed Him at another Feast, even as they had at previous Feasts.

How clearly John's Gospel shows that the Feasts had indeed become "Feasts of the Jews" instead of the Feasts of the **Lord**! Jewry kept the Feasts; the Feasts of Passover, Tabernacles and Dedication, but they missed the One to whom all Feasts pointed and in whom all would find fulfilment. They kept the letter and missed the spirit. They fulfilled the ritual and missed the reality. They fulfilled the type and missed the antitype. They followed the natural and missed the spiritual — Christ Himself!

Christ was the Temple-cleanser, and the Temple-illuminator. Thus the church may learn lessons from the failure of Jewry as set out in the Gospel of John in relation to the Feasts of Jehovah. The church as His Temple is dedicated to Him. Only as it is kept in this manner can there be the enjoyment of "The Feast of Dedication" (I Corinthians 3:16-17; Ephesians 2:19-22).

II. THE FEAST OF PURIM

The Feast of Purim is founded upon the story of the Feast of Esther, especially the events of Chapter 9. It is another Post-Mosaic Festival but no reference is found in the New Testament concerning it.

However, there are spiritual and moral lessons which the church may learn from this Feast which is still kept by modern Jewry.

Purim, after the name Pur, in the Persian language, signifies "lot". The Feast of Purim, or Feast of Lots has a reference to the time having been pitched upon Haman through the decision of the lot (Esther 3:7).

Although the Feast was a Post-Mosaic Festival, it was a yearly celebration and a joyous time in Jewry. As we consider the story of Esther and the inauguration of this Feast, we will discover spiritual truths for the church in these last days.

During the reign of Ahasuerus, the king of Persia, the queen Vashti had displeased the king and had been disposed from her royal throne. Certain virgins were chosen to go through months of purification and preparation out of which one would be chosen to replace Vashti. The fair and beautiful Esther was chosen to be the bride, the royal queen (Esther 1-2).

In the King's palace was an Agagite, a descendant of Amalek, of Esau, by the name of Haman. He carried within his heart a Satanic hatred for the Jewish nation. Mordecai, Esther's uncle, would in no way bow to this wicked Haman (Esther 3:1-6).

In the first month, that is, the month Nisan, which was the Feast of Passover, lots were cast before Haman from day to day and month to month through to the twelfth month, Adar (Esther 3:7).

Haman, at this time told King Ahasuerus that there was a certain people scattered throughout his **127** Provinces who had their own laws and who failed to keep the laws of the Persian kingdom. He suggested that the king write a decree that these people be destroyed. He himself would help finance the business. The king sealed the decree with his own ring. Letters were written throughout the Provinces that all Jews, men, woman and children, were to be destroyed on the 13th day of the month, Adar. The letters were delivered in haste by the posts to all Provinces (Esther 3:8-15).

Great mourning fell upon the Jews throughout the Provinces as they realized the death-decree which hung over their heads and their days were numbered.

When Mordecai found out he called upon Esther to endeavour to change the decree. He said to her that enlargement and deliverance could come from another place if she held her peace at this time. The great challenge to Esther was "And who knoweth whether thou art come to the kingdom for a time as this?" (Esther 4:1-14).

Esther, along with the Jews at Shushan, fasted 3 days and 3 nights without food or water. At the end of the days she would risk her life by appearing before King Ahasuerus (Esther 4:15-17).

On the third day she appeared before the King as he sat on his royal throne. She found favour in his sight and he held out to her the golden sceptre.

In the following days, upon her request, the King, along with Haman, attended banquets which Esther had prepared (Esther 5:1-14).

Providentially after the first banquet the king could not sleep. Someone was asked to read him some of the Chronicles of the kingdom. The account of Modecai saving the king from assassination was read. The king asked if this person had been rewarded at all. The answer was in the negative. In the morning the king called Haman in and asked him what he thought should be done to a person the king desired to honour. Haman, filled with pride and egotism thought the king would like to do honour to him. So he described in glowing terms what rewards should be given to such a person. With amazement and bitter disgust the king told him to to all he said to Mordecai *(Esther 6:1-14)*.

The next banquet the king and Haman attended, the king asked Esther what her request would be and it would be granted, even to half of the kingdom *(Esther 7:1-2)*. Queen Esther took advantage of the whole situation. She begged for her own life and the life of the Jewish people who had been sold to destruction. The king, horrified, asked who dared to do such a thing. The wicked Haman was pointed out. Haman stood to plead for his life, even throwing himself upon Esther's divan, which was the greatest of insults in a Persian palace *(Esther 7:3-8)*. The end result was that Haman hung from the very gallows which he had prepared for Mordecai to hang on *(Esther 7:9-10)*.

The king gave to Esther all of Haman's possessions and his own ring which he had given to Haman *(Esther 8:1-2)*.

However, the great problem remained and that was the saving of the Jews as a nation in the Provinces. The law of the Medes and Persians could not be reversed. The king therefore gave permission to write another law by which the Jews could stand to preserve their lives and to destroy all those who would seek to destroy or assault them *(Esther 8:3-14)*. Thus there was a counter-decree without nullifying the previous decree.

The Jews had great joy and gladness in the Provinces when they received this counter-decree. Great fear fell on the people and many became Jews when they saw this *(Esther 8:15-17)*.

On the 13th day and the 14th day of Adar, the Jews stood and defended their lives and possessions throughout the Provinces. Seventy five thousand people were slain. In Shushan palace 500 people were slain. Thus the Jewish nation was providentially preserved from annihilation. Haman's ten sons were slain and hung on gallows also.

The Jews at Shushan then set aside the 13th, 14th, and 15th day of Adar as days of feasting, resting and rejoicing and sending portions one to another to commemorate this great deliverance *(Esther 9:1-19)*. Mordecai wrote letters and made a decree that year by year the Jews should establish the 14th and 15th days of Adar as a Festival time, the Feast of Purim *(Esther 10:1-32; 11:1-3)*.

This is the story behind the Feast of Purim, the Feast of Esther, the Feast of Lots. Although the name of God is not mentioned in the Book of Esther, His providential hand is manifest throughout.

"The Jewish Catalogue", published by the Jewish Publishing Society of America (p. 136) writes concerning the modern keeping of this Feast.

"Of course, the most famous and delightful part of the reading involves the obligation to "blot out" Haman's name. Everytime the name is pronounced by the reader, it is an obligation to make noise, yell, stamp your feet."

The Jews read the Book of Esther or the Negillah in their Synagogues on this Feast day. Mordecai's name is cheered but whenever Haman's name is pronounced, the hearers make a terrible noise in the Synagogue.

Some suggestions are given by the Jews in the keeping of this Feast day. "Write Haman's name on the bottom of your shoes and then kick and stamp. Bang together rocks with his name on them. Blow a shofar. Blow a trumpet. Play appropriate organ music. Play inappropriate organ music. Beat on a drum, pots and pans, etc. Shake a tin can full of nails (this can be devastating). Be imaginative. Use your head. There is also the custom to make a dummy Haman and beat it, hang it, and then burn it."

Queen Esther may be pictured as a type of the church bringing deliverance to the people of God in the last days. Haman and his 10 sons typify the Antichristal spirit and kingdom which would arise against the church and seek to destroy the people of God.

As the church, like Esther, seeks the Lord in prayer and fasting and touches the Calvary experience of 3 days and 3 nights, God will providentially work mighty enlargement and deliverance.

Spiritually speaking, the lots will be cast, but the final disposing and decision will be of the Lord *(Proverbs 16:33)*. Lots were cast on the Day of Atonement over the two goats *(Leviticus 16:8)*. The land of Canaan was divided by the casting of lots before the Lord at the Tabernacle in Shiloh *(Joshua 18:10; Numbers 26:52-56)*. Jonathan was chosen by lot *(I Samuel 14:41)*. Jonah was chosen by lot *(Jonah 1:7)*. The soldiers cast lots over the seamless robe of Jesus at the cross *(Matthew 27:35)*. And the disciples cast lots before the Holy Spirit was outpoured at Pentecost *(Acts 1:26)*.

Proverbs 18:18 says: "The lot causes contentions to cease, and parteth between the mighty."

The significance of the lot is simply the making of a choice between one or another.

In the New Testament revelation, God has chosen the church, the bride of Christ, to be the instrument of judgment on the kingdom of Satan *(Genesis 3:15 with Romans 16:20)*.

The victory that the church brings to her people will result in a spiritual Feast of Purim. It will indeed be a Feast of "light, gladness, and joy, and honour" in which many of the people outside of the kingdom shall become believers *(Esther 8:16-17)*. It will be "a day of gladness and feasting, and a good day, and of sending portions to one another, and gifts to the poor." It will be rest from enemies and sorrow will be turned to joy *(Esther 9:17-19, 22)*.

This will be the spiritual fulfilment of the Feast of Purim in the church, the bride of the King of Kings and Lord of Lords. She will be the instrument that God uses to crush the head of the serpent in the last days *(Revelation 12 with Ephesians 5:23-32)*.

Chapter Twenty-One
MODERN JEWISH FESTIVALS

It is of interest to see how the Jews, generally the more Orthodox, keep the Feasts of the Lord in these modern times. Although some of the details may vary in different Jewish communities, the basic procedures are the same.

We will consider briefly the modern Jewish Festivals, comparing them with the Biblical commands, observing and learning what lessons may be gleaned therefrom.

I. THE FEAST OF PASSOVER

The Festival of the Pascal sacrifice took place in early Springtime. For the Jew it was the Feast of Spring when nature was in its spring-time after the death of winter. It symbolized the national birth and deliverance of Israel historically.

It was also the Feast of the offering of the firstfruits of the grain. The original Egyptian Passover varied much with the succeeding permanent Passover because one was kept in the exodus from Egypt, and the rest in memory of that exodus.

The Jewish custom in the keeping of the Passover today varies in a number of areas when compared with the Biblical commands and accounts. The modern custom has some interesting facets to it and although it may vary in different places, the basics are the same. For the Jew it is a season of liberation and a season of joy. We note in outline form the general order for the keeping of the Feast.

A. First of all, the house is cleansed from all leaven, and all pots and pans are cleansed.

B. Various symbols are placed on the table in their respective places in the Passover Feast.

1. A place is set for Elijah and an empty chair is set at the head of the table, while the door is opened to him. There is the "cup for Elijah". This is to fulfil *Malachi 4:5-6* concerning the expected coming of Elijah as Messiah's forerunner. The Rabbis believe that the Messiah, the Desire of all nations, and the Hope of Israel could come on a Passover night *(Acts 28:20; Haggai 2:7)*.

2. A bowl of salt water is placed on the table. This is symbolic of tears shed in Egypt and the crossing of the Red Sea.

3. Greens are set on the table — symbolic of Spring time.

4. One shank bone is there. This is symbolic of the Passover lamb, when not a bone was to be broken.

5. One egg is set there — symbolic of life and resurrection.

6. Candles are lighted — symbolic of light and glory in the Tabernacle of the Lord.

7. Four cups of red wine are set. This is symbolic of the blood of the lamb. These cups are drunk at specified times during the Feast.

8. A horse-radish is set on the table-symbolic of the bitter herbs and bitterness of bondage in Egypt.

9. Grated apples and nuts are there — symbolic of the clay bricks made while in Egyptian slavery.

10. The Afirkomen, or three pieces of unleavened bread with a white paper between each piece is set on the table. Symbolic of the kind of bread they ate when leaving Egypt.

11. The father as head of the house blesses all and all drink of the wine. Then there is the chanting of songs of deliverance from Egypt as the story of the Exodus is related. A dip is put into a cup of wine and one drop is allowed for each of the 10 plagues of Egypt as all count.

12. The Feast is closed with singing as Elijah's cup is poured out, while the door is opened for his coming.

The two most interesting parts of the Passover Supper are those that relate to the Bread and the Wine.

During the celebration of the Jewish Passover, three cakes of unleavened bread are placed one upon another, separated by a napkin between each. At a certain point in the Feast the middle cake is broken in two. One piece is distributed among those present and the other is hidden beneath a cushion. Toward the end of the Feast the hidden portion is brought to light and eaten by those surrounding the Passover table.

During the course of the Feast, the four cups of wine served to the family are used in the following manner. The cups are called:

The Cup of Blessing

All partake of this cup, even the babes (Compare *Luke 22:17; Ephesians 1:3; I Corinthians 10:16*).

The Cup of Wrath

This cup is not drunk but is poured out on the table as the plagues of Egypt are recited. Christ drunk this cup for us in Gethsemane and Calvary *(Luke 22:42-44)*.

The Cup of Salvation

This cup is filled to overflowing; Symbolic of an overflowing salvation *(Psalm 116:13)*.

The Cup of the Kingdom

This cup is poured out. Jesus spoke of His eating and drinking afresh in the kingdom with His disciples after His resurrection *(Matthew 26:26-28)*.

The Jew who is blind to the Christ of God does not understand the full significance of the Feast. For the believer all is clearly seen.

The three pieces of the Afirkomen symbolize the Godhead, as Father, Son and Holy Spirit. The central piece being broken, eaten, hidden and then brought forth symbolize the central One in the Godhead. It speaks of the death, burial, resurrection of Christ. It is suggested that the word "Afirkomen" means "The Coming One" and surely this points to the Lord Jesus Christ Himself.

Thus the New Covenant believer partakes of the bread of the New Covenant when he has the holy communion.

The Lord Jesus also took the cup of wrath and judgment for our sins in Gethsemane and on Calvary. He has provided the cup of blessing, and the cup of salvation. And He will drink anew with His redeemed the cup of the kingdom when He returns again.

Each time the believer partakes of the Lord's Supper he is fulfilling all that is symbolized in the Passover Supper.

The great tragedy in the modern Jewish Feast of Passover is that Christ the Passover Lamb has come and they, as a nation, missed Him. The thing that is missing from every Jewish Passover is **the blood!** The Lord said "When I see **the blood** I will passover you" *(Exodus 12:13)*. Not when I see all the other things on the table, but when I see the redeeming blood.

Hence no Jewish Passover today is acceptable to God, for Christ is God's Passover Lamb and the only hope for the Jew is in the reality which is in Christ. Otherwise all is but an empty form, lifeless because it is bloodless!

For the Jew and Gentile who have found Christ, all can meet around one common table, the Lord's table, and partake in spirit and in truth of the bread and the wine of New Covenant relationship *(I Corinthians 11:23-32; Matthew 26:26-28)*.

II. THE FEAST OF PENTECOST

The Jew celebrates yearly the Feast of Pentecost or the Feast of Weeks as commanded by the Lord *(Leviticus 23:15-17; Exodus 23:19; 34:22)*.

The Jews count Passover as the birth of the nation and Pentecost as encounter between God and the people. The two main features of the Feast are the Harvest rejoicing and the Celebration of the giving of the Law. Since Israel's dispersion, the latter has been more the emphasis in the keeping of this Feast.

A. Harvest Festival

The Jews read the Book of Ruth at this Feast. It is significant of the coming into Israel of the Gentiles by the function of a Kinsman Redeemer. It is prophetic to the Jew of the coming in of the Gentiles under Messiah's ministry. It is called the Festival of the Firstfruits, or Festival of the Harvest. It is a holy convocation.

Paul, in speaking of the Jew and Gentile coming together to form one body as the true Israel of God is applicable to this Pentecostal harvest *(Ephesians 2:11-22)*.

B. The Giving of the Law

The prevailing mood of the Jew during this period is one of semi-mourning. It is a period of apprehensive anticipation as they in spirit approach Mt. Sinai and the revelation of God. For, according to Hebrew reckoning, the Torah (the Law) was given at Mt. Sinai on this 50th day. Hence it is called the Feast of the Giving of the Law and as such is counted as the birthday of Judaism. Here also at Sinai the marriage of Israel and God took place and the Law became the wedding contract where Israel entered into Covenantal relationship with Jehovah.

Paul's reference to the giving of the Law Covenant and the New Covenant ministry is found in

II Corinthians 3, as already seen.

The general order for the celebration of the Feast is as follows:

1. The Jew counts 49 days from the second night of the Passover festivities.

2. Meditation, prayer and preparation for Pentecost take place.

3. The homes are decorated and Synagogues with branches, greens and flowers. Some spread grass on the Synagogue floor to represent the grass on which Israel stood while receiving the Torah. Some weave a crown of flowers and branches and place it over the Torah.

4. Jews stay up the entire night, discussing and studying the Law, taking a small portion from each Book of the Bible, from its three parts, the Torah, Prophets and Writings, and each section of the Talmud. The choice depends on the group.

5. Two loaves are baken — symbolic of the two tablets of the ten commandments on two tables of stone, and the two wave loaves which were offered in the Temple at this Feast.

6. Regular Synagogue services take place at this Feast.

Once again we note the things which are missing from the modern keeping of the Feast of Pentecost. The Temple is missing in which the blood sacrifices and the two wave loaves were to be offered. And the Law is still externalized as far as the unbelieving Jew is concerned. They continue the general form and memorial, even as many do in Christendom, but lack the Holy Spirit who is the Spirit of Pentecost. For, first it is the blood of the Lamb of God in Passover, then it is the Spirit of God in Pentecost. No blood, means no Spirit, for the Spirit and the blood agree in one *(I John 5:5-8).* Only as one accepts the blood of Jesus our Passover can one receive the Spirit of Pentecost. It is His ministry then to write the New Covenant commandments in our hearts and minds. Any other Pentecostal Feast is but the letter without the Spirit, the form without the reality, the shadow without the substance. What a tragedy that the orthodox Jew keeps the Passover with the Lamb of God, and Pentecost without the Spirit of God! What lessons this affords the church.

III. THE FEAST OF TABERNACLES

A. The Blowing of Trumpets

Judaism actually has two New Year's day. One in the first day of the month Abib or Nisan, which means Spring *(Exodus 12:1-2),* and the other New Year's Day is the first day of the seventh month, which is called Tishri *(Leviticus 23:24).* It is the latter reckoning that the Jewish calendar follows.

After the Jews came back from Babylon they began to observe New Year's Day more especially *(Nehemiah 8:1-12).* On this day, called Rosh Hashana, there is the blowing of the ram's horn with all of its significance. Under the Law of Moses trumpets were blown and special sacrifices were offered at this holy convocation *(Numbers 28:11-15).*

The general order for the keeping of this Day is as follows:

1. The blowing of horns and trumpets having a threefold purpose:

   a. A trumpet call to repentance, calling those dead in sin to awake to life by repentance and regeneration.

   b. A reminder to Israel of the mercy of God and the Covenantal relationship to the fathers and the nation.

   c. To confound and confuse Satan because of his accusations against Israel before the Lord for their sins.

   The horn used on this day is a ram's horn, reminding all of Abraham's supreme sacrifice of Isaac and the ram caught in the thicket by its horns *(Genesis 22:1-18).*

2. The solemn time of repentance and preparation for the coming Day of Atonement which follows 10 days later. The Rabbis believe and teach that three books are opened in this period of New Year. One book is for the righteous; one book is for the wicked; the other is for those who are neither righteous nor wicked, an intermediate group. The righteous are rewarded with good things of life while the wicked are rewarded condemnation and death. The intermediate group are given 10 days to repent. All their deeds, good and bad are in the book. If their repentance is genuine, then on the Day of Atonement they are judged accordingly. These 10 days are called "The Ten Awesome Days."

3. Prayers of humiliation and penitence are said in the Synagogue on New Year's Day, as all prepare for the Day of Atonement.

4. In the afternoon of New Year's Day the Jews perform symbolic washing away of their sins into the waters. The ceremony is based on *Micah 7:19* where the Lord said that He would cast their sins into the depths of the sea.

B. The Day of Atonement

The Jews call the Day of Atonement "Yom Kippur". It begins at sunset on the ninth day of Tishri and continues to sunset of the tenth day of the same month. This day is called "The Sabbath of Sabbaths." We note the procedure in Jewry for the keeping of this day in modern times.

1. The Day of Atonement is a solemn fast day, from sunset to sunset.

2. All assemble at the Synagogue and pray and seek God for the atonement and forgiveness of sin. The Day of Atonement is called the Day of Judgment and Reckoning.

3. Between New Year's Day and the Day of Atonement are the ten days of repentance and heart searching after reconciliation with God and man.

4. Because the Jews are without a Temple, Priesthood and sacrifice various substitutes have been brought in by the Rabbis. These are listed here:

    a. Repentance, prayer and charitable deeds are most important at this time.

    b. A rooster for the male and a hen for the female are used as substitutes for the atoning sacrifice and swung around the head as a symbol of expiating sins. The very Orthodox Jew does this and it is called "Kapporoth", meaning "propitiatory" or the atoning sacrifice. Others tie money in a handkerchief and swing it around the head and then give it to the poor.

    c. The personal sufferings and sacrifices of the Jews are also upheld as part of the atoning sacrifice.

    d. One's own death is used as a sacrifice based on *Psalm 116:15* which speaks of the preciousness of the death of the saints in the sight of the Lord.

    e. The study of the Torah, and more especially the Talmud is another substitute.

    f. A month of prayers for forgiveness offered at midnight is another substitute.

    g. Many Jews visit cemeteries and pray to the departed souls of the dead believing that they visit the graves at this time.

5. The Day of Atonement service in the Synagogue begins with a solemn declaration by the Rabbi and the congregation and then is followed by solemn prayer for forgiveness for all failures in every area of life.

6. The Day of Atonement is completed by the blowing of the ram's horn, the trumpet which is to declare the coming of the Messiah who will fulfil the Day of Atonement services.

    Again, as in the previous Feasts, the Jews are without the Temple, the Priesthood and the sacrifices and therefore without atonement.

    Thus "The Day" becomes merely a sad traditional form and mocks them because there is no atoning blood, no "Kapper", no covering for their sin *(Exodus 21:30; Leviticus 16:21-22)*.

    They continue to live in the shadow and miss the reality in Christ. They have an incomplete Bible; the Old Testament without the New Testament. They hold the promise without the fulfilment; the passing type without the eternal antitype.

    After the Day of Atonement is over they hold no assurance of sins forgiven. There can be no assurance without the Messiah. As they listen to the ram's horn at the close of the Day they look to Messiah's first coming.

    Yet all their questions and answers concerning the Atonement are found in the person and work of the Lord Jesus Christ. He has already come the first time and made the once-for-all atonement and sacrifice for sin. He has provided the atonement, the true covering and cleansing in His own body and blood. He is the High Priest after the order of Melchisedek and ministers for all who will believe and receive. From the heavenly Sanctuary He will return the second time without a sacrifice for sin and bring full salvation for His own at the last trumpet. He thus fulfills all the empty form the Jew carries on today without Him *(Hebrews 9:1-28)*.

C. The Feast of Tabernacles

The Orthodox Jew also keeps the Feast of Tabernacles or "Succoth" as it is called. "Succoth" means "Booths", hence Tabernacles is the Feast of Booths *(Leviticus 23:39-43; Deuteronomy 16:16)*. This Feast is held on the 15th day of Tishri, five days after the Day of Atonement. The general festivities at this time involved the following thoughts and deeds:

1. It is a Feast of Thanksgiving, or Israel's Harvest Festival. The harvest is in from the fields and orchards and it is a time of great rejoicing.

2. It is also a Feast of Commemoration as the people remember the exodus from Egypt and their 40

years wandering in the Wilderness when they lived in tents and tabernacles — symbolic of their pilgrimage stage enroute to Canaan land.

3. The Jews build little booths or tabernacles. These are made of plaited branches as to their walls and then thatched roofs, shading them from the sun by day but permitting the light of the stars to be seen at night.

4. After much controversy between the Pharisees and Sadducees another custom developed. The people were to bring to the Temple or the Synagogue a small handful of branches, made of palms, myrtles, and willows and wave them in specified directions during certain parts of the service. This was called the "lulav". Besides this the Jew brings some citrus fruit called "ethrog", symbolic of the fruit of the promised land. The three basic symbols of the Feast of Tabernacles were the booths, the lulav and the ethrog. The Feast pointed to the past, what God had done, and also to the future, what God will do.

5. In remembrance of the pouring out of the waters of Siloam the Jew offers in the Synagogue much prayer for rain.

6. The seventh or last day is called the Day of the Great Hosanna. At this time the Hallel *(Psalms 113-118)* is chanted. The closing words have Messianic implications. The word "Save now" means "Hoshanna." The Jews, during prayer, shake off the leaves of the branches of the willows to symbolize the shaking off of all their sins. Messianic prayers are also said at this time.

It is evident that the multitudes must have experienced a wave of the joy of the Feast of Tabernacles when Jesus rode into Jerusalem on the colt. Hence they cut down branches of various trees, and spread their garments in the road as they cried "Hosanna to the Son of David: Blessed is He that cometh in the Name of the Lord; Hosanna in the highest" *(Matthew 21:1-11).*

The Feast of Tabernacles therefore to the Jew is a Harvest Thanksgiving, a National Deliverance commemoration and a looking for the coming of the Messiah.

The One who can "Save now" has already come and they did to Him what they would. He was the Word who "tabernacles" among men in the tent of the human body. He made the atoning sacrifice for Trumpets, Atonement and Tabernacles. He is the propitiation for the sins of the Jewish nation and for the sins of the whole world *(I John 2:1-2).*

The Jew need no longer cling to the empty ritual looking for Messiah but may turn and find full reality in Christ **by faith,** even as every believer, Jew or Gentile, has already found.

The lessons have been observed already but bear repeating. Christians can fall into the same kind of ritualism and formalism and externalism and miss the spirit and reality in Christ unless true spiritual life and relationship with Christ is maintained. The church in her history, sad to say, has followed Jewish history and many many times become wrapped up in the external form and missed the knowledge and truth in the form *(Romans 2:20).* May the Lord preserve us unto reality is our prayer.

Chapter Twenty-Two
THE SABBATH AND THE LORD'S DAY

In our final chapter we consider the vital subject concerning the keeping of the Sabbath Day in the Synagogue and the keeping of the Lord's Day in the Christian Church.

The Sabbath became the focal point for all the Feast days and for this reason the chapter on the Feasts commences with the instruction for the keeping of the Sabbath (Leviticus 23:1-3). Here we consider the Old Covenant Sabbath and see how it is fulfilled in Christ and the New Covenant Lord's Day.

I. THE SABBATH DAY

The Sabbath day, as circumcision, was given as a sign between the Lord and the nation of Israel. It was given for a perpetual Covenant to the nation (Exodus 31:12-18). It was included in the Ten Commandments written on tables of stone (Exodus 20:1-21; Deuteronomy 5:1-21). These were written with the finger of God.

The Jews themselves say that it was never intended for the Gentile but was the heritage of Israel. Sabbath observances presuppose a Temple, a Priesthood and a sacrifice for on this day there were to be extra burnt offerings offered, besides the daily sacrifice (Numbers 28:9-10).

The word "Sabbath" simply means "Rest" or "Cessation from work." It is a cessation from the works of man. God worked six days in creation and rested the seventh day. He sanctified the seventh day, setting it apart from the rest of the working week. It became a day of rest and Israel's weekly Sabbath pointed back to the rest of God in creation (Genesis 2:1-3).

The Lord said through the Prophet Ezekiel that He had given His Sabbaths to be a sign to Israel (Ezekiel 20:12).

The Sabbath is called "a delight, the holy of the Lord and honourable" (Isaiah 58:13). Sabbath Psalms were composed for use on this holy day (Psalm 92).

The weekly Sabbaths in Israel pointed back to creation's rest but also forward to redemptive rest which would come at the close of God's working week (Hebrews 4:9). Also, as noted earlier, the Feast days were additional Sabbaths in whatever week they fell, besides the weekly Sabbath.

The Jew originally did have some beautiful thoughts about the Sabbath. The Jew saw that the whole week took its character from the Sabbath. They also taught that the whole week surrounded the Sabbath. Sunday, Monday and Tuesday belonged to the past Sabbath; while Wednesday, Thursday and Friday belonged to the coming Sabbath. The days of the week only exist because of the Sabbath. The Rabbis taught that "all the days of the week has God paired, except the Sabbath, which is alone, that it may be wedded to Israel" (Edersheim, in **"The Temple"** (p. 177).

Israel was to welcome the Sabbath as a bride; its advent as that of a king. Sabbath was a foretaste of Messianic life.

The way the Lord commanded Israel to keep the Sabbath was basically in the following manner. There was first, on the negative side, to be a cessation of work in general and the doing of one's own pleasures, and on the positive side, a holy convocation or a delighting oneself in the Lord and His Laws. No business was to be transacted on the Sabbath day (Nehemiah 10:31-33; 13:15-22).

The Shewbread was to be changed every Sabbath day (Leviticus 24:8; I Chronicles 9:32). They were "to **remember** the Sabbath" (Exodus 20:8). This spoke of the inward state of the heart, soul and mind. They were "to **observe** the Sabbath" (Deuteronomy 5:12). This spoke of the outward keeping of its laws and regulations.

Violations of the Sabbath day were judged by stoning to death (Exodus 35:1-3). No fires were to be lit on the Sabbath. Hence this man was stoned for gathering sticks on the Sabbath (Numbers 15:32-41).

However, over the years, the Sabbath keeping became polluted and a real mockery to God. He lamented a number of times through Ezekiel over the fact that Israel "polluted My Sabbaths" (Ezekiel 20:12-24).

Not only so, but the Talmud (Jewish Commentaries) had 39 categories of things forbidden on the Sabbath day, and then subdivided these 39 categories into 39 classes, thus totalling 1521 rules for the Sabbath (**"The Feasts of Israel"** by Victor Buksbazen (p. 80)). They fell to hair-splitting over rules which God never gave.

"The Jewish Catolgue" (P. 105) lists the 39 forbidden acts on the Sabbath. These are the following: "Ploughing, sowing, reaping, sheaf making, threshing, winnowing, selecting, sifting, grinding, kneading, baking, sheepshearing, bleaching, combing raw material, dyeing, spinning, inserting thread into a loom, weaving, removing the finished article, separating into threads, tying a knot, untying a knot, sewing, tearing, trapping, slaughtering, skinning or flaying, tanning, scraping, marking out, cutting to shape, writing, erasing, building, demolishing, kindling a fire, extinguishing a fire, the final hammer blow, carrying in a public place."

But the Rabbis created a ridiculous system of Sabbath prohibitions and then created subtle evasions of keeping these rules. All these things helped to bring the Sabbath into disrepute and made it a burdensome stone for all who tried to keep it. It was the Talmudic traditions and rules for the Sabbath that Jesus continually broke and for which the rulers hated Him (Mark 7:1-13).

At one time the disciples plucked ears of corn on the Sabbath and the Pharisees challenged Jesus that they were breaking the Sabbath. Jesus used two illustrations of violations of Old Testament law to refute their argument. David partook of the Shewbread which was only lawful for the priests to eat and the priests in the Temple off the Sabbath sacrifices, yet neither are counted as Sabbath violations. Hence neither were the disciples violating the Sabbath by eating a little plucked corn (Matthew 12:1-8; Luke 6:1-5).

Immediately following this incident, Jesus went into the Synagogue on the Sabbath where there was a man with a withered hand. They asked Him was it lawful to heal on the Sabbath days. Their motive was to have something wherewith to accuse Him. Jesus threw the challenge back into their face. Would they lift a sheep out of the pit it had fallen into on the Sabbath, or loose an ox or an ass for watering and not count this as work? Then He told them it was lawful to do good on the Sabbath and then healed the man. The Pharisees went out and held council how they might destroy Him. They were more interested in the keeping of a day, or their interpretation of it, than the healing of the sick and suffering (Matthew 12:9-14; Luke 6:6-12).

Jesus healed the woman of her infirmity on the Sabbath also. The ruler of the Synagogue was furious and told her that there were six other days in which to be healed, not the Sabbath. Jesus plainly called him a hypocrite (Luke 13:10-17).

Jesus also healed a man of dropsy on the Sabbath day and silenced the Pharisees by doing such (Luke 14:1-6).

When the impotent man was healed by Jesus at the pool of Bethsaida, the Jews told him that it was unlawful to carry his bed on the Sabbath. They persecuted Jesus and sought to kill Him for doing these good works on their Sabbath rest (John 5:1-20). The man born blind was also healed on the Sabbath day (John 9:13-16).

A study of the Gospels show the hypocritical inconsistency of Christ's times as to the keeping of the Sabbath. The Jews would lead an ox or an ass to watering on the Sabbath and not count that work. They would offer sacrifices in the Temple yet not count that work. They would even circumcise a man on the Sabbath yet not count it a violation of Sabbath rest (John 7:22-23). Yet when Jesus loosed people from their sicknesses or infirmities the Jews charged Him with violation of the Sabbath rules. When He taught and healed and did good deeds on the Sabbath they accused Him of breaking the Law and were angry with Him.

All of this proves how the Law of God concerning the Sabbath had been corrupted by Talmudic traditions and interpretations of the Law never commanded by the Lord God. Jesus came to show them what it truly meant to keep Sabbath, by worshipping the Lord God, teaching, preaching, healing and blessing those in spiritual and physical need.

He gave two fundamental statements concerning the Sabbath and these are found in Mark 2:27-28.

A. The Sabbath was made for man and not man for the Sabbath. Thus the day was given for man's benefit, not man given for the benefit of a day. Man needs physical rest and recuperation, as well as time for spiritual refreshment.

B. The Son of Man is **Lord** of the Sabbath. He is over and above the keeping of a day. The Jews kept the letter of the Sabbath, with numerous additions, and missed the spirit of the Sabbath and crucified the **Lord** of the Sabbath.

The way the average Jew keeps the Sabbath today is very simple. Sabbath begins at sunset Friday evening. A service takes place in the Synagogue involving reading from the Torah and special prayers of welcome for the coming Sabbath, the Bride and Queen. Jewish homes are decorated as for a Feast, tables decked, candles lit and a special meal is prepared for the family on returning from the Synagogue. The cup of wine is blessed and passed around the family members. Then after supper is finished, a thanksgiving prayer is said and Sabbath hymns are chanted. Sabbath day itself is to be a time of rejoicing and a time to provide charity for the poor and needy.

The things that are lacking from every Jewish Sabbath are twofold; the sacrifice and the One who gives true Sabbath.

The Sabbath to be kept properly had to have the Sabbath sacrifices, the body and blood of the two lambs. By this the Lord was teaching Israel that true rest can only be upon the basis of the atoning blood. And of course this necessitated an officiating Priesthood to offer the sacrifices. But the Jew today is devoid of these things, not having their Temple. Hence there can be no true Sabbath without blood atonement.

Then on the other hand, the Sabbath rest pointed to Messiah Jesus who alone could give true rest. The day pointed to the Person. The Jews in Christ's time became so wrapped up in the day of rest with its distortions that they crucified the One who could give them rest. They crucified Him while at the same time professing to keep the Feast and the Sabbath days *(John 18:28; 19:31; Acts 13:27)*.

The Lord Jesus Christ is **the sacrifice** and **the rest** of God. All is fulfilled in His person and work. By receiving Him there is cleansing from sin in His blood and one finds true Sabbath, true rest. For this reason He calls us to come to Him and He will give us rest and to learn of Him and we will find rest *(Matthew 11:28-30)*.

When sin is ultimately dealt with and made an end of, then Messiah will bring in the seventh Day of Rest as in the Millenniel Kingdom Rest. This is **the Sabbath** that remaineth for the people of God but can only be entered into and enjoyed by accepting the blood of redemption *(Hebrews 4:9)*.

II. THE LORD'S DAY

The controversy over Sabbath keeping and the keeping of the Lord's Day has been one of the greatest between both the Synagogues and the Church, as well as in the Church itself. The result has been confusion all around. The question of the Pharisees is still asked, even of Christians, today. "Why do thy disciples not keep the Sabbath?"

As already seen, Christ did not repudiate the observance of the Sabbath but He did repudiate the traditions and burdens which the Rabbis had placed on the people. Christ showed them what true Sabbath keeping was and declared that He was Lord even of the Sabbath day *(Matthew 12:28)*. Because He is Lord of the Sabbath day, He is Lord of every other day.

The early church was vexed by these type of questions, especially with the coming in of the Gentiles. The Judaizing teachers endeavoured to bring the Gentiles under the Law by the rite of circumcision and Sabbath keeping. The Apostle Paul dealt specifically with both of these things and showed that the Christian is under a New Covenant.

There are believers today who would seek to impose Sabbath keeping, along with other ceremonial laws, on the church. Thus the Gospel of the Galatians became a mixture of Law and Grace, Moses and Jesus, and brought believers into legalistic and ceremonial bondages, robbing them of their liberty in Christ.

We note some of the major questions and points about Sabbath keeping and whether the believer in Christ is under obligation to keep such.

A. Why did Christ keep the Sabbath?

1. Christ kept the Sabbath as God intended it to be kept; not in the letter but in the spirit. This he did by worshipping the Father, teaching and preaching and healing the sick and diseased and ministering to the poor and needy.

2. Christ also kept the Sabbath because He was born under the Law to redeem them that were under the Law *(Galatians 4:4-5)*. The moment Christ was circumcised He became debtor to do the whole Law *(Galatians 5:3)*. Sabbath keeping and circumcision were two of the greatest signs of God's covenant with the chosen nation of Israel. These signs were not given to the Gentiles.

B. Why did the Apostles keep the Sabbath?

1. The Book of Acts shows that the Apostles kept the Sabbath. The Apostle Paul made it a practice to preach and teach in the Jewish Synagogues on the Sabbath day *(Acts 13:14, 27, 42-44; 15:21; 16:13; 17:2; 18:4)*.

   The reason Paul especially did this was to fulfil the Gospel commission "To the Jew first, and then to the Gentile" *(Romans 1:17)*. Paul went to the Synagogues because he was a Jew and knew that that was the best time to get the Gospel to the Jews as they assembled in the Synagogues.

2. The second reason is that the Apostles were in the great transitory period from the Old Covenant to the New Covenant. For this reason we see the same Apostle Paul keeping the first day of the week and speaking about it in his writings *(Acts 20:7 with I Corinthians 16:2)*.

C. When were the Sabbaths to cease?

1. Even under the Old Covenant when Israel was keeping the Sabbaths, God spoke in no uncertain terms concerning their hypocritical observances *(Isaiah 1:10-17; Lamentations 2:6)*. He spoke through the prophet Hosea that He would cause their Feast days, and Sabbaths to cease *(Hosea 2:11)*. This He did at the Cross when Christ fulfilled them as a passing shadow.

2. The Apostle Paul devotes two passages concerning the subject of the keeping of days. He told the Colossians that no man was to judge them in meat, or in drink, or in respect of an holy day, or of the new moon, or of the Sabbath days. All were but a shadow of things to come. Christ Himself is the substance of the shadow *(Colossians 2:11, 16-17)*.

   He also wrote to the Romans that one man esteems one day better than another, another man esteems every day alike. This covered the attitude of Jews and Greeks. He said for every man to be fully persuaded in his mind and regard their days as unto the Lord *(Romans 14:5-7)*. Paul never imposed on Jew or Gentile the keeping of a certain day.

D. Which Covenant is the believer under today?

The Sabbath is the sign and seal of the Old or Mosaic Covenant *(Exodus 31:12-18; Ezekiel 20:1-12)*. It was not the sign or seal of any of the previous Covenants nor of any Covenants which followed.

When Jesus came, He was born under the Old Covenant to fulfil it and abolish it at the Cross, as to its ceremonial laws. Just before His death He established the New Covenant in His own body and blood *(Matthew 26:26-28)*.

Paul clearly tells us that the Old Covenant was old, and decaying, and ready to vanish away; that it was a ministration of death and to be done away *(II Corinthians 3:1-18; Hebrews 8:6-13)*.

The New Covenant had its own sign and seal, even the true and spiritual rest, which is the baptism of the Holy Spirit *(Isaiah 28:9-11; Acts 2:1-4)*. To take the Sabbath day and impose the keeping thereof upon Christians today, Jew or Gentile, is to take the sign and seal of the Old Covenant and add it to the sign and seal of the New Covenant. It is confusion of Covenants. This is why Paul wrote to the Galatians, under the New Covenant, yet allowing the Judaizers to teach them that they were under Old Covenant laws. He wrote to them saying: "Ye observe **days,** and **months,** and **times** and **years.** I am afraid of you, lest I have bestowed upon you labour in vain" *(Galatians 4:10-11)*.

Once a beliver knows which Covenant he is under it settles for him the matter of Sabbath keeping. To say that all other Sabbaths, and Festival Sabbaths were nailed to the cross, but not the weekly Sabbath, because it was in the Decalogue, is inconsistent interpretation. The Mosaic Covenant was fulfilled and abolished at the Cross. The believer is under the New Covenant and has its sign and seal placed upon the heart.

E. Why the New Testament Believer keeps the Lord's Day.

Following is a summary of some of the more important facts as to why the believer keeps the Lord's Day as a loving privilege and not a legal obligation.

The New Testament Christian keeps the Lord's Day:

1. Because the waving of the Sheaf of Firstfruits took place on the morrow after the Sabbath. This pointed to the fact that Christ's resurrection took place on the first day of the week, not the Jewish Sabbath *(Leviticus 23:11; Luke 23:54; John 19:31; I Corinthians 15:20-23)*. Christ rose from the dead the first day of the week.

2. Because the Feast of Pentecost took place on the morrow after the seventh Sabbath, which was the first day of the week. This pointed to the fact that the Holy Spirit was to come on the first day of the new week, not on the Sabbath *(Leviticus 23:15-16; Acts 2:1)*. The Holy Spirit was outpoured on the first day of the week.

3. Because the disciples met to break bread on the first day of the week and to hear preaching of the Word *(Acts 20:7)*.

4. Because the believers gathered together and took their offerings as God had prospered them on the first day of the week *(I Corinthians 16:2)*.

5. Because the Sabbath day was the rest of Creation, and the Lord's Day is the rest of redemption *(Genesis 2:1-3; Matthew 28:1-6)*.

6. Because the Sabbath day was the sign and seal of the Mosaic or Old Covenant and the believer is under the New Covenant sign and seal.

7. Because the Sabbath day in the Old Testament was obligatory on pain of death. Under the New Testament there is absolutely no command to keep any special day. The keeping of the Lord's day was a voluntary, spontaneous day of worship and service to the Lord. The day was kept, not because it was a legal obligation but because they loved to keep it. This should be the attitude of believers today, according to the Government they may be under.

8. Because all the moral commandments of the Decalogue are repeated, in one form or another, by Christ and the Apostles in the New Testament; the one exception is the keeping of the fourth commandment which is never once commanded in the New Testament.

9. Because in the early Church the Christian was eventually forced out of the Synagogue by persecution, for he could not have Christ in one hand and Moses in the other hand *(Acts 8:3-4)*. God allowed this to come to force the separation between the Synagogue and the Church. For a while Jewish Christians kept both the Sabbath and the Lord's Day, but the two were incompatible and had to be separated

(Acts 15:24-29). The Sabbath was never enforced on the Gentile believers after this, only by Judaizing teachers of the Law. The early believers who did keep Sabbath were Judaizing believers, a mixture of Law and Grace. They were cut off from the main flow of the Christian Church and despised by the Synagogue. Hence it is wrong for legalizers today to use these people as a "proof" that early believers kept the Sabbath.

10. Because Church History confirms the fact that Christians kept the Lord's Day.

    a. Barnabas, one of the Apostolic Fathers of the First Century A.D., writes: "We keep the Lord's Day with joyfulness, the day on which Jesus rose from the dead."

    b. The "Didache of the Apostles", one of the earliest Christian Documents states: "On the Lord's Day gather yourselves together and break bread and give thanks. This is also of the first Century.

    c. Ignatius, Bishop of Antioch, in the year 110 A.D., says: "Those who have walked in ancient practices attain unto newness of hope, no longer observing Sabbaths, but fashioning their lives after the Lord's Day, that we may be found disciples of Jesus Christ, our only teacher."

    d. Justin Martyr, in the year 135 A.D., says "Sunday is the day on which we all hold common assembly, because it is the first day on which God having wrought a change in the darkness and matter made the world, and Jesus Christ our Saviour on the same day rose from the dead. And on the day called Sunday all who live in cities or in the country gather together to one place and the memoirs of the Apostles or the writings of the prophetic Word are read as long as time permits."

    e. According to Iranaeus in 155 A.D., Tertullian, 200 A.D., and Eusebius 315 A.D., Christians repudiated the seventh day Sabbath and recognized the first day of the week as the Lord's Day.

Thus Sunday observance, or the keeping of the Lord's Day was already in vogue before the rise of the Popes or Constantine the Great, when he in 321 A.D., made "Sunday Law" observance obligatory. Judaizing Christians kept the Sabbath day, while the Christian Church kept the Lord's Day *(Revelation 1:10)*. Christ did not change the Sabbath to Sunday. Sunday is not the Sabbath. It never was and never can be.

All the Old Testament types of rest pointed to Christ and then to the Millenniel rest, and Eternal rest. Noah, whose name means "Rest" found rest in the Ark of God *(Genesis 6:13-16)*. Ruth the Moabitess found "rest" in the land of Bethlehem-Judah, "the house of bread and praise" *(Ruth 1:9)*. Israel found "rest" in the land of promise, in Canaan land *(Hebrews 3:11, 18)*. The Ark of the Covenant sought "rest" for Israel in their journeys *(Numbers 10:12, 33-36)*.

The Temple of God was built by King Solomon, a man of rest, wisdom and peace and it was here the Ark eventually found "rest" *(II Chronicles 6:41-42)*. The Sabbath day was a day of rest for Israel *(Exodus 31:15)*. The seventh month, Tabernacles, was a month of rest *(Leviticus 23)*. The seventh year was a year of rest and release for the land and people *(Leviticus 25:4-5)*. The fiftieth year was a Jubilee year and also a year of rest for the land and the people *(Leviticus 26:34-35)*.

All point to **rest in Christ.** He is the Rest-bringer and Rest-giver. And when sin, sickness, disease and death, and Satan and his hosts are cast into the bottomless pit and finally into the Lake of Fire, then there will be true rest, eternal rest. Until then, the believer enjoys that spiritual rest which alone is found in the Christ of God *(Matthew 11:28-30; Hebrews 3-4)*. Sin broke God's rest and man's rest in creation, and when sin is dealt with in redemption, then and then alone will perfect rest be found!

In conclusion, the believer should be fully persuaded in his own mind as to the setting aside of a day unto the Lord. Salvation is not dependent on the keeping of any day of the week, whatever day it may be. All depends on Christ and His finished work and our relationship with Him *(Romans 14:5-7)*.

Various countries have different days of the week set aside for rest and recuperation and the believer will do well to take advantage of this and make it a time of spiritual rest and worship. He will stand fast in the liberty wherewith he has been made free. He will serve the Lord Christ every day of the week and avail himself of one of these days to worship the Christ of God.

In Christ the believer finds true Sabbath rest. He ceases from his own works and rests in the finished work of Christ. It is in Christ there is everlasting rest, thus fulfilling the "perpetual Covenant" of Sabbath rest. It is not in the keeping of **a day** but in the receiving of **a person** — Christ Jesus our Lord — that one finds the rest of God!

SUMMARY AND CONCLUSION

We have concluded our study on the Feasts, both Mosaic and Post-Mosaic. We have considered in brief the modern Jewish Festivals.

All may be summarized by two observations. First, ceremonies and all that pertains to the letter and ritual of the Law, are empty and vain apart from the reality in Christ. Jewish history becomes a real warning and example of that which has happened in church history. It shows how one may hold the shadow, the type, the promise and the prophecy and never come to the antitype, the substance and the fulfilment. It is sadly possible to know the letter of the Law and that which kills and miss the Spirit which gives the life.

The second major observation is that the Lord desires all of His people to enter in and enjoy the spiritual realities in all three Feasts. In Solomon's reign Israel kept the three Feasts in the year (II Chronicles 8:13). The three Feasts speak of the Fulness of the Godhead which all believers may enjoy. Passover is the Feast of the Son, Pentecost is the Feast of the Holy Spirit, and Tabernacles brings us to the Father and the Fulness of the Godhead (Ephesians 1:10-18; 3:17-21).

The church is living in the last of the last days when the Feasts will be entered into. None need stay at any one Feast but all may, if they will, experience all Feasts!

Therefore **"Let us keep the Feasts."**

FEASTS OF THE LORD

FEAST	MONTH OBSERVED	MEMORIAL ASPECT	PROPHETIC ASPECT	DOCTRINAL AND EXPERIENTAL ASPECT
I. Passover	First Month, 14th Day (April 14)	Israel's Deliverance out of Egyptian bondage	Death of the true Lamb of God on the Cross	Justification by faith in the Blood. Repentance, regeneration, redemption adoption
Unleavened Bread	First Month, 15th-22nd Day	The going out of Egypt	The burial of Christ	Sanctification and Separation from evil. Water Baptism
Firstfruits	First Month, 18th Day	Crossing the Red Sea	The Resurrection of Christ	Walking in resurrection and newness of life
II. Pentecost	50 Days after Waving Sheaf of Firstfruits	Giving of the Law at Mt. Sinai	Pouring out of the Holy Spirit on Day of Pentecost Birth of Church	Baptism of the Holy Spirit Earnest, Firstfruits, Seal of the Spirit
III. Tabernacles Blowing of Trumpets	Seventh Month, 1st Day	To prepare people for Atonement and Tabernacles	To prepare God's people for the end-time	Revivals, Awakenings. Call of Spirit. Preparation for Coming of Christ
Day of Atonement	Seventh Month, 19th Day	Priest opened Holy of Holies. Cleansing of sins of people	The cleansing of the Church in the end-time	Purification, Reconciliation, Maturity, Perfection. Sin judged
Tabernacles	Seventh Month, 15th Day	Entering into the Promised Land, great rejoicing	Final ingathering of souls. Ultimately Second Coming	The Rest of God. Kingdom Rest. Christ Tabernacles in His people.

THE HEBREW CALENDAR
SHOWING THE "TIMES & SEASONS"

YEAR SACRED	YEAR CIVIL	MONTH	DAYS	ENGLISH	FESTIVAL	SEASONS AND PRODUCTIONS
1.	7.	Abib, or Nisan. (Green ears) Ex. 12:3	30	April 14th 15-21st 18th	Passover 14th — Unleavened Bread 15th Sheaf of Firstfruits 18th — Firstfruits of Barley Harv. Pres. Ex. 12-13; Lev. 23:10	Fall of Latter or Spring Rains. Deut. 11:14. Floods Josh. 3:15. Barley ripe at Jericho. Wheat partly in the ear.
2.	8.	Zif. (Blossom) I Kgs. 6:1	29	May	Second Passover for those who could not keep first. Num. 9:10-11; II Chron. 29:2 & 30:2.	Barley Harvest general. Ruth 1:22 Wheat ripens.
3.	9.	Sivan. Esther 8:9	30	June 8th	Pentecost or the Harvest, or Feast of weeks. Firstfruits of wheat harv. Lev. 23:17-20. Firstfruits of all the ground. Ex. 23:19. Deut. 26.	Wheat Harvest. Summer begins.
4.	10.	Thammuz. Zech. 8:19	29	July		No rain from April till Sept. I Sam. 12:17
5.	11.	Ab. Ezra 7:9	30	August		The Streams dry up. Heat intense. Vintage. Lev. 26:5.
6.	12.	Elul. Nehm. 6:15	29	September		Heat still intense. II Kings 4:18-20
7.	1.	Tisri or Ethanim I Kgs. 8:2.2 II Chr. 5:3	30	October 1st, 10th 15-21st	1st Feast of the Trumpets. Num. 29:1 Day of Atonement. Lev. 16. 15th Feast of Tabernacles Lev. 23:34	Former or Early Rains begin, Joel 2:23, Grape Harvest general. Num. 13:23, Firstfruits of Wine & Oil. Deut. 16:13, Ploughing & Sowing begin.
8.	2.	Bul. (Rain) I Kgs. 6:38	29	November		Rain continues. Wheat & Barley sown. Vintage in N. Palestine.
9.	3.	Chisleu. Neh. 1:1	30	December 25th	Feast of Dedication. I Macc. 4:52-59 Jn. 10:22-23.	Winter begins. Snow on the Mountains.
10.	4.	Tebeth. Esther 2:16	29	January		Oddest month. Hail and snow. Josh. 10:11
11.	5.	Shebat. Zech. 7:10	30	February		Weather gradually becomes warmer.
12.	6.	Adar.	29	March 14-15th	Feast of Purim. Esther 3:7; 9:1-32	Thunder & Hail frequent.

—*Adapted by K.J. Conner*

13. Ve-Adar. A 13th month called Ve-Adar (the 2nd Adar) was inserted on the months about once in three years. (7 times in 19 years) to make up the difference between the Jewish year and the Solar year, the one now in general use. The length of the Hebrew month was regulated by the changes of the Moon, and was reckoned from one New Moon to the Next New Moon. Their months were usually designated by numbers, i.e., the 1st, 2nd Month etc.

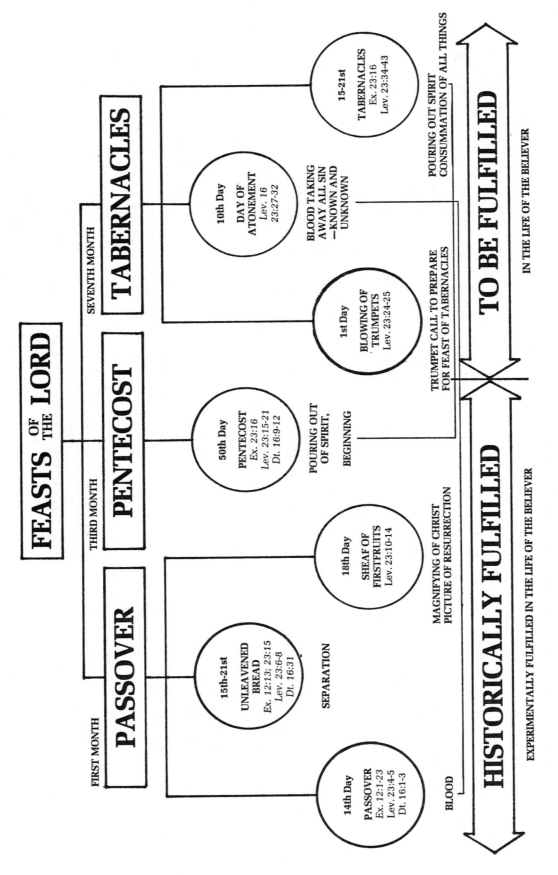

FEASTS OF THE LORD

FIRST MONTH   **THIRD MONTH**   **SEVENTH MONTH**

PASSOVER   PENTECOST   TABERNACLES

14th Day
PASSOVER
Ex. 12:1-23
Lev. 23:4-5
Dt. 16:1-3

15th-21st
UNLEAVENED BREAD
Ex. 12:13; 23:15
Lev. 23:6-8
Dt. 16:31

18th Day
SHEAF OF FIRSTFRUITS
Lev. 23:10-14

50th Day
PENTECOST
Ex. 23:16
Lev. 23:15-21
Dt. 16:9-12

1st Day
BLOWING OF TRUMPETS
Lev. 23:24-25

10th Day
DAY OF ATONEMENT
Lev. 16
23:27-32

15-21st
TABERNACLES
Ex. 23:16
Lev. 23:34-43

BLOOD

SEPARATION

MAGNIFYING OF CHRIST
PICTURE OF RESURRECTION

POURING OUT OF SPIRIT, BEGINNING

TRUMPET CALL TO PREPARE FOR FEAST OF TABERNACLES

BLOOD TAKING AWAY ALL SIN — KNOWN AND UNKNOWN

POURING OUT SPIRIT
CONSUMMATION OF ALL THINGS

HISTORICALLY FULFILLED   TO BE FULFILLED

EXPERIMENTALLY FULFILLED IN THE LIFE OF THE BELIEVER

IN THE LIFE OF THE BELIEVER

PASSOVER: Shadow of the Crucifixion and a type of Salvation.
PENTECOST: Shadow of Acts 2 Pentecost and a type of the Baptism of the Holy Ghost.
TABERNACLES: Symbolic of what God wants to do at the end of the Age & the coming of the **Lord Jesus Christ.**

(Chart by Richard Holland)

BIBLIOGRAPHY

1) Buksbazen, Victor., *The Gospel in the Feasts of Israel.* The Friends of Israel Missionary and Relief Society, Inc., 1218 Chestnut Street, Philadelphia 7., 1974.

2) Coates, C.A., *An Outline of the Book of Leviticus.* Stow Hill Bible & Tract Depot. 2 Upper Teddington Road, Hampton Wick, Kingston-on-Thames, Surrey., 1919-20.

3) Coates, C.A., *An Outline of the Book of Deuteronomy.* Stow Hill Bible & Tract Depot. 2 Upper Teddington Road, Hampton Wick, Kingston-on-Thames, Surrey, 1919-20.

4) Edersheim, Alfred., *The Temple-It's Ministry and Services as they were in the Time of Christ.* Wm. B. Eerdmans Publishing Co., Grand Rapids, Michigan, 1951.

5) Gustafson, Roy. L., *Feasting on the Feasts.* Dunham Publishing Co., Grand Rapids, Michigan, 49506., 1958.

6) Larkin, Clarence., *Dispensational Truth.,* 2802 N. Park Ave., Philadelphia 32, PA., 1918.

7) Mackintosh, C.H., *Notes on Leviticus.* The Bible Truth Press, New York., 1879.

8 Mackintosh, C.H., *Notes on Deuteronomy.* The Bible Truth Press, New York., 1879.

9) Ritchie, John., *The Feasts of Jehovah.* Kilmarnoch, Scotland. John Ritchie, Ltd., Printers and Publishers, 1895.

19) Shepherd, Coulson., *Jewish Holy Days.* Loizeaux Brothers, New York., 1961.

11) *The Jewish Catalogue.,* Compiled and Edited by Richard Siegel, Michael and Sharon Strassfeld. The Jewish Publication Society of America, Philadelphia. 1976.

12) Van Ryn, August., *His Appointments* (Lectures on the "Feasts of the Lord" as recorded in *Leviticus 23).* Loizeaux Brothers, Bible Truth Depot, New York 10., 1944, 1954.

13) Warnock, George H., *The Feast of Tabernacles.,* Sharon Star Publishers, Saskatechewan, Canada, 1951.